INVENTING THE VICTORIANS

INVENTING
THE VICTORIANS

Matthew Sweet

faber and faber

First published in 2001
by Faber and Faber Limited
3 Queen Square London WC1N 3AU

Photoset by Wilmaset Ltd, Birkenhead, Wirral
Printed in England by
Clays Ltd, St Ives plc

Matthew Sweet is hereby identified as author
of this work in accordance with Section 77
of the Copyright, Designs and Patents Act 1988

A CIP record for this book
is available from the British Library

ISBN 0-571-20658-1

2 4 6 8 10 9 7 5 3 1

Contents

List of Illustrations

Inventing the Victorians

'You'll adore my Aunt Jane,' said Raymond. 'She's what I should describe as a perfect Period Piece. Victorian to the core. All her dressing-tables have their legs swathed in chintz.'
  Agatha Christie, *Sleeping Murder* (1976)

Suppose that everything we think we know about the Victorians is wrong. That, in the century which has elapsed since 1901, we have misread their culture, their history, their lives – perhaps deliberately, in order to satisfy our sense of ourselves as liberated Moderns. It comforts us to imagine that we have escaped their influence, freed ourselves from their corseted, high-collared world, cast off their puritanisms and prejudices. But what if they were substantially different from the people we imagine them to have been? What if they were more liberal and less neurotic than us? Had more fun than us, and were less hypocritical about sex than us? What if the popular images of the Victorian period – straitlaced patriarchs making their wives and children miserable, vicious showmen beating their freak exhibits, whaleboned women shrouding the piano legs for decency's sake, then lying back and thinking of England – obscure a very different truth?

  This book is an attempt to re-imagine the Victorians: to suggest new ways of looking at received ideas about their culture; to distinguish myth from reality; to generate the possibility of a new relationship between the lives of nineteenth-century people and our own. It aims to break up the stereotypes which have shaped our thinking about the Victorians for the last hundred years: the belief that they were forced into silence on certain subjects; that they led secret lives; that their culture was defined – to an extent which ours is not – by a divide between its respectable surface and dark underworld. It aims to surprise by exhuming Victorian texts which question our preconceptions about the culture that produced them: the bisexual pornography in which the two heroes indulge in guiltless sex with each other before climbing into bed with the two heroines; the

[ix]

1 Victorians enjoying the nakedness of their piano legs (advertisement for the John Brinsmead piano company, *Illustrated London News*, 1889)

children's adventure serial starring a cross-dressing teenage boy; the advertisements that wooed people like you and me into meetings with personalities like Julia Pastrana the Baboon Lady, Miss Atkinson the Pig Woman and the Bipenis Boy. It also aims to challenge the assumption that nineteenth-century culture was less sophisticated than ours; that the Victorians were people with sensibilities irremediably different from our own; that they were no good in bed and no fun at parties; that we should consider them our moral inferiors – our enemies.

Most of the pleasures we imagine to be our own, the Victorians enjoyed first. They invented the theme park, the shopping mall, the movies, the amusement arcade, the roller-coaster, the crime novel and the sensational newspaper story. They were engaged in a continuous search for bigger and better thrills. The Victorians took their pleasures in private fetish clubs and at terrifying magic lantern displays. They watched death-defying tightrope acts, played mechanical arcade games and were dazzled by the spectacles offered by panoramas, dioramas, neoramas, nausor-amas, physioramas and kinematographs. The Cremorne Gardens – a pleasure park near Battersea Bridge – were more of a meat market than the sleaziest twenty-first-century club. The sensation drama – a theatrical genre reliant on spectacular stage tricks – created high-tech simulations of waterfalls, burning buildings, horse races and avalanches over a century before the 'helicopter moment' in *Miss Saigon*. The Burlington Arcade was a swanky mall where sex and shopping were pursued with equal enthusiasm – and transvestite boys were its speciality. Sensation novels books such as *The Woman in White* (1860) and *Lady Audley's Secret* (1862) – offered pleasures so intense that their detractors claimed they could drive you to drink, insanity or copycat crime. Newsagents sold pin-ups of serial killers; chemists dispensed mind-altering drugs, no ques-tions asked. If Queen Victoria wasn't amused, then she was in a very small minority.

We think of the Victorians as racists, yet they had no anti-immigration laws and elected Britain's first Asian Members of Parliament. We think of them as religiose, yet church attendance figures fell just as dramatically in the nineteenth century as in the twentieth. We think of their society as violent, yet their crime figures were lower than ours. We think of them as misogynist, but – with the shameful exception of the Contagious Diseases Acts, which subjected suspected prostitutes to forcible medical examina-tion for venereal disorders – the statute books describe a fairly linear narrative of female emancipation. We think of them as royalist, when the period was the zenith of British republicanism. We think of them as puritanical, and when mountains of evidence are produced to the contrary, we insist that they were forced to conduct clandestine sex lives and use it to amplify their reputation for hypocrisy. We can just about bring ourselves to give the Victorians the credit for building the houses in which we live, the railway tunnels through which we commute, the pubs in which we drink, the sewers which funnel away our excrement, the museums and galleries in which we spend our Sunday afternoons. We are less inclined to acknowledge their responsibility for an almost uncountable number of other important innovations: both for concepts which are often believed to be ahistorical – such as the inherent goodness of children, homosexuality and heterosexuality, the notion that family members, ideally, should like each other – and for a huge roster of inventions usually assumed to be of more recent origin. Blame them, or thank them, for the suburban housing estate. For the fax machine. For the football league, political spin-doctoring, heated curling tongs, vending machines, the electric iron, the petrol-driven car, feminism, the London Underground, DIY, investigative journalism, commercially-produced hardcore pornography, instantaneous transcontinental communications networks, high-rise public housing, plastic, free universal education, product placement, industrial pollution, environmentalism, fish and chips, X-ray technology, sex contact ads, paper bags, Christmas crackers, junk e-mail (by telegram, but still just as annoying), global capitalism, interior design and Sanatogen – the stuff that surrounds us in the early twenty-first-century world, both the good and the bad. Despite such evidence, we have chosen to remember the Victorians not as our benefactors, but as sentimentalists, bigots, Jingoists and hypocrites. The Victorians invented us, and we in our turn invented the Victorians.

Sexuality was the principal territory upon which this body of myth and misinformation was constructed. 'Lie back and think of England' is a phrase often used to characterise Victorian women's attitude to sex – despite the fact that its first recorded instance is in a private diary from 1912.[1] That old chestnut about draped piano legs is quoted with even greater regularity. The Victorians, the orthodox view goes, were so afraid of the power of sexuality that they felt compelled to cover up the legs of their pianos; they obscured signs of the body even where they existed only by inference. It has become the perfect exemplum of their prudishness, cited with impressive regularity in both popular and scholarly writings.[2]

The piano leg question took on its emblematic status in 1947, when it was debated in a series of radio programmes which aimed to summarise nineteenth-century ideas and beliefs. The socialist historian H. L. Beales, addressing Victorian attitudes to sex, pictured nineteenth-century housewives in a state of panic over the rudery embodied in their home furnishings: 'Out came the drapings for the piano-legs – was it the high polish which was vulnerable, or were legs just such things that should not be seen? A conspiracy of silence was established on the subject of sex which has never been completely broken up.'[3] The following week, the psychoanalyst Edward Glover returned to the same subject, taking issue with Beales's conclusions but adding a Freudian flavour which only served to intensify Beales's repressive hypothesis: 'The woman who draped the legs of her piano, so far from concealing her conscious and unconscious exhibitionism, ended by sexualising the piano; no mean feat.'[4] Glover's interpretation is alive and well today. An article in the *Radio Times*, publicising a similar BBC radio season marking the centenary of Queen Victoria's death, asked, 'Does it not take a mind somewhat preoccupied by sex to imagine knickers on a piano?'[5]

This fiction, so attuned to post-Victorian prejudices about the nineteenth century, continues to proliferate, not just in popular journalism and gossip, but in the work of serious-minded academics and historians. Rosemarie Morgan in her Penguin edition of Thomas Hardy's *Far from the Madding Crowd* (2000), asserts that, for the Victorians, the 'specific curvature of a piano leg [was] matched to the erotic body'.[6] Stephen Bayley's book *General Knowledge* (1999) argues that 'The icons of the modern movement were as historically specific as the nineteenth-century obsession with modesty, which led the Victorians to dress table legs in pantaloons. Just as they felt it necessary to disguise household apparatus and buildings, so the modern movement demanded the clear articulation of an internal mechanism through external forms.'[7] Richard Sennett, in *The Fall of Public Man* (1986), traces a similar argument. 'The idiocy of such prudery can so cloud the mind that its source is forgotten,' he writes. 'All appearances have personal meanings: if you believe that little gestures with the eyes may involuntarily betray feelings of sexual license, it becomes equally rational to feel that the exposed legs of a piano are provocative.' Sennett argues 'that cultural change, leading to the covering of the piano legs, has its roots in the very notion that all appearances speak, that human meanings are immanent in all phenomena'.[8]

The voice of this particular appearance, however, is an act of historical ventriloquism. There is no evidence that the custom was ever practised in the period, except as a means of protecting valued furniture from damage – in much the same way that antimacassars defended upholstery from dirt and hair-cream.[9] Moreover, this little paradigm of prudishness existed for the Victorians much as it exists for us – only they told it as a joke against the perceived over-refinement of middle-class Americans. British readers were introduced to the idea by *A Diary in America* (1839), Captain Frederick Marryat's credulous and antagonistic account of life in the New

World. Marryat describes how he visited Niagara Falls with a female friend, who slipped on a rock and grazed her shin. 'Did you hurt your leg much?' he asked.

> She turned from me, evidently much shocked, or much offended; and not being aware that I had committed any very heinous offence, I begged to know what was the reason of her displeasure. After some hesitation, she said that as she knew me well, she would tell me that the word *leg* was never mentioned before ladies. I apologized for my want of refinement, which was attributable to my having been accustomed only to *English* society, and added, that as such articles must occasionally be referred to, even in the most polite circles of America, perhaps she would inform me by what name I might mention them without shocking the company. Her reply was, that the word *limb* was used; 'nay,' continued she, 'I am not as particular as some people are, for I know those who always say limb of a table, or limb of a piano-forte.'[10]

Marryat was even more surprised when he encountered the limbs of a piano at a seminary for young ladies. His guide informed him that the mistress of this establishment, in order to demonstrate 'her care to preserve in their utmost purity the ideas of the young ladies under her charge ... had dressed all these four limbs in modest little trousers, with frills at the bottom of them!'[11]

Back home, the Captain's anecdotes were adopted as proverbial examples of American reserve. On the stage of the Haymarket Theatre, London, a satirical song in J. R. Planché's burlesque *Mr Buckstone's Voyage Round the Globe* (1854) declared:

> 'To the West, to the West, to the land of the free –'
> Which means those that happen white people to be –
> 'Where a man is a man –' if his skin isn't black –
> If it is, he's a nigger, to sell or to whack ...
> Where the legs of the table in trowsers are drest:
> Away, far away, to the land of the west.[12]

On 29 December 1856, the naturalist Richard Owen wrote to John Murray, the publisher, complaining that the editor of the *Quarterly Review* was being unreasonably squeamish about the terms used in an article about sexual reproduction in bees and moths. 'This sensitiveness,' Owen grumbled, 'truly akin to the Yankee nether-clothing of the pianoforte legs, is shutting out a vast and rapidly increasing store of most interesting and important knowledge.'[13] By the following decade, the image was transforming into a standard satirical shorthand for the notion of prudery – an 1868 cartoon attacking the conservatism of the author Eliza Lynn Linton, for instance, depicted her at an easel whose legs were wrapped in frilled pantalettes.[14]

Was this practice ever pursued, even in America? Probably not. The most likely explanation for the origins of the story is that the Captain's friends were simply pulling his limb. Marryat himself was doubtful about some of his conclusions, suspecting that he may have been deliberately misinformed by those hoping to undermine his work. After the publication of Frances Trollope's *Domestic Manners of the Americans* (1832) and Harriet Martineau's *Society in America* (1837), few were minded to help another English writer libel their country. 'If they have the slightest suspicion that a foreigner is about to write a book,' he reflected, 'nothing appears to give them so much pleasure as to try and mislead him.'[15] More evidence that Marryat was the victim of a hoax comes from a knuckle-headed parody of his work, *Lie-ary on America, with Yarns on its Institutions* (1840) by 'Captain Marry-It'. The pseudonymous American author rewrites the Englishman's account in the most ludicrous manner, but seems satisfied to rehearse the grazed knee incident at Niagara Falls more or less as Marryat tells it, describing how the L-word ruined a pleasant afternoon of sightseeing: 'Sink my hull if she didn't instanterly capsize in a swoon; and her mammy told me never to mention that wulger thing "leg" in the presence of a Yankee female, or I might endanger their lives and their modesty for ever.'[16] The joke is essentially unchanged, suggesting that most American readers would find this genuphobia as ridiculous as those in England. Whatever the case, the synecdochic relationship that now exists between Victorian sensibilities and the clothed piano leg is wholly fraudulent. It persists, however, because the story is useful as a way of dismissing the Victorians' experience as less honest, less sophisticated, less self-cognisant than our own.

How did the Victorians fall victim to what E. P. Thompson called 'the enormous condescension of posterity'?[17] It was a speedy and subtle process, the most visible aspect of which was a battle fought in the early years of the twentieth century between the more ironical members of the Bloomsbury set and an ageing cohort of nineteenth-century survivors. The opening shots were fired in *Eminent Victorians* (1918), Lytton

Strachey's persuasive and witty debunking of four nineteenth-century worthies: Cardinal Manning, Florence Nightingale, General Gordon of Khartoum and Dr Thomas Arnold, headmaster of Rugby – a group of sacred cows which Strachey determined to milk for laughs. To ensure that his subjects appeared sufficiently silly or callous, he even produced a few fictional factoids. He decided that Manning never spoke of his wife after her death. He claimed that Arnold's legs were 'shorter than they should have been'.[18] He implied that Gordon was a drunkard (but chose not to elucidate his sexual interest in young men – perhaps because he shared it).

It was Arnold's granddaughter, Mary Ward, a novelist born in Tasmania in 1851, who led a feeble resistance movement against the book, condemning its 'coarse caricature' and 'sheer brutality' from the pages of the *Times Literary Supplement*.[19] For those in and around the Bloomsbury circle, bashing her in print then became a kind of team sport. 'How this lights up the stuffed world of the first class railway carriage that she lives in!' shrieked Virginia Woolf, momentarily forgetting, perhaps, her own distaste for travelling in the same compartments as the working classes.[20] The Bloomsberries' contempt for Ward killed her posthumous reputation. Today, she is chiefly remembered as an opponent of women's suffrage, but it is not perverse to argue that Ward made as concrete a contribution to the advancement of women's rights as the iconised author of *A Room of One's Own* (1929). Ward was an active member of the committee that brought women students to Oxford University, established an education centre for working Londoners in Gordon Square, set up a network of child-care facilities for the capital's working women, founded Britain's first school for disabled children, and became the first female journalist to file a story from the trenches of the First World War. Now relocated to Queen Square, the Mary Ward Centre remains an important adult education institution, but the guides who escort crocodiles of tourists on walks around literary Bloomsbury prefer to concentrate on the numerous shifts in Woolf and Strachey's living arrangements than on the transformative effect Ward exerted upon the lives of the working-class women with whom they shared a postal district.

Bloomsbury's poison-pen letter to the past arrived at the perfect moment. The reviews were extremely positive – although one in the *TLS* introduced an element of doubt which reflects one of the key themes of this book: 'We live in a world that they [the Victorians] built for us, and though we may laugh at them, we should love them, too.'[21] Strachey's opinion of the Victorians as 'a set of mouthing bungling hypocrites' was, however, being echoed throughout Edwardian culture.[22] Growing awareness of Freud's work, which offered the twentieth century a system of sexual signification unavailable to its predecessor, amplified the belief that the Victorians were fundamentally ignorant about the workings of their own sensibilities. As Michael Mason notes in *The Making of Victorian Sexuality* (1994), the epithet 'Victorian' had already begun to acquire a pejorative edge by the time Strachey's book was published. *Eminent Victorians*, however, did more than any other text to fix the twentieth century's attitude to the nineteenth – and the indignant counterblasts came quickly. In 1919, the poet and MP J. A. Bridges took issue with 'the slighting way in which people, who very likely know little about the matter, are accustomed to write and talk about the Victorian era, as if everything done during that period by those whom we had been brought up to honour and respect was quite futile and absurd.'[23] He suspected that 'Probably the same class of people will – if the earth should last so long – in the twenty-first century be disparaging and sneering at the present era, with as much or as little reason'.[24]

From this point on, it was open season on the Victorians. They became the favourite comic stereotype of the age. In Grace James's musical comedy *The Pork Pie Hat* (1922), a phalanx of nineteenth-century schoolgirls chorus their adherence to a twentieth-century caricature of Victorian virtue:

First Boarder: I am a gentle, good Victorian child,
  Obedient, patient, modest, meek and mild.
Miss Pinkerton. Speak when you're spoken to and then be quiet
  Content with simple joys and simple diet.
Second Boarder: Dear ma'am, I'll always try to do my duty,
  Morality attracts me more than beauty.[25]

Less Eminent Victorians (1927) parodied Victorian mores in limerick form:

  There was a young Lady of Dover
  Who started to read Casanova.
  She hadn't gone far
  When she told her papa
  That she felt she was blushing all over.[26]

Strachey's allies Osbert Sitwell and Margaret Barton collated *Victoriana: A Symposium of Victorian Wisdom* (1931), which gloated over absurdly old-fashioned journalistic diatribes against Ibsen, Wilkie Collins and women's suffrage. The phrase 'mid-Victorian' became a sly social put-down. Cecily Sidgwick's novel *Victorian* (1922) has its heroine worrying that a new arrival at her home will be 'mid-Victorian', and not a subscriber to her own more liberal views.[27] Caryl Brahms and S. J. Simon's *Don't Mr Disraeli* (1940) and Barbara Shaw's play *A Mid-Victorian Trifle* (1940) encapsulated the silliness and social conservatism which Moderns expected their predecessors to embody. In *Don't Mr Disraeli*, Aunt Laetitia pronounces that 'ankles ... can inflame the basest passions,' and an 'Observation Scout from the Society for the Stimulation of Morality and the Encouragement of Good Taste' wakes up with a prostitute in a stucco love-nest in St John's Wood and wonders whether to report himself to his superiors.[28] Shaw's play, written during the Second World War for a cast of women, is set during the Crimean War:

> *Mrs Cameron*: Oh, dear, if her papa hadn't been such a clever physician and amused himself teaching Caroline a lot of things she ought never to have known, she wouldn't have dreamed of following that unprincipled Nightingale woman to the Crimea and then got married to a black man! (*Hysterics*).[29]

In the 1930s and 1940s, the nineteenth century became a popular setting for lightly satiric sentimental fiction, such as *The Frozen Heart* (1935) by Amy Strachey, widow of Lytton Strachey's cousin, Catherine Gayton's *Those Sinning Girls* (1940) and Amy Jay Baker's *Those Victorians* (1947) – hindsighted romantic sagas cluttered with embroidered mob caps, bamboo work boxes and knowingly rebellious heroines. Self-consciously period thrillers also appeared. In 1922, the actor-manager Tod Slaughter took over the Elephant and Castle Theatre in south-east London and initiated a programme of emphatically retro revivals of Victorian melodrama standards. In doing so, he nurtured – or perhaps even created – the popular notion of what constituted the nineteenth-century theatre's melodramatic style. Patrick Hamilton's play *Angel Street* (1938) brought a more understated version of Slaughter's Victorian hypocrite to the West End and Broadway, and when it was filmed (for the second time) as *Gaslight* (1944), cinemagoers saw Charles Boyer's high-collared, cravat-wrapped tyrant undone by Joseph Cotten's dickie-wearing,

American-accented detective, and cheered the extinction of old-style villainy. *The Adventures of Sherlock Holmes* (1939) became the first Conan Doyle adaptation to portray Holmes in a specifically Victorian London. With the period setting came Nigel Bruce's bumbling, fusty, Stracheyite Watson: an image that subsequent incumbents of the role would find hard to erase. British films with nineteenth-century subjects reinforced the association of the period with themes of brutality and hypocrisy. In 1935, Slaughter's company made a surprisingly successful transfer to the cinema, mining their repertoire to furnish material for a number of 1930s quota quickies. Slaughter's posturing, lip-smacking, moustache-twirling characters were all of the same type: monsters of hypocrisy. In *The Crimes of Stephen Hawke* (1931) – a pastiche described by Slaughter in the film's prologue as 'a new old melodrama' – the titular character is a respected money-lender who lives a double life as a murderous burglar named The Spinebreaker. In *Maria Marten or Murder in the Red Barn* (1935), he plays William Corder, an outwardly respectable man exposed as a seducer and a killer.

As Jeffrey Richards has noted, Slaughter's films established a critique of Victorianism that was developed with enthusiasm in the popular cinema of the following decades. In *Great Expectations* (1946) and *Oliver Twist* (1948), David Lean imported the techniques of German Expressionist film-making into the depiction of Victorian narratives, and created a kind of nineteenth-century *noir* that remains a touchstone for any director tackling stories set in the period. It was the Hammer horror cycle, however – which rolled from the late 1950s to the mid-1970s – which did the most to shape the popular perception of Victorian sensibility.[30] *The Curse of Frankenstein* (1957) and *Dracula* (1958) were the first versions of these narratives to be set firmly in the nineteenth century. The Universal horror films from which they were remade have no obvious period content: the lab equipment in *Frankenstein* (1936) was high-tech enough to be reused in the sci-fi epic *Flash Gordon* five years later. Hammer used the historical setting to tell parables about the pleasures of the Permissive Society, which it dramatised as a battle between the promiscuous Undead and conservative Victorians – which is why the company took such delight in stories involving lesbian vampires in nineteenth-century Swiss finishing schools and tight-laced virgins being transformed into carnal monsters after a nocturnal visit from Christopher Lee. The subtext of these movies doesn't lie very deep below the surface: when Hammer transported Dracula to Swinging

London for the final films of the series, he became high priest of an orgiastic gang of vampire hippie bikers.

By the time the Count came to Carnaby Street, voices dissenting from Hammer's view of the nineteenth century had long fallen silent. Even in the aftermath of the publication of *Eminent Victorians*, protests against anti-Victorianism were weak and marginal. In 1928, the poet and prominent anti-vivisection campaigner Stephen Coleridge complained in his volume of personal reminiscences that 'We ... are a little apt to look back at the Victorians with a superior smile.'[31] The title chosen by the illustrator James Thorpe for his own memoirs, *Happy Days: Recollections of an Unrepentant Victorian* (1931), suggests that surviving Victorians were expected to be apologetic about the age into which they were born. In the year of his death, the architect, clubman and aristocratic roister-doister Ralph Nevill published an account of nineteenth-century pleasures, *The Gay Victorians* (1930), with the explicit intention of debunking the debunkers who characterised his youth as a time of austerity and prohibition. Victorian London was 'much more free in its life and amusements' than its 1930s counterpart, run by the 'hypocritical [and] canting present generation'. He blamed 'Ultra-respectability, the great fetish of modern England' and 'Puritan fanatics' for this sad decline. Nevill, with the roseate nostalgia of a dying man looking back at past hedonisms, recalled a world of pre-Edwardian all-night partying: music hall lounges; free and easy supper places; Barrer's Oyster Rooms on the Haymarket; the Alhambra on Charing Cross Road, with its obliging chorus girls; the Shades, a club which stood in Leicester Square on the spot now occupied by the Empire cinema, where the cutlery was stamped 'Stolen from the Shades'; the Gardenia Club around the corner, where 'five shillings to the porter and any name you fancied scribbled in a book made you free of the place, as long as you did not throw glasses about, or quarrel with lady members'.[32] Nobody listened to him, however. As the Canadian historian Herman Ausubel reflected in 1955, 'Anti-Stracheyite Victorians have failed notoriously, for *Eminent Victorians* gives every sign of enduring for a long time.'[33]

Now that over a century has elapsed since Queen Victoria's death, it is time to rethink our assumptions about life in her reign; to question the validity of texts that we have decided typify nineteenth-century attitudes; to test our beliefs about the era against comparable phenomena in our own times. A whole canon of morally prescriptive writing, for instance, has been assumed to be reflective of the real lives and attitudes of Victorian people. William Acton's *The Functions and Disorders of the Reproductive Organs* (1857) – in which he famously remarked that 'The majority of women (happily for them) are not very much troubled by sexual feelings of any kind' – is frequently cited as the defining slogan of Victorian attitudes to female sexuality.[34] Daniel Pool, in his popular guide *What Jane Austen Ate and Charles Dickens Knew* (1998), contends that Acton's works 'suggest how much truth there was in our stereotypes of the constrained character of nineteenth-century English sexual behaviour'.[35] Sources concurring with Acton, however, are rather less easy to find than those arguing exactly the opposite – that women's erotic appetites were strong, and that sexual abstinence could harm the health of the female subject. Sara Stickney Ellis's *The Wives of England* (1843) occupies a similarly prominent position in discussions of the domestic lives of nineteenth-century women. Selective quotation from her didactic writing has launched a thousand critiques of the power of Victorian patriarchy, yet such studies rarely acknowledge that allusions to her work in more mainstream literature – in the works of Wilkie Collins and Geraldine Jewsbury, for example – are invariably dismissive. How do we know that using Ellis or Acton as keys to the nineteenth-century mindset is not like using *Men are from Mars, Women are from Venus* (1992) or *The Surrendered Wife* (2001) to explain the complexity of our own? Why should we assume that the Victorians' self-help books and sex manuals were any less silly, flaky or ephemeral than those that fill today's bookshops?

Above all, perhaps, we should acknowledge the hypocrisies and inconsistencies present in our relationship with the Victorians. When we see, for instance, David Lynch's *The Elephant Man* (1979) or one of David Lean's Dickens adaptations, we congratulate ourselves for having escaped the feculent horror-show of the Victorian city – a black and white world of bad drains and brick alleys, which modern plumbing and sodium lights have successfully banished. Yet, since the 1980s, these Gothicised industrial spaces have been converted into chi-chi apartment blocks, and out in the new middle-class suburbs, contractors are busily assembling neo-Gothic and Tudorbethan environments of which Charles and Carrie Pooter would have heartily approved. Similarly, when we see period musicals such as Lerner and Loewe's *My Fair Lady* (1956) or Vivian Ellis's *Bless the Bride* (1947), we use the Victorian period to indulge escapist fantasies about romance uncomplicated by anxiety about sexual equality – equality which most of us would be unwilling to relinquish. A political adaptation of that same nostalgia was deployed by Margaret Thatcher's Conservative Party in 1983, when it made enormous electoral capital from its invocation of a mythic nineteenth century of Tory content: a utopia of personal thrift, ruined by the foundation of the welfare state and the promulgation of Keynesian economics. However, most of those people who voted for the Tories throughout the 1980s remained part of a broad consensus which celebrated the modern world's distance from an age in which women were unenfranchised and, it is imagined, tyrannised by their husbands and suffocated by their under-wear.

Readers hoping to find any right-wing nostalgia in these pages will, I hope, be disappointed: it is not my intention to suggest that the nineteenth century was a low-tax, free-trade paradise from which we have all been expelled by social democracy. What follows is an attempt to undermine the orthodox views of the nineteenth century offered by progressive and reactionary traditions; to suggest how we might liberate the Victorians from Stracheyite, Thatcherite and Freudian prejudices; how we might learn to live with them on better terms. It is not a conventional history book; not a comprehensive survey of the period, decade by decade, social class by social class. It is an attempt to conjure up the excitement, the permissiveness, the sense of pleasurable velocity that was central to the Victorian experience; to demolish the notion that the nineteenth century was an era best characterised by reticence, stability, sobriety and conservatism. Some members of the cast of characters who populate this book – Lucia Zarate the celebrity dwarf, Ah Sing the Stepney opium master, William Dugdale the Chartist pornographer, Dr William Palmer the serial killer – will be unfamiliar to many readers. Others – Aubrey Beardsley, Josephine Butler, Oscar Wilde, Queen Victoria – will, I hope, seem unfamiliar in the light of its contents. The fieldwork on these pages, which has taken me to (among other places) the edge of the Niagara Falls, a strip club in Sheffield, a freak show on Coney Island and a concrete housing block in Shadwell, aims to expose the Victorian-ness of the world in which we live; to demonstrate that the nineteenth century is still out there, ready to be explored. A less obviously geographical journey will be described in the progress of the chapters, which follow the Victorians as they engage with their popular culture, go shopping, gossip, visit the movies, eat dinner, redecorate their homes, take drugs, have sex, negotiate the daily business of their lives. And, as the story moves on, the connections between the hundreds of disparate anecdotes, histories, texts and lives recorded in this book will, I hope, begin to make a broader claim about the nature of Victorian sensibility.

By the time you've read this book, I believe you will be convinced of a number of relatively minor points: that the exhibition of human oddities had its positive side; that recreational drug use in the nineteenth century was widespread and socially acceptable; that far from being a Modern marooned in the past, Oscar Wilde was – sexually at least – a fairly typical Victorian man. I hope you will also be convinced of some rather wider assertions: that Victorian culture was as rich and difficult and complex and pleasurable as our own; that the Victorians shaped our lives and sensibilities in countless unacknowledged ways; that they are still with us, walking our pavements, drinking in our bars, living in our houses, reading our newspapers, inhabiting our bodies.

CHAPTER ONE

The Sensation Seekers

Outside amusements were few: hence the frequency with which
the piano figured in the home.

T. K. Derry and T. L. Jarman, *The Making of Modern Britain* (1956)

The front page of a nineteenth-century copy of *The Times* is a printed
rebuttal to the received image of Victorian entertainment. The edition for
1 January 1861 carries 179 advertisements on its cover. There are sixty
relating to shipping, rail travel, haulage; seven personal announcements;
twenty-three lost and found dogs, watches and relations; five legal
notices; one each advertising the sale of picture frames, bottles and
Christmas trees. But the remaining eighty-one are all related to entertainments and leisure: either for products such as toys, games, conjuring sets,
skates and magic lanterns; or events such as concerts, theatricals,
acrobatic displays, panoramas, pantomimes, waxwork shows and phreno-
logical demonstrations. There are four ventriloquists, three magicians,
two dancing dog acts, a spiritualist and a pianist for hire, and ten
announcements from ticket agencies offering to secure admittance to
any show in London.

A breathless excitement gasps from these advertisements, as if their
hyperbole can hardly hope to keep pace with the appetite it feeds. Every
product, every event, every novelty is too big, too massive, too wondrous
for any sensible person to ignore. It suggests a culture drunk with a sense
of its own success, its dizzying complexity; a population goggling at the
endless opportunities for spectacular pleasure made possible by those
qualities. An ad for the 'Juvenile Fete' at the Royal Colosseum, for
instance, announces that 'the Giant Christmas Tree will bloom with
watches, cutlery, jewellery and countless toys for gratuitous distribution'.
There will be 'Modern Magic by Mr Taylor' and a demonstration of a
'New and powerful Oxyhydrogen Microscope, with its Myriad of Living
Wonders'. A 'Photo-stereoscopic Exhibition', 'Cosmoramic Views' and
'Colossal Dioramas of London & Paris, Stalactite Caverns, Swiss
Cottages and Mountain Torrents' can be experienced, along with the

[1]

2 The death of Madame Genieve (*Punch*, 1863)

novel promise that 'Mr Morris will perform on the Crystal-ophonic and Musical Rocks'. Science-fiction technology, coupled with aggressive marketing techniques, produces boasts of volume and richness too gigantic to represent, too extensive to consume. The magic is modern, the dioramas are colossal, the views are cosmoramic and the distribution is gratuitous. The children of Londoners at the turn of the twentieth century yelled for Playstations, Pokemon and Buzz Lightyear. At the 1861 Juvenile Fete, hundreds of young Victorians scrabbled for spoons and paste diamonds, wild with an identical desire for instant gratification.

There were other, more complex objects of desire: Victorian children wanted to get their hands on the new generation of domestic gadgets formulated with only pleasure in mind; machines that would import the visual thrills of the diorama, the Cosmorama and the photo-stereroscope into the drawing rooms and parlours of England. Sir Charles Wheatstone had devised the stereoscope – a device for viewing three-dimensional images – in 1833. By the 1860s, improved, compact models by Sir David Brewster and Oliver Wendell Holmes had made the machine a mass-market home entertainment system. The London Stereoscopic Company claimed a stock of 100,000 machines, and their advertising slogan 'No Home Without a Stereoscope' made a familiar play upon fears of parental inadequacy. The magic lantern, known since the seventeenth century, enjoyed a concurrent vogue. The first practical handbook on the domestic operation of such devices was published in Britain in 1866, and celebrated 'the increased use of the Magic Lantern, as a means of beguiling the long evenings of winter'.[1] For those parents of more modest means, the Zoetrope – invented in 1834 by William George Horner – was a cheap substitute. It may not have offered the spectacular dissolving views of the destruction of Pompeii provided by the more expensive models of magic lantern, but its revolving drum conjured something more genuinely magical: a series of images printed on a strip of paper, which strobed into vigorous life. Lions leaping over the backs of galloping horses, couples swirling about a dance floor, red devils jumping through hoops, an infinite number of monkeys exchanging stovepipe hats in a continuous loop. The Zoetrope brought the movies to England. The Victorians gazed into the machine, thrilled with the knowledge that, thanks to these new visual technologies, it was no longer possible for them to believe their eyes. One of their many innovations in this field, the cinematograph, remains quite popular today.

There were social and economic factors determining the increasingly elaborate, technological and systematised nature of having fun. The Factory Act (1847) prescribed statutory holidays, giving precise delineation to the boundary between work and leisure time. Crudely speaking, work patterns shifted from those following the rhythms established by families and communities to those timetabled by managements keen to optimise the productivity of their workforces. At the same time, traditional leisure pursuits were being undermined by a new body of public order legislation which still maps the limits of acceptable behaviour on our streets. The 1834 Poor Law Act meant that travelling balladeers and entertainers could be arrested for vagrancy; the 1835 Highways Act allowed street entertainments and sports to be reclassified as nuisances; the 1835 Cruelty to Animals Act outlawed cock-fighting and dog-fighting – but preserved aristocratic blood sports. There was a switch from locally-generated activities and community-based entertainments to increasingly officialised ones: national cricket and football leagues, public swimming baths, dance clubs, museums, exhibitions, arcade games, ticket-only entertainment events – the repertoire of public recreations to which we still adhere. Visual spectacles took on a new primacy. Like us, the Victorians loved staring at things with their mouths open.

The historian Thomas Richards traces this quest for stimulation to the theatre in the first full decade of the Victorian era. 'The spectacle of the early Victorian stage conditioned their audiences always to expect more ... Indeed, one reason Prince Albert's idea for a Great Exhibition was so well received is that by the late 1840s, the escalation of spectacle had gotten so out of hand that it was evident nothing short of a massive collective effort could possibly come close to satisfying the well-nigh universal public craving for monster displays of special effects.'[2] Some of the Crystal Palace exhibits might now seem rather peculiar – a brace of stuffed ermine nailed into position at a taxidermal tea-party, a precursor of the fax machine, gigantic butter sculptures, a roll of paper 1.5 miles long – but these attractions were viewed by a daily average of 43,000 visitors (easily double the figure for its modern equivalent, the Millennium Dome) and helped to inaugurate the first great boom in British consumerism. When Mr Sleary, the lisping circus ringmaster of Dickens's *Hard Times*, reflected that 'people mutht be amuthed', he was acknowledging that the frantic mass consumption of novelty was one of the defining qualities of the nineteenth-century experience. Always more, always bigger, always increasingly exciting, extravagant, pleasurable; entertainments which dispensed thrills that were powerful enough to overwhelm the senses. And it was in the Crystal Palace that the Victorian public submitted to the most overpowering spectacle of their age – but they had to wait until 1861, when Joseph Paxton's flatpack glass cathedral to global capitalism had been dismantled, removed from its first home in Hyde Park and reassembled in a semi-rural suburb of south-east London.

In the early years of the 1860s, a term began to appear in journalistic writing that described a new type of cultural product, one which embodied the mid-Victorian predilection for spectacular thrills: sensation. By the end of the decade, the public had experienced sensation trials, novels, paragraphs, dramas, contortionists, diplomacy, and – in a burlesque version of *The Hunchback of Notre Dame* – a sensation goat. The word had been in use since the last quarter of the eighteenth century to describe a violent or excited feeling produced within an individual or community. (The OED's first recorded use of this sense is found in Lord John Malmesbury's diary for 1779. Malmesbury, the celebrated diplomat, wrote of 'a great sensation in the foreign courts'.) Its use as an attributive noun, however, does not seem to have occurred until the 1860s, when a plethora of examples appeared in print for the first time. In 1861, the *Illustrated London News* observed the prevalence of the ' "sensation" paragraphs' of modern crime reporting. The epithet was being applied to fiction by 1861, when a reviewer in the *Spectator* referred to Francis Browne's *The Castleford Case* (1861) as 'a new variety of sensation novel'. Wilkie Collins and Mary Elizabeth Braddon – who favoured plots involving bigamy, murder, poisoning, insanity and theft – were regarded as the chief exponents of the form. In 1864, a critic in the *Edinburgh Review* commented that 'two or three years ago … nobody would have known what was meant by a sensation novel', and claimed that the term had evolved from the status of 'jocular use' to one of a 'regular commercial name'. It was attached to 'drama' and 'scene' in print by 1860 – William Makepeace Thackeray noting in 1861 that 'at the theatres they have a new name for their melodramatic pieces, and call them "Sensation Dramas" '. In his column in the *Cornhill*, Thackeray considered an infamous murder in Northumberland Street, arguing that the incident was a greater sensation drama than the most celebrated of the genre, Dion Boucicault's *The Colleen Bawn* (1860).[3]

In terms of plot, characters and dialogue, the sensation drama was not significantly different from the melodramatic pieces that Boucicault and other writers had been producing since the 1840s. Indeed, many were versions of older material, rewritten and repackaged to include extra novelty elements. The reason for the astonishing success and popularity of plays such as *The Colleen Bawn* and *The Octoroon* (1859) lay in their overwhelming emphasis on arresting stage mechanics, their aggressive progress towards what became known as the 'sensation scene' – the Victorian equivalent of today's 'helicopter moment'. These works, and those of Boucicault's imitators, constructed a dramatic plot around a series of thrilling stage effects which relied on elaborate theatrical technology and acrobatic performances from the actors. Boucicault first realised that audiences appreciated touches of arresting realism in 1841, when he decided to abandon the traditional painted drapes and dress the set of his farce *London Assurance* with real windows, mirrors and chandeliers – and elicited a spontaneous round of applause simply by raising the curtain. By the 1850s, his techniques had achieved extraordinary levels of complexity. *The Poor of New York* (1857) – the title of which Boucicault altered to fit wherever his company happened to be playing – amazed audiences with its forced-perspective gaslit street and its burning building licked by real flames. *The Colleen Bawn* used gauze waves flapped by twenty stage hands to create the illusion of a cave filled with lapping water. *The Octoroon* reconstructed a burning riverboat and a thrillingly lifelike Southern plantation, and used a camera to catch its villain. *Pauvrette* (1858) boasted an onstage avalanche and the collapse of a rope bridge over a crevasse. *The Flying Scud* (1866) simulated Derby Day with cardboard horses, and concluded by leading the genuine article on to the stage for the finale. (In the Théâtre des Variétés in Paris, they went one better and engaged real horses to gallop and pant away on a concealed treadmill.)[4]

It was, however, the final act of *The Colleen Bawn* – which witnessed the near-drowning of the heroine and her dramatic rescue from an underground river – that delivered the most profound sensation. Henry Morley, the theatre critic of *The Times*, reflected that by September 1860 ' "Have you seen the *Colleen Bawn*?" ' became one of the questions which everybody asked and which nobody cared to answer in the negative.' 'He Who Pays' of *Punch* protested, 'Of course I went to the *Colleen Bawn*. I couldn't help myself. Everyone was bothering me about it.' The magazine published a cartoon satirising its modishness with the leisured classes, in which a young woman affirms her familiarity with the piece in a tone that speaks volumes about the rapidity with which some Victorians moved from one novelty to the next:

> *Horrid Girl (with extreme velocity)*: 'SEEN "THE COLLEEN BAWN"! DEAR, DEAR! YES, OF COURSE. SAW IT LAST OCTOBER! AND I'VE BEEN TO THE CRYSTAL PALACE, AND I'VE READ THE GORILLA BOOK!'[5]

Queen Victoria went to see the production twice during its initial run. (She also paid dozens of visits to the Crystal Palace, but it is not known whether she was enough like the Horrid Girl to have read Paul Belloni Du Chaillu's *Explorations and Adventures in Equatorial Africa* [1861], the first published account of gorillas in the wild.) Full of admiration for Boucicault's work, she wrote to the Princess Royal to say that 'People are wild about it – and the scene when the poor Colleen is thrown into the water and all but drowned is wonderfully done.'[6] So intense was the response of its audience that the play generated a plethora of cross-media spin-offs, some produced with Boucicault's co-operation, others maintaining a more piratical relationship with their source. In December 1861, it would have been possible to see the morning performance of the equestrian version of the show at Astley's Amphitheatre, travel to the Gallery of Illustration on Regent Street to hear Mr John Orlando Parry 'Relate, Musically, the Vicissitudes of "The Colleen Bawn"', catch the original at the New Adelphi, cross the Thames for a late performance of the Surrey Theatre's burlesque version – *The Cooleen, Drawn (from a novel source), or The Great Sensation Diving Belle* – and round off the evening by dancing to *The Colleen Bawn Galop*, *The Colleen Bawn Polka Mazurka* and *The Octoroon Valses*. Six months later, those not entirely satiated could roll up at Covent Garden for *The Lily of Killarney*, the grand opera rewrite, crafted in collaboration with John Oxenford and Julius Benedict.

Sensation was a physical effect upon the body – a book, play or event which made the heart beat faster, the pupils dilate, the eyes follow the performer or the plot with hysterical urgency – but it also implied a wide and swift circulation throughout culture. Even as it engendered a somatic response in its audiences, the work of Dion Boucicault, Mary Elizabeth Braddon and Wilkie Collins was crackling through Victorian culture like an electric shock.

There was one name, however, that was more perfectly synonymous with the Victorians' craving for sensation: Blondin. Born Jean François Gravelet in the Normandy town of Hesdin, in 1824, Blondin was unquestionably the nineteenth century's greatest icon of spectacular entertainment. His acrobatic performances at Niagara Falls in 1859 were reported all over the globe; his displays at the Crystal Palace two years later made him one of the most celebrated personalities in England. The secret of his success was simple. He risked a sudden and messy death for a paying public who found themselves mesmerised, appalled, transported to a state of irresistible agony, by his feats of skill and nerve. Watching his act must have been a furiously difficult pleasure – accounts of audience members fainting half-way through were routine – but hundreds of thousands of spectators found it impossible to tear their eyes away from him. There will never be another Blondin. Even if what he did was still legal, it is doubtful whether any living person would be capable of repeating his stunts.

Stand on the midway point of the Rainbow Bridge, the great metal arch which connects Ontario, Canada, with Buffalo, USA, and you begin to appreciate the extraordinary nature of Blondin's talent. One hundred and fifty feet below, the copper-blue rapids of the Niagara river surge northwards. At this height, you can see little constellations of white gulls dotted on the surface. The fisherman casting their lines from the rocks on the Canadian side are impossibly tiny. Up ahead, the twin monsters of the Horseshoe and the American Falls appear as two white walls of thunder and spray. Even from this vantage point – a chunky arm of steel and concrete, two thick lines of traffic wide – the view is enough to make you feel sick and dizzy, to grip the rail more tightly. The courage required to walk across this chasm on a length of rope two inches thick can scarcely be imagined. But to make the trip blindfolded? Or pushing a wheel-barrow? Or riding a bicycle? Or carrying a man on your back? No wonder many Britons suspected that reports of Blondin's activities were some sort of hoax, 'an idle phantom floating in the imaginative brain of the New York penny-a-liners'.[7]

Today, perhaps, he might as well have been a hack's fiction. Many inhabitants of Niagara Falls have never heard of Blondin. When I visited the scene of his triumphs, my questions about him drew blank looks or, at best, vague noises about a waxwork that was once suspended from a wire stretched across Clifton Hill, a mile of neon-lit tourist attractions and fast-food joints which slopes from the railroad line to Queen Victoria Park. This, it seems, was the property of Louis Tussaud's English Wax Museum, an institution which once housed a whole reliquary of Blondin artefacts. According to a file of clippings in the public library on the Ontario side, Blondin's bicycle and his wheelbarrow – always referred to in the publicity by the baffling phrase 'Irishman's buggy' – were rediscovered in the late 1950s by the acrobat's grandson, F. J. Blondin, in an antique shop in Ship Alley, Stepney, in the parish of St George's-in-the-East, London. The owner of the shop, Jack Miller, recalled that his father had bought these items of memorabilia at auction, after Blondin's death – since which time they had only gathered dust in the cellar. In January 1960, the *Niagara Falls Gazette* carried a photograph of Miller astride the bicycle, trundling over the pavement in front of his shop, and, a few months later, celebrated the vehicle's Canadian homecoming by positioning the bandleader Rudy Vallee on the saddle, with the Falls crashing down in the background. The waxworks, however, was closed by its owners shortly after Labour Day, 2000. When I visited, it was a hole in the ground opposite a branch of Wendy's Old-Fashioned Hamburgers. A Rainforest Café is slated to take its place.

Giving up these objects for lost, I wandered up the street to visit the Ripley's Believe It or Not Museum. In one of the final cases in the exhibition, after the parade of shrunken heads and torture instruments and patent vampire-killing kits, I came upon the missing Blondin waxwork, lit atmospherically, with a little group of objects ranged around him: the bicycle and the wheelbarrow, scuffed and battered; his white tunic, with a blue collar-piece studded with gold stars; a length of the rope upon which he walked across the torrent, risking utter annihilation.

Blondin's father, André Gravelet, spent most of his life as a professional soldier. A loyal Bonapartist and member of the Grande Armée, he fought for Napoleon at Austerlitz and Wagram, survived the retreat from Moscow and the battle of Waterloo. However, the occupation that he gave to the Hesdin registrar on the birth of his son signals his attachment to a career that predated his military experience. The word in the book is *funambule* – tightrope walker. The father was clearly eager that the son should follow in his footsteps: Jean François Gravelet was enrolled at the École de Gymnase at Lyons at the age of five, and had begun to perform professionally – as 'The Little Wonder' – before his sixth birthday. By the time he was ten, and orphaned, the boy was already able to support himself with money from rope-walking performances. Soon he was performing under the name 'Blondin', his father's old professional *nom-de-plume*. After eighteen years of travelling Europe with a number of circus outfits, he was signed by Gabriel Ravel, head of a popular troupe of acrobats, for a tour of the United States under a two-year contract with the celebrated showman Phineas Taylor Barnum. The company sailed for New York in 1851, and the trip changed Blondin's life for ever. He was able to use his physical skills in the daring rescue of a man who fell overboard during the rough sea crossing, but more significantly for his career, he was able to demonstrate that his talent was of a higher order than that of the group by which he was employed. In the finale of the show, Antoine Ravel made a daring leap over a group of twenty men holding fixed bayonets. At least, that's how it appeared to the audience. Actually, Ravel choreographed the armed extras so that he only had to clear two of the bayonets to avoid being kebabbed. During a rehearsal, Blondin casually threw a backward somersault over the whole company, and in that cocky act, secured himself a lifetime at the top of the bill.

At Niagara Falls on the last day of June 1859, Blondin performed the stunt that would cause his name to be telegraphed across the globe. There had been acres of pre-publicity for the event, most of it bad. His original intention had been to string his tightrope through the cloud of mist surrounding the Falls, but the landowner on the American side, a General Porter, would not give his consent. Porter's father had allowed the first Niagara Daredevil, Sam Patch, to erect a diving platform on his property, and the family had no wish to involve itself in another elaborate suicide. Reluctantly, Blondin secured his 1,300-foot cable further downstream, as Niagara townspeople placed bets on his likely demise, and local newspapers announced that they would be sending their obituarists to cover the event. As it transpired, these journalists had to file a rather different kind of copy for the following day's papers. In the process, they discovered that Blondin was as much an exponent of the media circus as of the more traditional kind.

'Precisely at a quarter to five o'clock,' wrote the *Toronto Globe*, 'he seized his balancing pole, weighing about fifty pounds, and although the sun was shining in his eyes, he tripped forward, and almost before the people were aware he had cleared the American land, nothing intervened between him and his destruction but a two-inch rope.' The Niagara *Daily Gazette* correspondent continued: 'He walked out about 100 feet, sat down, laid down lengthwise with his back on the rope, stood on one foot, and then pursued his journey stopping about every 150 feet and going through similar acts until he reached the center of the cable.' The reporter from the Troy *Daily Times* observed: 'Here, standing on the rope, with as much indifference as if it were a solid platform, he deliberately lowered a small line to the little steamboat, the *Maid of the Mist*, that had steamed out to that point; to the line was attached a bottle of wine by the captain of the boat, and the bottle of wine being drawn up by the adventurer, he opened it, and, making a comprehensive bow to both crowds on the sides of the river, he drank the health of all present.' Then, according to the *Gazette*, 'From this point he made no stops and reached the opposite side of the river in two minutes. He was greeted on the Canada side with cheer upon cheer, waving of handkerchiefs, and other demonstrations of joy.' The *Globe* recorded his words to the crowd: 'My dear friends – I have got across safe. I hope you will remember me, for I am poor. I cannot tell you any more in English, but it is all right.' Half an hour later, he was tripping back to the American side. 'Thus', reflected the *Times*, 'was successfully accomplished one of the most daring and useless feats that even this fast age has ever witnessed.'[8]

Blondin, however, was only warming up. The following Monday, he crossed the gorge with his body enveloped in a sack. The week after, he walked over backwards and returned pushing a wheelbarrow. On 3 August, he varied the programme by hanging by his hands, hanging by his feet, hanging by one ankle, and by lying across the rope and moving his arms and legs in a swimming motion. Over the course of the next two seasons, he made the crossing shackled by the ankles (in the manner of a 'Siberian slave'); in the dark, amid squalls of fireworks; on stilts; blindfolded; in a monkey suit; playing a drum; and dressed as a French chef, carrying a portable stove on his back. 'It must not be imagined that the stove he bore upon his back was a full-sized cast iron "Victor", neither must it be fancied a miniature affair,' noted the reporter from the Buffalo *Morning Express*. 'It was a goodly sized, properly fashioned cooking stove, made of Russia sheet iron, and boasting a smoke pipe about two feet in height.' It needed to be. 'Arrived at the centre of the rope,' continued the *Express*, 'Blondin secured his pole and proceeded with great nonchalance to make preparations for "camping". Unslinging his stove he placed it upon the rope before him, sat down, and with some pitchey, combustible material built his fire, exciting it with the bellows, and soon raising a smoke which proved the genuineness of the preparations for cooking. When a proper degree of heat had been attained he produced his eggs, broke them into his dish and threw the shells into the river. The omelette was prepared with all the skill of a *chef de cuisine*, and when it was complete he lowered it to the deck of the *Maid of the Mist*, where, we doubt not, it was divided into the smallest possible shares, and eagerly treasured by the passengers.'[9] (Actually, the passengers scuffed and scrabbled like pigeons after peanuts, not knowing whether to down the eggy scraps or simply gaze upon them in admiration.)

On 17 August 1859, Blondin attempted what was probably the most dangerous stunt of his career. His manager, Harry Colcord – taller and several pounds heavier than his client – had little notice that he was to be the human cargo for this crossing, and it was only when the pair were a hundred or so feet out over the rope that the Frenchman informed his passenger that he would be forced to dismount several times in order for the acrobat to take a rest. Colcord described his voyage in an interview conducted in the late 1890s: 'Just think of the situation – getting down off a man's back, feeling with your foot for a taut, vibrating rope, then standing on the same, while it swung to and fro, some hundreds of feet in [the air], and holding on to a man in front of you clad in slippery tights, when the least false move or loss of presence of mind of either might plunge you both into eternity, and then climbing again upon his back – and this had to be repeated seven times!'[10]

After this performance, Blondin struggled to find other routines that would increase the audience's palpitating appreciation. With Colcord's involvement, the Niagara citizens' sense of pleasurable anxiety had peaked, and making the crossing in a series of funny costumes was no substitute for the possibility of two people ending their lives pureed by the Rapids. So elaborate and peculiar did these permutations become, that they eventually became the object of journalistic satire. This mock challenge was issued to Blondin in September 1859 by a reporter from the McKean *Citizen*:

A single telegraph wire shall be extended from the American to the Canada shore, without a single guy, directly over the cataract at Niagara Falls. The 'local' [correspondent] of this paper wearing cowhide boots and dressed in the costume of a female Dutch cook, will proceed to the middle of the wire, with a common clay pipe as a balancing pole, driving before him a hog and a cow, and carrying on his back a cooking-stove, a coop of chickens, a bed and bedding, a keg of lager beer, a barber's chair, and various cooking utensils. He will then unload himself and immediately go to bed. After a snooze of fifteen minutes he will rise, dress himself, take a glass of beer, milk the cow, kill the hog and dress it, cook fresh pork for breakfast, after which he will eat a wolf's meal. He will then throw one hundred and thirty summersaults [*sic*], sucking an egg while in the air at each evolution, alighting the last time on the tip of the cow's horn, and while in this position will take the chicken-coop, and after having taken the chickens out one at a time and wrung their necks consecutively, will balance the cooking-stove on his right-hand thumb, balance the bedstead on his left thumb at the same time finishing the beer and making a Dutch speech to the admiring crowds on either shore ... The foreman of this paper will then come out on the wire, blindfolded and shackled, walking on his hands. There will then be a representation of Heenan and

Morrissey's prize-fight, in which the 'local' and foreman will exchange sundry knocks and kicks and black eyes. The whole to conclude with a representation of some of the loving scenes in Romeo and Juliet.[11]

As this sarcasm indicates, Blondin's nonchalance on the high wire was being replicated in his audiences. Crowds dwindled from 25,000 to 6,000. A second season at Niagara demonstrated that he had a better head for heights than for business, and, after making several unwise financial decisions, Blondin soon found himself out of pocket. Moreover, he had competition – rivals began to undermine the uniqueness of his act. Some, like 'Professor Shields', a self-proclaimed professional jumper who leapt from Blondin's rope and was smashed to pieces on the rocks below, were not a serious threat. However, in 1860 a ropewalker calling himself Signor Guillermo Antonio Farini (but christened plain William L. Hunt in Lockport, New York) secured permission to cross the ravine in a location much nearer to the American Falls, and made the trip in the person of 'Biddy O'Flaherty, the Irish Washerwoman', with a patent Empire Washing Machine strapped to his back. Blondin sensed that he should terminate his association with Niagara as soon as the 1860 season was concluded. Harry Colcord had come to the same decision, and used the money he had made from his association with Blondin to set up his own portrait studio in Chicago. The acrobat gave one final exhibition, a Royal Command performance in the presence of Edward, Prince of Wales, sold up his house and considered his next move. Gabriel Ravel, his former employer, offered him a European tour. But another manager, Henry Coleman, had a better proposition: a thousand-pound-a-gig contract for twelve performances in London. The venue was to be the Crystal Palace, now relocated from Hyde Park to the developing suburb of Sydenham.

As well as the financial reward, there was another advantage to a season in London. It might finally convince the British public that such a person as Blondin actually existed. As late as January 1860, *The Times* felt it necessary to report that a resident of Bedfordshire had recently received 'a reliable letter from Canada' which insisted upon the veracity of his achievements. The Niagara media had sniggered over initial English scepticism about these events, but the London press was correct to be cautious. As Captain Marryat had discovered, American hoaxes had a habit of making it across the Atlantic undetected. In September 1855, reports of the discovery of a monster in Silver Lake, New York, slipped through the net – despite the creature being nothing more than an inflatable prop constructed by a canny hotelier named Artemus B. Walker. ('He is 59 feet 8 inches in length,' gushed the paper, 'and has a most disgusting look.') More embarrassingly, a *Times* correspondent named John Arrowsmith filed an account of a train ride he had taken through the state of Georgia, in which he claimed the hot-headed Southern passengers fought regular duels to the death. His report was published in October 1856, and received with satisfaction by British readers as a prime example of the lawlessness they associated with American culture. The president of the railroad company lodged a complaint, but it took the intervention of the British consul in Georgia for *The Times* to concede that Arrowsmith had been duped. More pertinent to the Blondin report, *The Times* had in April 1859 been fooled into printing a phoney story about a daring stilt-walk across the Niagara Rapids by a Signor Gaspa Morelli – a story which shared many details with the news from Niagara later that same year. 'Once or twice he seemed to lose his balance, and a sickening shudder ran through each one of the beholders. Recovering himself, he still kept on – still receded, until, to our straining eyes, he could scarcely be distinguished from the foaming waters.'[12]

When Blondin docked in Southampton on May Day 1861, he was entering a culture both hungry for sensational novelty – books, stunts, plays, outrageous press stories – and deeply absorbed in a debate about the rights and wrongs of that predilection: a debate which rumbles on to this day. Like *The Colleen Bawn* , Blondin immediately became the focus of a merchandising industry. The Bush Hotel at Niagara Falls had put Blondin Soup on its menu before the acrobat had made his first crossing, and by the end of the 1860 season, that establishment's regular newspaper advertisement featured him crossing the gorge with a barrel of their branded oysters secured to his back. Stallholders in Niagara had also been known to flog Blondin Lemonade for a dollar a glass. British commercialism, however, was much more energetic and comprehensive. In 1862, George Linnaeus Banks, Blondin's first biographer, described the appearance of 'coats, hats, cigars, neckties, perfumes, Manchester prints, Limerick lace, Paisley shawls, articles of confectionery, stationery and millinery' all bearing the acrobat's name. Stringed puppets and figurines also went on sale, their makers eager to cash in on the intense enthusiasm for the little Frenchman. 'If you entered the boudoir of a lady of fashion,' noted Banks, 'the first question was sure to be "Shall you see Blondin?"' The proverbial gossip of the tea-tables, and the small-talk of the smoke rooms, gave place to similar enquiry.' Banks, the husband of Isabella Varley, who would later achieve recognition as the author of a popular novel, *The Manchester Man* (1874), had some misgivings about Blondin's sensational associations:

> People did not, then, go to see Blondin for the mere sake of a 'sensation', as if such things were confined to the Crystal Palace; as if we had not 'sensation' preachers and writers, 'sensation' theatres and concert rooms, 'sensation' steamers and exhibitions, – all well enough in their respective spheres, yet all liable, like Blondin, to this one objection, that they are out of the common way. Whatever is extravagant or eccentric is a 'sensation'. It may be a comet, a curricle, or a crinoline; it may be a Japanese ambassador, or a Blondin.[13]

As this semantic wriggling suggests, the status of such events was being hotly contested. Whereas Blondin's official publicity emphasised the leisurely, elegant nature of his performances – the 'wonderful' manner in which he went calmly through the motions of ordinary domestic activities (sitting, lounging, cooking, eating) while suspended on a hundred-foot highrope – audiences and journalists were more ready to engage with their deadly possibilities. From his grandstand seat at the Crystal Palace, Dickens observed that 'Half London is here, eager for a dreadful accident,' and admitted that he was 'rather ashamed of [him]self' that 'thousands of us, have come to see an acrobat perform a feat of imminent danger' for the sake of 'an exquisite and new sensation'. A skit in *Punch* took Samuel Johnson and James Boswell to the show, in which the amanuensis is upbraided for his pretension: ' "You are a humbug," said my venerated friend. "You care nothing for the fellow's courage or skill, but you have a vulgar desire to go with the multitude, and perhaps a concealed hope that you may be present at a painful catastrophe." ' The most honest appraisal of the performance, however, was printed in the pages of a small regional newspaper: 'Not to "put too fine a point on it",' wrote the reporter from the *Oxford Chronicle*, 'we like to be *in at the death*, it is a confession humiliating to our higher humanity, but it is the truth, and that is the reason why thousands, who would be ashamed to confess the instinctive motive even to themselves, rush to the Crystal

Palace to see M. Blondin. They say a sensation is worth any money, and certainly the sensation of the spectator is indescribable during this remarkable performance.'[14]

'Sensational' is still a pejorative term today. It bespeaks the inaccurate, the hyperbolic, the uncritical, the irrational. 'We live in an age of sensation, rather than reason,' mourned the *Daily Telegraph* in 1993; 'Welcome to London's Age of Sensation,' exclaimed a 1999 edition of the *London Evening Standard* – just as, 130-odd years earlier, a music hall singer in a penny dreadful opined:

> In Eighteen Hundred and Sixty-five.
>   Of progress much we boast,
> Yet we may find, if we but mind,
>   Abuses by the host.
> And now-a-day's 'tis very sad,
>   Our noble boys to find
> So morbid and sensation mad,
>   To truth and nature blind.[15]

On a rope strung across the heights of Paxton's glasshouse, Blondin gave the Victorians their sensations until they were sick with pleasure. He repeated the business with the sack, the omelettes, the ape suit and the shackles, and added a new routine in a suit of armour. He pushed a lion across the rope in a wheelbarrow, as fireworks exploded overhead. He even crossed the rope carrying his five-year-old daughter Adèle on his shoulders, until the Lord Chamberlain prohibited a repeat of this feat.

Blondin's arrival in Britain gave rise to many rival acts, employed by competing entertainment managements to capitalise upon the vogue for highwire walking which he had created. Selina Young, a ropewalker since her childhood, established herself as 'The Female Blondin' with a daring highrope walk across the Thames from Battersea Bridge to the Cremorne Gardens. Twenty thousand spectators watched her make the three-quarter-of-a-mile trip – which, for some undisclosed reason, she completed in Albanian national costume. The event produced an outpouring of bad journalism ('She stood forth in the light of the declining sun, her gold-broidered dress and white pole gleaming refulgently') and secured her a season at the Alhambra Theatre on Leicester Square. Here in the domed auditorium, on a site where an

Odeon cinema now stands, she gave nightly shows on a wire 150 feet in the air – the same height at which Blondin had crossed the Niagara Gorge – and shared the bill with two other notables: M. Dupont the great Sensation Contortionist, who 'Although 5 feet 9 inches high ... issues from a hamper 26 inches long by 10 inches deep', and 'the marvellous, the thrilling, the wondrous Leotard'. Leotard's speciality was the trapeze, and his talent made him the original subject of George Leybourne's 1861 song about the 'Daring Young Man'. His appearances were advertised alongside those of Blondin on the front page of numerous editions of *The Times*, and he even received billing over the ropewalker on the cover of a pop-up book for children. He was one of the decade's most significant figures, still well known enough in 1869 for *Fun* magazine to parody Disraeli's problems with the Irish Church Bill as a slip for a daring PM on a flying trapeze. His name, of course, survives in the term still used for a one-piece suit worn by gymnasts.[16]

Such was the air of seriousness surrounding the acts of these performers that during December 1861 the Polytechnic Institution in London held a series of lectures on the technicalities of highwire walking and trapeze artistry, augmented by diagrams and models of Blondin and Leotard. Towards the end of his career, Blondin's gentle respectability only seems to have increased. In 1887, 'his marvellous performance on the High-Rope' was advertised as part of a 'garden party, fête and temperance demonstration' in the grounds of Carron House, Birmingham. There was strong pressure to maintain a dignified atmosphere at such displays after the bad publicity generated by a spate of accidents involving Blondin imitators in the early 1860s. In July 1861, a tightrope prepared for Selina Young at the Alhambra snapped before she stepped out upon it. 'If the law cannot hinder such dangerous exhibitions,' muttered *The Times*, 'it should, at any rate, be able to control the conditions under which they are produced.' Young narrowly avoided death for a second time in December 1861, when, at a display at St George's Hall, Stonehouse, the rope broke beneath her. 'For our own part,' admitted one reporter, 'we confess that a sickening sensation at the sight prevented us from seeing.' A third fall, at Highbury Barn in August 1862, left her permanently disabled and declared a 'poor victim of the morbid taste of the present day' by Felix Joseph, the co-ordinator of the appeal fund in her name. She had stumbled and plummeted to the ground when a firework display during the performance produced some unexpectedly loud bangs. The incident nearly claimed the life of Leotard, who slipped from his trapeze when a member of the audience shouted news of Young's injury around the Alhambra auditorium. A few weeks later, Young hobbled out of hospital, and with the money raised by Joseph, established her own public house on the south bank of the Thames.[17]

Not all her colleagues were so fortunate. In January 1863, the wife of a tightrope walker named Farini (no relation to Blondin's Niagara rival) was killed when she fell from her husband's shoulders; the circus family continued working on the wire until the end of the century. The most significant public outcry came after the death of Mme Genieve, who also styled herself as the 'Female Blondin'. Genieve's rope broke as she reproduced Blondin's blindfolded crossing at a fête in Aston Park, Birmingham. The accident was made more dreadful by the revelation that the acrobat had been eight months pregnant. Queen Victoria sent a letter to the mayor of Birmingham, condemning such displays. *Punch* commented upon the tragedy with a grim cartoon of Genieve making blithe progress through the sky, as a skull-faced representation of Death swoops down towards her, knife in hand, to slice through the supporting cable. (Below, a phoney advertisement announces that 'An Infant Ten Months Old Will Be Discharged From A Catapult [Registered] Above A Regiment of Soldiers with Fixed Bayonets.)[18] A third 'Female Blondin' suffered a near-fatal accident in Bolton on 4 May 1869, and another at Dundee in July 1870. In the latter case, a press report reflected that the accident would be 'a spice of sensation that would be considered a windfall by those who are ever on the outlook for the wonderful, and that would have done a heart good not altogether jaded by sensation'.[19] Blondin suffered no such fate. He died in his bed at the age of seventy-three, in happy retirement with his chickens and his dogs and a new wife, Katherine James, a nurse some forty years his junior. In over sixty-five years of stunts, he had only suffered one fall – and in that case he had grabbed a guy rope and swung back on to the main cable. Perhaps he was such a sensation that even Death stood gripping the balcony rail at the Crystal Palace, unable to avert his gaze from the figure high above, pushing something ludicrously dangerous – a lion-filled wheelbarrow, say – across the glassy abyss.

So successful were the Crystal Palace seasons that Blondin decided to make England his home, performing around the country until he had reached his seventieth year, buying property in Ealing and christening it 'Niagara House'. The place is long gone now, but if you stand outside the

Plough Inn near Northfields underground station, you face the site upon which it once stood. If you had walked past here in 1895, when back strain finally forced the septuagenarian acrobat to live out his life at ground level, you may well have been lucky enough to see him turn a somersault – he remained obliging to his admirers to the end. This suburban idyll did not last long, however: two years later, the 'Hero of Niagara' died from the effects of diabetes – cancer took Katherine in 1901. They were buried together in Kensal Green Cemetery, with Blondin's first wife Charlotte to keep them company, in a grave just a few plots away from Wilkie Collins. The weather has turned the marble cameos on the grave the same coppery hue as the waters of the Niagara River.

A couple of years after Blondin's remains were sunk in the west London soil, Jarvis Blume, a judge from Chicago, attended a dinner party at which the guest of honour, an elderly portrait and landscape artist, astounded the company with an anecdote of his youth. The artist's name was Harry M. Colcord. Jarvis decided to record and publish the story, as *Across Niagara on Man's Back* (c. 1899). 'Although nearly forty years have elapsed since the thing occurred,' Colcord recalled, 'the thought of it haunts me as closely as if it happened yesterday. Often in my dreams it all comes back to me. Again I sway from side to side and lay myself like a dead weight as Blondin goes onward step by step, the rope swaying and his balancing pole oscillating; again I see the shores black with people and look down upon the swirling river, far below, until we seem to be rushing up stream; again I descend from his back and stand on the taut, vibrating rope, so near to Death, that his skeleton head seems grinning at my shoulder. . . and I jump in nervous terror and spring coldly perspiring from my couch. It is like living the horror over and over again.'[20]

A few blocks past the offices of the Niagara Falls *Gazette*, on the New York side of the gorge, lies the concrete monster of the Niagara Falls Public Library. Here, in a neat plastic wallet, is an autographed cabinet photograph of Colcord. He is wrapped up in a big fur coat, a huge moustache thriving under his nose. Appropriately enough, the shot was taken in the Crystal Palace Photographic Studio, a faux-Paxtonian shop on North Clark Street, Chicago, run by a pair of Hungarian brothers. There are other pictures in the file. One of Colcord, perched on Blondin's back, making the perilous journey; one depicting the acrobat with the pole lodged at his feet, its owner standing casually, arms folded, gazing over the water like a complacent tourist. The image which caught my attention most powerfully, however, was a photograph to which a colourist had added tones and hues, studding the blue collar-piece of his costume with cheerful yellow stars, and touching up the blurred parts of the exposure. The doctoring process has enacted a strange transformation upon the subject. He has a flat, white brow, dark socket-like eyes, high cheekbones, a thin crease of a mouth. Inadvertently, Blondin's face has become a ghostly skull.

3 Blondin crossing the Niagara rapids (stereoscopic card, c.1859)

CHAPTER TWO

The First Picture Show

Although the kinetoscope and cinématograph are regarded as
distinctively modern contrivances, it should be borne in mind
that they represent only the recent development of a principle
that has long been familiar to students of optical science.

J. Miller Barr, 'Animated Pictures', *Popular Science Monthly* (1897)

In the backroom of a trattoria tucked behind the Grand Hotel in Cannes,
I witnessed a little piece of movie history. A wave of heat from the pizza
oven made the little gaggle of hacks assembled for the show drip quietly
into their Diet Cokes. A screen was unfurled in front of us. A man with a
standard personal computer, linked to a smart little video projector with a
domed top, fussed away at his desktop, clicked on an icon and attempted
to play a length of digital video footage – which seized up immediately. As
he had the volume turned up to maximum, the machine's clanging error
message made everybody in the room wince. Another attempt – and
success. On the white screen, in the juddering entryphone aesthetic of
Internet moving pictures c. 2000, there appeared an interior scene, set in
a car driving through an American city. The scene had been shot from
the back of the vehicle, and a middle-aged couple were seated in the
front, occasionally turning round to address an unseen passenger. This
mystery figure, in whose position the audience was placed, was then
plonked into a wheelchair and trundled down the corridors of a geriatric
home, before being lifted on to the bed. Whereupon the audience
glimpsed this central character in a dressing table mirror. A television set.

The revolutionary quality of this short work seemed utterly elusive
until it was screened for a second time. The plot, dialogue and
performances were all as before; we were clearly watching the same
footage once again. But the images on the screen were very different. The
panning camera followed a new set of subjects: instead of concentrating
on the old couple sitting in the car, we were staring out of the window at
the traffic. As the patient was pushed down the corridor, the gaze of the
camera fell upon a different combination of passers-by. It was then that it

[21]

4 A still from George Albert Smith's *Kiss in the Tunnel*, 1899 (courtesy the BFI)

became clear that the picture was being manipulated by the man at the keyboard, who was pushing his mouse from side to side, determining the compass of the frame; as if he was the character in the wheelchair, moving his eyes to whatever caught his attention. We were watching the world's first 360° digital movie. And were we impressed? Well, a bit. But not that much. Nobody ran screaming from the restaurant, unable to cope with the concept.

The movie camera occupies a special and symbolic place in contemporary culture. The moment of its invention is often used to mark the end of the past and the beginning of the present – a *cordon sanitaire* between the last moments of History and the first moments of Modernity. For the most part, our evidence of the nineteenth century is a collage of sepia photographs, which suggest a frock-coated, straight-backed sort of place – still, stiff, stern, silent, with a horizon painted on a studio canvas and a potted aspidistra somewhere in the background. With the birth of cinema, it is as if the world sprang suddenly into animation. From the moment the Lumière Brothers dimmed the lights and set their cinematograph whirring, life became a luminous progress of flappers and tanks and Charlie Chaplin. Film ushered in a new and distinctly modern visual culture that was more kinetic and plausible than anything which had existed before. Its ability to reorder, repace and rewind time helped to transform the structure of the novel. Although Virginia Woolf claimed to have found her visit to the movies in January 1915 'very boring', it is doubtful whether she would have found the freedom to cut and splice the chronology of her narratives without the example of the cinematograph.[1]

A celluloid curtain has descended between the cine-literate moderns and pre-cinematic Victorians – impressionable types who ran yelping from the room thinking that the train on the screen was going to grind them up under its wheels. And this moment of panic has become the key element in considerations of nineteenth-century attitudes to the arrival of the new medium – the quality that marks the movies out as a harbinger of the future. In most accounts of the Lumières' first screening to a paying audience on 28 December 1895, it is claimed that *L'Arrivée d'un train à la Ciotat*, the brothers' study of an express train coming to a halt at a railway station in Lyons, caused an outbreak of terror. *Brewer's Cinema* (1995) claims that it 'sent frightened viewers fleeing to the exit'; David Thomson's *Biographical Dictionary of Film* (1994) that 'some spectators ran fearfully away'. George Méliès, however, one of the audience of thirty-three at that first picture show in the Salon Indien – under the Grand Café on the boulevard des Capucines, Paris – does not mention any such exodus in his account of the evening, only the wild enthusiasm of the spectators: 'At this sight, we sat with our mouths open, thunderstruck, speechless with amazement. At the end of the screening, all was madness, and everyone wanted to know how they might obtain the same results.' Engagement, excitement, pleasure, yes, but there is nothing to suggest that these nineteenth-century punters at the first picture show believed that the objects represented on the screen were about to be imported physically into the room. The British film-maker Robert Paul suggested that only the doziest hicks might respond to the cinematograph in such a way. His *The Countryman's First Sight of the Animated Pictures* (1901), in which a smocked bumpkin reacts with terror to film footage of an approaching train, amused precisely because this was not the way in which most early cinemagoers would have reacted to such a spectacle. The medium produced thrills, not blind fear: a reviewer of Paul's *Rough Sea at Ramsgate* (1896) enthused that 'the spray is thrown up in so realistic a fashion as to make the people in the stalls actually start involuntarily, lest they should be drenched!' Many audience members responded to Wolfgang Petersen's *The Perfect Storm* (2000) in the same way.[2]

As the Victorians were already accustomed to viewing a plethora of mechanical processes for producing moving images, it would be wrong to think of the cinematograph as one of those technologies that was without precedent, which immediately brought about some radical shift in perspective. For those who had been cranking away at the penny gaffs, viewing What the Butler Saw peepshows like *Five Girls in One Bed* and *Why Marie Put Out the Light*, the cinematograph would have appeared as a diverting combination of the magic lantern and the Mutoscope, a clever refinement of technology which had been in development for their entire lifetime. Indeed, when the Lumière devices began touring the world in 1896, many thought them inferior to Eadweard Muybridge's zoopraxiscope, a projecting variation on the zoetrope which threw up looped images of excellent quality. The *Popular Science Monthly*, however, was confident that one day the technology would 'ultimately be rendered as free from defects as are ordinary stereopticon views'.[3] *The Times* introduced its readers to the machine as 'a contrivance belonging to the same family as Edison's kinetoscope and the old "Wheel of Life", but in a rather higher stage of development. The spectator no longer gazes through a narrow aperture at the changing picture, but has it presented to him full size on a large screen. The principle, however, is much the same, consisting simply of passing rapidly before the eyes a series of pictures representing the successive stages of the action.'[4]

This coolness is not affectation. As the previous chapter has suggested, nineteenth-century audiences had long been wowing their senses with a progress of visual entertainments – the phenakistoscope, the eidophusikon, the kineorama, the kalorama. For most Victorians, moving pictures captured on reels of celluloid film and projected on to a screen were just another sideshow trick. A brilliant one, mind you. One that caught on with amazing speed. Twelve months after that first thirty-minute show in the basement of the Grand Café, the medium had reached almost every corner of the globe, and the Lumières had acquired a chain of picture houses in Europe and America. And, as the public became hungry for more of these entertainments, exhibitors demanded new subjects to fill their schedules. Trains pulling out of stations and children playing with cats were not going to amuse for very long. Plots and scenarios and dramatic situations, however, would keep the audience coming back each week. Novels and the theatre could supply them ready-made. Between 1896 and 1915, there were fifty-six adaptations of Dickens, twenty-one based on the novels of Edward Bulwer-Lytton (including six versions of

The Last Days of Pompeii) and seventeen different takes on Washington Irving's *Rip van Winkle*. The catalogue reads like some eccentric rewrite of the 'Twelve Days of Christmas': six *Jane Eyre*s, nine *Dr Jekyll and Mr Hyde*s, ten *Uncle Tom's Cabin*s, ten *East Lynne*s. By the time cinematograph shows had become part of the British recreational diet, most of these novels' authors were dead. But for some Victorian novelists – Thomas Hardy, Marie Corelli, Arthur Conan Doyle and Mary Elizabeth Braddon for four – the moving pictures were to become a smart way of making cash and selling books. At the close of the nineteenth century, the uneasy relationship that exists today between writers and movie-makers had already been established.

London, 1863. This year, Mary Elizabeth Braddon is one of Britain's most celebrated novelists. Celebrated by her readers, that is. Churchmen and snooty reviewers can't bear her: the Archbishop of York tut-tuts about the 'deep feeling of overwrought interest' her fiction is exciting; *Punch* jokes that her books seem intended for 'Harrowing the Mind, making the Flesh Creep, Causing the Hair to Stand on end, Giving Shocks to the Nervous System ... and generally Unfitting the Public for the Prosaic Avocations of Life'.[5] Margaret Oliphant, a prolific – but less financially successful – novelist is pursuing a vendetta against her in the press, dropping hints about her rival's pseudonymous work for cheap, bloodthirsty periodicals. In short, Mary Braddon is a hot property. Her first best-seller, *Lady Audley's Secret* – in which the heroine pushes her husband down a well to prevent her exposure as a bigamist – is being discussed in the drawing rooms and back kitchens of England. *Aurora Floyd* (1863) is now just as successful, largely because of a set-piece scene in which the heroine attacks her stableman with a horsewhip. 'An event in literature,' according to one critic. 'Depraved,' according to another.

Cut to Mary Elizabeth Braddon in 1913. Fifty years on, she is a grand old lady living in a grand new house in Richmond, and still turning out a novel every year. Her husband and publisher John Maxwell – whom she married in 1874, after fourteen years of cohabitation and childbearing – is long dead. Tonight, she is giving her handful of servants the night off. She is taking them to the pictures. Top of the bill is a movie from the Thanhouser company of America: a sensational two-reeler with a violent, passionate subject perfectly suited to twentieth-century appetites. The title is *Aurora Floyd*. Mary Braddon, who has passed from a world of bonnets and broughams to one of biplanes and poison gas, gazes up at the flickering screen as her heroine raises her horsewhip and sinks it into the flesh of her enemy.

The film is lost, although a few scattered details are preserved in reviews and advertisements. Thanhouser placed announcements in the trade press, assuring exhibitors that the popularity of the novel would ensure them large audiences. Just as some conservative critics disapproved of the novel's subject matter when it was reviewed in the 1860s, the *New York Dramatic Mirror* took issue with the representation of bigamy. 'For a girl to find herself married to two men is not the most pleasant sensation in the world – either for her or the spectator. There is an unsavory flavor vitiating almost every turn in the theme. That there is a situation, we admit, but what an unwholesome one it is.'[6] Louis Reeves Harrison in *Moving Picture World* praised the performance of the lead Florence LaBadie, one of Thanhouser's signature stars, an actor as 'fast' as a Braddon heroine: she loved riding, swimming and speedboats, and died at the age of twenty-nine from post-operative blood poisoning, following an injury sustained when the brakes of her automobile failed as she drove down a steep hill near Ossining, New York.

LaBadie was not the first screen Aurora Floyd. A month prior to the Thanhouser adaptation's release in America, the Selig company produced a one-reel version of the novel, under the title *Her Bitter Lesson* (1912). And Braddon's screen history went back further than this. In 1906, the British firm Walturdaw, founded by a pair of travelling showmen named J. D. Walker and Edward George Turner and a schoolteacher named G. H. Dawson, shot the first documented adaptation of *Lady Audley's Secret*, a year before they developed a synchronised sound-and-image system which would have allowed them to add dialogue to the picture. The Chicago-based Kalem film company made the first American version of the novel in the summer of 1908, probably with their in-house star and screenwriter Gene Gauntier in the title role. In May 1912, the popular matinee idol King Baggot starred in the Independent Motion Picture Company's rendering of the same book, in a critically acclaimed version directed by Otis Turner.

None of these films exists today. Indeed, much of our earliest cinematic heritage has been comprehensively lost. Films were burned or discarded, studios demolished, lives and careers forgotten. In 1897, for example, the Mutoscope and Biograph Company built a film studio behind the Tivoli Theatre on the Strand. The stage had removable glass walls, could be rocked for movement effects and rotated towards the sun to maximise available light. Not a trace of it remains. But there are vestiges of this past here and there, if you know where to look. Stand in front of the Las Vegas amusement arcade on Wardour Street, Soho, and look up to the top of the building, and you will see the name 'Urbanora House' inscribed on the brickwork, signalling its identity as the first of many film production companies to set up home on this thoroughfare. Travel by train from Brighton to Hove and look through the window facing the south side of the track, and you will see a one-storey shed that was once a powerhouse of British movie-making. On it, you can still read the faded word KINEMACOLOR, the name of the colour process invented by George Albert Smith, director, producer, theme-park owner, mind-reader, author of *Experiments in Thought Transference* (1888) and, in the words of Michael Balcon, 'the father of the British Film Industry.' Walk from the station to St Ann's Well Park, and – if you've chosen to arrive on a hot summer day – you may be able to see the outline of the foundations of the studio building in which he shot his films, etched into the turf of the rose garden.

Smith began his career as a stage hypnotist. The telepathy act he performed with his partner Douglas Blackburn was phoney, but so good that the leading lights of the Society for Psychical Research were all convinced of its authenticity, and persuaded him to become a member. In March 1896, Smith saw a programme of the Lumière Brothers' films in Leicester Square. Enthused, he turned over a section of land in his popular theme park in Hove to film production. Before 1899, he had either mastered or invented most of the techniques of editing, close-ups, point-of-view shots and continuity upon which cinema still relies, and had helped to make Hove the centre of film production in Britain, an English Hollywood. At 120 Western Road, in what is now a kitchen showroom, Esmé Collings shot the first British blue movie, *Woman Undressing* (1897); on the other side of the street, at number fifty-five, the magic lanternist James Williamson established a rival film works, from which he produced hundreds of one-minute subjects, including *The Big Swallow* (1901), a trick movie in which Williamson appears as a man whose mouth appears to gulp down both camera and cameraman. A small exhibition in the Hove Museum commemorates these pioneers, but beyond a circle of specialists and enthusiasts, their names are not well known. Even if he had been a genuine psychic, Smith could not have foreseen how comprehensively their legacy would be forgotten.

In Bath, there are other ghosts to be hunted. If you wander down the

Corridor, a nineteenth-century shopping arcade with an elaborate glass canopy, entering from the side nearest the Abbey and stopping just before you get to number nine, a shop selling garish gifts and stationery, you'll see on your left the entrance to a narrow side-corridor. Walk down here to the end, and a gated staircase marks the entrance to what was once the photographic workshop of William Friese Greene. At the top of these stairs, Friese Greene and a local instrument maker named John Arthur Roebuck Rudge began a series of experiments that resulted in the production of a primitive motion picture camera. Rudge had already invented a device named the Bio-phantoscope which could display seven slides in quick succession, giving a zoetrope-like illusion of movement. Friese Greene believed that whoever could bring this process to perfection would achieve something of global importance. His biographer Ray Allister claimed that he expressed it to his wife in these terms: 'It is movement which compels attention ... Movement is life. Moving pictures will satisfy something deep inside all the people in the world.'[7] By this time, his machine – a foot-square box with a crank handle, very recognisably a motion picture camera – was ready for action. Early one Sunday morning in January 1889, he took the device down to Hyde Park and shot twenty feet of film, recording the progress of the traffic. Whether the process truly worked is doubtful, but Friese Greene claimed that in the small hours of Monday morning, on a screen in his studio in Piccadilly, he watched the first ever British movie: 'hansoms, buses and those tottering pedestrians passing along the pavement' flickered into life on the screen before him.[8] The development of the machine, however, had bankrupted him. He was forced to sell the patent for £500, and its new owners allowed it to lapse. By March 1895, the Lumière Brothers had patented their cinematograph, and Friese Greene's obscurity was sealed. This failure, however, didn't halt his research into other areas. Between 1889 and 1921 he took out more than seventy patents for other inventions including inkless printing, gyroscopic airships, a version of the fax machine and a colour film process. But he remained a disappointed man. In 1921, he dropped dead at a meeting of movie professionals in the Connaught Rooms, after giving a speech on the decline of the British film industry. Those present sent a floral wreath in the shape of a movie projector, with the words 'The End' spelt out in flowers. Friese Greene's Bath studio was empty when I visisted – but the premises were, until quite recently, a photographer's shop, so something of its past must be retained up there, behind the locked doors and inside the dusty cupboards.

For a more obvious sign of the past, take the train to Bushey in Hertfordshire. Stand on the corner of Melbourne Road and the High Street, and you'll see a large, barn-like building with a raised glass roof: the remains of the oldest daylight film studio in Europe. For most of the nineteenth century, Bushey was an insanitary little village with a poor population. These days, it is a mouldering adjunct of Watford with pretensions to gentility – a shabby bolt-hole for middle-class pensioners who can't afford Eastbourne. But while Sir Hubert von Herkomer made the place his home, it was a significant centre of British film production. Herkomer was a Bavarian-born painter who founded an art school in Bushey in the 1880s, and can also claim the distinction of having concocted, in a series of narrative paintings, all the Welsh druidic paraphernalia we now associate with that country's Celtic prehistory. Herkomer made it all up in his studio, and his clients, rich Welsh industrialists, propagated his work at *ersatz* jamborees like the National Eisteddfod.

A tragic accident in 1885 overshadowed the rest of Herkomer's life. His second wife Lulu Griffiths – whom he employed to nurse his first wife through her last illness – died after saving a small child from being run over by a carriage on the streets of York. She was several months pregnant, and the shock of the incident killed her baby. A traumatic still birth brought on a fatal bout of rheumatic fever. Herkomer was profoundly affected, and became obsessed with her memory. So obsessed, in fact, that three years later he married her sister, Margaret Griffiths, in a secret ceremony on the Continent (as this was technically incest until 1907), and built a gigantic Bavarian-Gothic mansion in Bushey, which he named after his dead spouse. Lululaund [*sic*] stood until 1938, when the local council – inspired, no doubt, by a surge of patriotic racism – declined to accept the house as a gift from its new owner, a developer from Watford, and allowed him to dynamite the Teutonic aberration at the heart of the town. For some reason, they left a corner wall standing, which has now been absorbed into an office complex named after its first occupant. There are other fragments of the past still to be seen. The Bushey Museum holds a few remnants of Lululaund's specially designed mock-medieval furniture, some of the most extravagant light-switch covers you'll ever see and a case of souvenirs relating to Herkomer's film company.

The company produced only a handful of movies, all of which have now been lost – despite a recent world-wide effort to locate any stray cans of Herkomer's work. But contemporary reviews and a lavish photo-graphic souvenir book of his costume drama *The Old Wood Carver* (1913) suggest that he applied the compositional techniques of his painting to the new art form, constructing shots with a painterly eye in an age when many directors just pointed the camera at whoever was running the fastest. He was widely credited with pushing cinema to new artistic heights, with bringing down the pace of the action to a more realistic speed and with taking more care than most with his period costumes and settings. He was especially enthusiastic about employing literary sources, and seems to have been the first British film-maker to commission a script directly from a novelist, in this case Marie Corelli.

Oscar Wilde is said to have dismissed Marie Corelli's novels from his Reading Gaol cell: 'Now don't think I've anything against her *moral* character,' he sneered, 'but from the way she writes *she ought to be here*.'[9] His wasn't an eccentric opinion. Journalists sent her poison-pen letters. The grammarian Henry Watson Fowler (of *Fowler's Usage*) cited her work as a perfect example of 'horrible' writing. And yet, despite this hostility, Corelli was once Britain's best-selling novelist, who counted Queen Victoria, Gladstone and the Prince of Wales among her admirers. In the 1890s, her brand of quasi-religious romance – in which, typically, beautiful heroines with names like Zara and Thelma conduct telepathic love affairs with Ancient Egyptians and scoot through outer space by means of 'spiritual electric force' – touched the imagination of an English public besotted with phenomena such as table-rapping, hypnotism and hunting for fairies at the bottom of the garden. Her fiction seduced with the kind of power wielded today by Angel Theology, New Age Christianity and all those rigourless pseudo-religions that appeal to daytime TV audiences, and her public image was mediated through a fog of glamour and mystery. In middle age, she doctored her publicity photographs to make herself appear to be a teenager. She owned her own gondola and imported a Venetian gondolier to ferry her up and down the river Avon. She was so self-conscious about her lack of height that she greeted her house guests while standing on a raised dais hidden under the long train of her dress. She was also fascinated by electrical technology, and the presence in her books of descriptions of wireless methods of communication may explain why, in the early days of the BBC, her name was used as Cockney rhyming slang for 'telly'.

By the time she received her commission from Herkomer, Corelli and the cinema were already intimate. In 1911, she had successfully suppressed the Dreadnought Film Company's unauthorised adaptation of her novel *The Sorrows of Satan* (1895), offering to give them permission on the condition that she be permitted to write the scenario. A British version, filmed by the Samuelson company in 1917 – starring every Somme bombardier's favourite pin-up, Gladys Cooper – seems to have received her seal of approval. Negotiations with the I. B. Davidson company produced authorised adaptations of her novels *Thelma* (1887) and *Holy Orders* (1908), although a further option on *Vendetta* (1886) was not exploited. What happened to Herkomer's collaboration with Corelli is uncertain. It was announced as being in pre-production in August 1914, but there is no evidence that the script was ever filmed, or even completed.

The work that did emerge from the Bushey studio, however, is evidence of Herkomer's importance in the history of British film. He planned to devote himself to the 'revivifying of the great works of literature' through the cinematic medium, and invented that tradition of glossy literary adaptation which we now associate with Merchant-Ivory. He also had profound, prophetic notions about the directions in which this new medium might grow. 'If one might indulge in a little chimerical phantasy,' he wrote in 1912, 'I should say the day will come when the one film will take up form, colour, and sound, and reproduce all these simultaneously; that a cinematograph will be laid on in every home, as your gas or electricity is now laid on; that the world's stories will be brought to you in a pictorial and dramatic form, such as one has not yet dreamed of.'[10]

Hubert von Herkomer first came to prominence in the 1870s, as an illustrator for the *Graphic* magazine. He provided accompanying engravings for Thomas Hardy's *Tess of the d'Urbervilles* (1891), and also painted the novelist's portrait. So when Herkomer decided to build a motion picture studio on his estate in 1912, it was to Hardy that he turned for inspiration. The following year, he approached the author for the rights to film *Far from the Madding Crowd* (1874), and even agreed to write a synopsis of the story for the press release. Hardy accepted Herkomer's cheque for £150, and informed his agent, 'Also please accept the Herkomer offer for 'The Mayor of Casterbridge' for £25 – which can do no harm even if not carried out.' Four weeks later, Herkomer's son Siegfried was down at Hardy's Dorset home having lunch and 'getting local colour' for the proposed movie. But by this time, Hardy was already an old hand at the game. His relationship with the cinema began in

February 1911, when he received a letter from a Mr Louis Vincent of the Warwick Trading Company, requesting his permission to make a film of *Tess of the d'Urbervilles*. Hardy immediately saw the company's offer as a potential commercial opportunity. 'I do not feel quite sure whether this is the wild idea of an irresponsible enthusiast or whether he is authorized by any of the Cinematograph Companies to make the application,' he wrote to his agent Frederick Macmillan. 'I should imagine that an exhibition of successive scenes from *Tess* (which is, I suppose, what is meant) could do no harm to the book, & might possibly advertise it among a new class.'[11]

Although Hardy seemed unaware of it, the Warwick Trading Company was the most respected movie outfit in England. It had been established in 1897 by the pioneering film producer Charles Urban, in offices at 4–5 Warwick Court, close by Chancery Lane, and had made a name for itself shooting newsreels of the Boer War. Indeed, Joseph Rosenthal's footage of the British flag rising over Pretoria was one of the most celebrated images of the conflict. The company built George Albert Smith's studio in Hove, and made a distribution deal with him for a series of fiction films. Its output included a string of comedies starring two tramp characters from the pages of *Chips* comic, Weary Willie and Tired Tim, and a burst of activity in 1910 produced *Two Beautiful Cracksmen*, *The Life of a Hired Bicycle* and *A Marriage of Convenience*.

The company offered Hardy ten per cent of the gross turnover for the right to film *Tess of the d'Urbervilles*. Macmillan vetted the company and its managing director, and accepted the deal on Hardy's behalf. 'It will be interesting to see what comes of this,' mused the novelist. 'I confess that my chief thought was whether it would affect book-sales.' As Warwick failed to act upon their purchase of these rights, Hardy didn't get the opportunity to find out. Herkomer's script for *Far from the Madding Crowd* seems also to have become stuck in Development Hell. A deal struck with Adolf Zukor's New York-based Famous Players company, however, did bring the novelist more than just a fat fee. At 11.30 in the morning on 21 October 1913, Hardy settled down in his seat at Pyke's Cinematograph Theatre, Cambridge Circus, London, to watch the press screening of Famous Players' *Tess of the d'Urbervilles*. Shot in the New England countryside, the film starred the formidable Broadway actress Minnie Madden Fiske, who – as Zukor pointed out, rather bitchily, in his autobiography *The Public is Never Wrong* (1954) – was nearly fifty when she went before the camera as Hardy's teenage dairymaid. 'It was a curious production,' noted Hardy, two days after the show, '& I was interested in it as a scientific toy; but I can say nothing as to its relation to, or rendering of, the story.' He was, however, quite happy to keep cashing the royalty cheques.[12]

From this point on, the movies became an important source of income for Hardy. In June 1915, he signed a contract with the Turner Film Company for the rights to film *Far from the Madding Crowd*. The firm was owned by Florence Turner, formerly known as the 'Vitagraph Girl', a star who had migrated from Hollywood to Walton-on-Thames to set up her own film studio. The five-reel movie was widely screened, but critics considered the lack of Wessex locations to be a fatal flaw. More deals followed: in 1915, Hardy discussed a film adaptation of *The Dynasts* with the playwright Albert Drinkwater, but advised him to go for the more sensational *Desperate Remedies* (1871) instead. In 1919, the Metro Pictures Corporation – one of the companies that later merged to form MGM – stumped up $50,000 for an option on *Tess*. In 1922 there were negotiations with the International Story Company for the rights to several of the novels, and, in 1925, with a Mr Golding Bright for a possible movie version of the marketably-titled short story 'The Romantic Adventures of a Milkmaid' (1883).

A 1921 adaptation of *The Mayor of Casterbridge* (1886) was the first to achieve a degree of authenticity by going on location in Dorset. Sidney Morgan of the Progress Film Company made the trip to Hardy's home, Max Gate, to discuss how to turn the novel into a cinematographic narrative, and solicited Hardy's help in getting the correct dialect words on to the title cards. Hardy read the script, made notes and corrections, and told no one, presumably, of his habit of inventing dialect terms. At dawn on the morning of 2 July, the author met Morgan and his crew, and together they made their way to Maiden Castle, where Hardy watched the company performing in the early light. 'This morning we have had an odd experience,' he wrote, later that day. 'The film-makers are here doing scenes for "The Mayor of C." & they asked us to come & see the process. The result is that I have been talking to the Mayor, Mrs Henchard, Eliz. Jane, & the rest, in the Flesh. The company arrived here at 1 o'clock this morning, & leave again tomorrow. It is a strange business to be engaged in.'[13]

He also spent time with the crew of the Metro Pictures version of *Tess* when they came to shoot in Dorchester during October 1922. Hardy did not bother seeing the film – which starred the silent heroine Blanche Sweet – but his wife Florence Dugdale did make it to a screening. An amateur actor, visiting Max Gate in the 1920s, remembers discussing the film with her. It was 'a quaint mixture of Victorian England brought up to date. Tess was depicted as meeting Alec d'Urberville in a night club and there was [*sic*] other odd arrangements. I had seen this film and was horrified – it was so utterly ludicrous and out-of-keeping with the play or book. But Mrs Hardy laughed heartily, though her husband gave me one of his rare shy smiles and shook his head when I asked if he had seen the film. Mrs Hardy enjoyed the occasional visit to the cinema and always referred to it as the KIN-E-MA.'[14]

Hardy, like many who came after him, attempted vainly to assert some form of artistic control over movie adaptations of his work. After poring over his agreement with Famous Players, he wrote to his agent, 'Does this confer a power to tamper with the story to any extent, such as might injure its circulation? e.g. changing it from a tragedy to a story in which everything ends happily.' The Progress contract also stipulated that the company should make 'No alteration or adaptation being such as to burlesque or otherwise misrepresent the general character of the novel.' These were precautions, he argued, 'in order to run no risk of injuring the sale of the book,' and he was sensible to try to make them. With most films running under half an hour, there was little time to explore the complexity of a 600-page source text. As one commentator noted in 1914, 'Every studio employs its quota of photo-play writers – men and women who condense or "bovrilise" some well-known story.'[15]

There was a fine line, however, between bovrilisation, bowdlerisation and burlesque. From around 1896, a whole genre of one-reel quickies sprang up that deliberately set out to parody popular literary hits. There was nothing, for instance, that George du Maurier's family could do to stop his novel *Trilby* (1895) being travestied by the Crystal Film Company as *Miss Trillie's Big Feet* (1915). The director, Charles Hutchison, reconstructed du Maurier's high Romantic tale of music and mesmerism as a loopy plot about chiropody, and subjected other nineteenth-century classics to the same process as *The Corsican Brothers Up to Date* and *Rip Van Winkle Badly Ripped* (both 1915). Miss Trillie was a clear pun on du Maurier's heroine, but the name also made reference to Tillie, a character played by Marie Dressler in a popular series of Mack Sennett comedies of the same year. (In 1897, Dressler had appeared at Proctor's Pleasure Palace, New York, in a 'musical and farcical spasm' entitled *Tess of the Vaudevilles*, second on the bill to a 'Scientific Marvel, the Lumière Cinematograph'.) The magazine *Film Fun* gave away the salient details of

Hutchison's one-reeler: 'Trillie is affected by a pair of tremendous feet. At the party which Little Billee gives her, she stubs her toe and runs a splinter into it. No coaxing will draw the splinter out, until Svengali, the weird hypnotist, charms it out. As a consequence he obtains power over Trillie, and many complications arise.' A dish of ice cream soon snaps the heroine out of her trance. 'All ends less unhappily than the original,' *Film Fun* informed its readers, somewhat unnecessarily.[16]

Even if they sometimes signalled it with parody, early film-makers were heavily dependent on Victorian authors for plots and situations that were workable, familiar and therefore marketable to their audiences. It's the same process that allows literary adaptations to figure so highly in our own film culture: a tried and tested plot is always considered a better bet than something original. And did the new medium allow film-makers to take these old stories into new areas of explicitness? To depict Tess's seduction by, or murder of, Alec d'Urberville, for example? Not quite. Cinema was subject to more moral strictures in the twentieth century than the novel ever had to endure in the nineteenth. Much has been made of Charles Mudie's attempts to use the economic power of his lending library system to censor improper subjects from the novels on his bookshelves, but these were amateur tactics compared with the restrictions that were soon placed upon film-makers.

In 1912, to discourage local councils from taking independent action against films of which they disapproved, the Cinematograph Exhibitors Association established the British Board of Film Censors, which centralised the process of vetting cinematic entertainments for public consumption. It drew up a list of twenty-two grounds on which films might be cut or suppressed – including 'medical operations', 'indecorous dancing', 'cruelty to women', 'executions', 'native customs in foreign lands abhorrent to British ideas' and 'vulgarity and impropriety in conduct and dress'. In 1913, C. L. Graham, who ran the Cinema Playwriting School from an unglamorous address in west London, warned his students to 'avoid scenes of murder, suicide, robbery, kidnapping, harrowing deathbeds, horrible accidents, persons being tortured, scenes attending an execution, violent fights showing strangling, shooting or stabbing, staggering drunkards, depraved or wayward women, rioting strikers, funerals, and all scenes of a depressing or unpleasant tone.'[17] According to a 1916 issue of *Picturegoer*, a filmed version of Henrietta Palmer's Victorian farce *Bootle's Baby* was banned in Philadelphia 'because a man got a letter from his wife, and burned it.

[35]

Tearing it would have been permissible, said the censors, but burning showed a contempt of the married relation.'[18] When the play was running in London in 1889, the decadent poet and little girl enthusiast Ernest Dowson kept up a dubious correspondence with its seven-year-old star Minnie Terry, and collected an album of souvenirs of her. The notion of censoring the destruction of a married couple's correspondence would have seemed as comical to him as it does to us.

Advocates of film censorship, however, celebrated this new atmosphere of restraint. In an influential trade publication, the *Kinematography Yearbook, Program, Diary and Directory*, Edward Heron hailed 1913 as 'a year of new-found purity for the picture theatre'. Marking the British Board of Film Censors' first full year of operation, Heron reflected happily on the demise of 'that crop of really shocking films, which were literally spurted out on to the projection screen the month before Mr Redford took up the reins of office'.[19] George Alexander Redford, previously the Lord Chamberlain's Examiner of Plays – in which capacity he became George Bernard Shaw's arch-enemy – was the BBFC's first chairman. The stink that arose when representatives of the British cheese industry called for the suppression of Charles Urban and F. Martin-Duncan's microcinematographic film *Cheese Mites* (1903) – in which a diner examines a piece of Stilton with a magnifying glass, and discovers the ecosystem within – could now be made sweet by an official body.

During their writing careers, both Mary Braddon and Thomas Hardy suffered their fair share of moral condemnation. Hardy had occasional run-ins with editors over questions of sexual explicitness, and such conflicts eventually turned him from novel-writing altogether; Braddon circumvented the problem by writing for periodicals which she edited herself. But none of their books was ever locked away in a vault on grounds of obscenity, nor did representatives of the dairy industry try to ban *Tess of the d'Urbervilles* on the grounds that it suggested dairymaids were easy prey for seducers. With that in mind, it's harder to see the rise of filmed narrative as the vehicle of new freedoms, and consequently, it is harder to see the movie camera as the machine that marks the boundary between an ignorant, innocent, steam-driven Victorian world and the modern electric technocracy in which we still live.

This seems all the more clear at the current stage in the development of the motion picture, when the dominance of celluloid is being challenged by a huge number of new digital media. Roasting in that trattoria in Cannes, as unimpressive an environment as the Salon Indien – a venue which was so unsuccessful that the Lumières managed to rent it at a reduced rate – it seemed very clear that cinema was being returned to the circumstances of its birth. In the 1890s, audiences experienced the movies through a variety of different media: kinematographs, choreuto-scopes, biophantascopes. They did not much care about the niceties of the apparatus: they just watched the images and accepted the textural differences between the movies produced. This sensibility is returning. For half a century, cinema attempted to counter the threat of television by making an emphatic commitment to lushness, scale, saturation. Cinema-scope, 3-D, Smell-o-Vision, 'Emergo' (in which a twelve-foot plastic skeleton whizzed over the heads of the audience) and 'Percepto' (in which audiences were treated to a mild electric shock) were products of this anxiety, as were the fetishistically lush and decorative surfaces of the David Lean and Merchant-Ivory schools of cinema. Now digital techniques have enabled the cheapest TV soap operas to ape that cinematic gloss, the quality of the image is no longer an essential characteristic of the moviegoing experience. That audiences happily watched the low-tech, raw images of *The Blair Witch Project* (1999) without asking for their money back indicates that the definition of what makes a movie is becoming as wide as it was for the Victorians. Download a movie from the Internet, and you're staring into a digital Nickelodeon. What was the 360° movie about the TV set but the kind of trick film which George Méliès was making in the 1890s: a one-shot amusement built around a technical gag? If the next stage of the movies has more in common with pre-cinematic visual entertainments, then that grand narrative of the birth of cinema will have to be substantially rewritten.

The traditional view of motion picture history, I think, would have baffled Mary Elizabeth Braddon (born 1835) and Thomas Hardy (born 1840), nineteenth-century survivors who participated in a medium adopted by the twentieth century as its own. But they must have been quietly flattered by the attentions of the film-makers. You can imagine them sitting on the back row of the Cinematograph Theatre, eating their vanilla ice-cream with little wooden spoons; feeling pleased that the movies have decided to launch a new publicity campaign for the novels they wrote thirty, forty or fifty years before; watching their work on the screen before them, transfigured into light.

CHAPTER THREE

The Boer War, Brought to You by Bovril

I lay in the ambulance and sucked down some of his excellent
Bovril.
  Robert Baden-Powell, Bovril advertisement, 1900

Late in the evening of 29 May 1864, a number of Members of Parliament
and former Members of Parliament received an unexpected knock at the
door. There, on the front step of a series of grand Belgravian residences,
stood a boy from the London District Telegraph Company, proffering a
sealed envelope from his bag. 'Having only arrived from the country on
the previous day,' reflected one distinguished gentleman, who was just
about to depart for the theatre, 'I feared that a fire or some other casualty
had occurred subsequent to my departure.' He – and others like him –
ripped open the communication at once. But the message did not relate a
narrative of death, disaster or financial loss. Instead of anxiety or grief, it
inspired bafflement, indignation and a couple of red-faced letters to *The
Times*. It read: 'Messrs Gabriel, dentists, Harley-street, Cavendish-
square. Until October Messrs. Gabriel's professional attendance at 27,
Harley-street, will be 10 till 5.' 'I have never had any dealings with Messrs
Gabriel', grumbled another recipient, 'and beg to know by what right do
they disturb me by a telegram which is simply the medium of
advertisement?'[1] Would the anger of this anonymous Parliamentarian
have been assuaged, I wonder, if he had realised that he had just opened
the first junk e-mail in history?

Messrs Gabriel were not registered dentists. They had received no
diploma from the Royal College of Surgeons. Indeed, their energetic
work in the field of self-publicity – much more revolutionary than
anything they accomplished during their incursions into Londoners'
mouths – precluded them from taking the examination. They may have
been happy that way. The Gabriels produced their own compendious
range of branded products – including patent 'self-adhesive indestructible mineral teeth and gums', Antiseptic Toothpaste and Royal Tooth
Powder ('prepared from a Recipe as used by Her Majesty ... whitens and

[38]

preserves the teeth and imparts a luscious fragrance to the breath') – from which they derived enough profit to open practices on Harley Street and Ludgate Hill. They were so proud of their commercial strategies that they even sponsored the frontispiece of one of the first manuals of advertising technique published in this country, and were doubtless delighted that their electric-mail campaign soon became a standard commercial practice. That same year, the National Provincial Clothing Depot in Bristol sent out telegrams to a swathe of potential customers, advising them that a thirty-nine-shilling Clifton suit – which they had not ordered – was ready for collection at the firm's premises. 'The servant, of course,' complained a recipient, 'takes it in and brings it into the parlour, and I being out my wife opens it at once, fancying all sorts of things, and, I need not say, is infinitely disgusted at the "sell".'[2] Although such incidents are recorded mainly through irritated outbursts in the press, firms obviously considered this method an effective way of creating new clients. During 1875, one enterprising furniture company simultaneously telegraphed messages to five thousand households at eight o'clock on the same evening – to advise them that twenty thousand bedsteads were always available for purchase at their depot.

Most of the techniques used today for circulating commercial information were founded during the nineteenth century. The Victorians inaugurated merchandising tie-ins with books and plays: loyal Wilkie Collins fans, for instance, could spray themselves with *Woman in White* perfume, wrap up in *Woman in White* cloaks and bonnets, and dance to various *Woman in White* waltzes and quadrilles; admirers of George du Maurier were sold *Trilby* sausages, *Trilby* ice-cream moulds, *Trilby* lapel pins and – rather more durably – *Trilby* hats. Product placement was pioneered by French novels in which the characters would call into real shops and celebrate the qualities of their products. (This technique was imitated by British penny serials – in which illustrations of street scenes might feature billboard advertisements for other publications.) Proprietary brand-names were first constructed by Victorian firms (the handle for Bovril beef extract, for instance, was formed from the Latin *bovus* and the word 'vrilya', a life-giving substance consumed by the protagonists in Edward Bulwer-Lytton's 1871 science fiction novel *The Coming Race*). Eco-marketing was invented by Crosse and Blackwell on 2 July 1855, when they took out an advertisement in the *Morning Chronicle* to announce that their company was removing artificial colouring from its popular range of preserved foods. The cinema advert had arrived by 1897

SAVED BY "BEECHAM'S PILLS."

5 Beechams blur the line between advertising and news: 'On Monday a serious accident happened off Southsea beach ... their chance of life seemed a bad one, as none of them appeared able to swim. *Beecham's Pills*, however, tacked and picked them up.' (*The Graphic*, 1899)

– one surviving example from this date features a chorus line of reeling Scotsmen whooping up the virtues of Dewar's Whisky.

Contact ads also flourished from the mid-century. In 1850, the *London Journal* began publishing personal announcements for the unattached, and by the 1870s, dedicated publications such as *Matrimonial News* went on sale, with ads displaying the same mixture of pretension, naïvety, pathos and weak humour familiar from the genre's modern forms: 'Adam Bede would like to marry "Kate Aubrey"'; 'Laha, tired of the quiet and monotonous life of a country girl, wishes to become the wife of an actor, and go upon the stage. She is nineteen, pretty, more fair than dark, and rather brilliant-looking by candlelight'; 'Frank, tall, passable-looking, and very affectionate, aged twenty-four, wishes to correspond with a view to an early marriage with a lady proprietor of a good hotel and posting house'; 'G. F. H. . . . is four feet high, hump-backed, bandy-legged, with squinting eyes, arms as long as a kangaroo's hind-legs, flat-nosed, red-haired, and with a mouth as big as the devil's punch-bowl.'[3]

The contact ad was not the creation of a periodical publisher keen to turn loneliness into cash – it was the subscribers of the *London Journal* themselves who turned its correspondence column into a textual dating agency. 'We have no ambition to act the part of an amateur Hymen in concocting such marriages,' the newspaper declared in June 1850 – but its readers had determined otherwise.[4] Similarly, *The Times* did not encourage the fashion for encrypted advertisements that blossomed on its front pages during the early 1850s. This little boom was probably inspired by the practice of sending intimate telegrams in code to avoid embarrassment at the telegraph office – and was swiftly concluded when it became clear that cracking these secret messages was developing into a national hobby. By the end of the decade, no pair of clandestine lovers was foolish enough to entrust their innermost thoughts to such a leaky medium. Between 1853 and 1854, however, A and W.M. made several passionate exchanges, Dominoes plotted an extra-marital affair, two young persons with the smutty monikers of Willie and Fanny related their mutual desires and, on 2 February 1853, a nameless cryptographer made this asseveration to his beloved: 'CENERENTOLA. N bnxm yt ywd nk dtz hfs wjfi ymnx fsi fr rtxy fscntzx yt mjfw ymf esi bmjs dtz wjyzws, f imtb qtsldtz wjrfns, mjwj It bwnyf f kjb qnsjx jfwqnsl uqjfxj : N mfaj gjjs ajwd kfw kwtr mfund xnshy dtz bjsy fbfd.'[5] *Times* readers familiar with alphabet substitution codes did not have to work hard to establish that if f stood for a, g for b, h for c and so on, the message, once the mistakes were pruned out, resolved as: 'Cenerentola, I wish to try if you can read this, and am most anxious to hear the end, when you return, and how long you remain here. Do write a few lines, darling, please. I have been very far from happy since you went away.' On 11 February, another encrypted message appeared from Cenerentola's Prince Charming: 'Zsyq rd mjfwy nx xnhp mfaj ywnji yt kwfrj fs jcugfifynts kwt dtz gzy hfssty. Xnqjshj nx xfs jxy nk ymf ywzj hfzxj nx sty xzx jhyji; nk ny nx fgg xytwnjx bngg gj xnkyji yt ymj gtyytr. It dtz wjrjrgjw tzw htzxns'x knwxy uwtutxnyynts: ymnsp tk ny.'[6] The clandestine lovers must have been horrified when, four days later, a rendering of this message appeared in the same column, correcting the errors in transcription: '... until my heart is sick have I tried to frame an explanation for you, but cannot. Silence is safest, if the true cause is not suspected: if it is all stories will be sifted to the bottom. Do you remember our cousin's first proposition? Think of it. N pstb Dtz.' The last three encoded words were particularly ominous: 'I know You.'

The rumbling of the Cenerentolans did not dissuade others from attempting the same form of communication. It was a correspondence addressed to 'Flo', which began in the personal column of *The Times* later that same year, that brought the vogue for amatory encryption to an end. Flo's communicant, 'Indian Shawl', employed a more complex system, based on the random allocation of numbers to letters of the alphabet, but it was soon cracked by Sir Charles Wheatstone – inventor of the concertina, the stereoscope and the ticker-tape machine – who inserted his own parody of the Flo-Shawl correspondence on 6 January 1854. A single further message appeared, on the following day: 'FLO. - 8 9454 6454401 214 739844 30 6307284446. 84314 51 2274 12 0214 943426 '326352 08585,' 9. 2., 8177327853. 81770'. This translates as: 'Flo. - I fear, dearest, our cipher is discovered. Write at once to your friend, 'Indian Shawl', P.O., Buckingham, Bucks.'[7]

After this exposure, the Victorians seemed happy to compose more gently cryptic personal ads. The repertoire of announcements remains familiar: the pathetic ('The one-winged DOVE must die unless the CRANE returns to be a shield against her enemies'); the romantic ('THE lady who travelled from Bedford to London by Midland train on the night of the 4th inst., can now MEET the GENTLEMAN who shared the contents of his railway luncheon basket'); the conciliatory ('MARY ANN C.- Do return home. You labour under an illusion. What you wish to accuse me of does not exist. This I solemnly declare.'); and the indignant ('SHOULD this meet the eye of the lady who got into the 12.30 train at New Cross Station on Friday, May 15, with two boys, one of whom was evidently just recovering from an illness, she may be pleased to learn that three of the four young ladies who were in the carriage are very ill with the measles, and the health of the fourth is far from what her relations could desire').[8]

Private advertisers were usually keen to obscure their identities. Commercial advertisers worked towards the opposite ends, and many chose to bask in the reflected glory of the celebrity endorsement. Bovril enlisted the help of Baden-Powell and Rudyard Kipling to sell beef extract. A prominent grocer attempted to sign two well-known figures of scandal to promote his imported cheese: Arthur Orton, a butcher from Wagga Wagga who attempted to pass himself off as the heir to the vast fortune of the Tichborne family, declined to participate, but Viscount Hinton, a notorious aristocratic swindler, agreed to take the fee, and would have willingly marched through the streets of Glasgow at the head of a line of pigs, had the police not arrested him on firearms charges just before the gig. Georgina Weldon, a celebrated litigant, monkey-fancier and collector of musical orphans, was the face of Pears Soap in 1888. Sarah Grand, author of the phenomenal best-seller *The Heavenly Twins* (1893), lent her name to an 1890s campaign for Sanatogen vitamin tonic. Oscar Wilde fronted publicity for Madame Fontaine's Bosom Beautifier ('Just as sure as the sun will rise tomorrow, just so sure it will enlarge and beautify the bosom,' read the tagline).[9] By the time these personalities were boosting their income with such deals, music hall performers had been in on the game for several decades. The cross-dressing comedian Miss St George Hussey – 'The Female Irishman' – advised readers of the *Era* that 'Comfortable Lodging, Cleanliness, a nicely cooked Dinner; every attendance, Gas, Fire, and no grumbling' was available from Mrs Nicholl of Belfast, while Leglere's Acrobatic Troupe thumped the tub for her rival, Mrs Moran.[10] George Leybourne, the original *lion comique*, had contracts to plug companies and products in his stage act, and wrote songs which became the world's first advertising jingles. His famous number 'Champagne Charlie' (1868) is an extended sales pitch for a certain company of wine makers:

> Some epicures like Burgundy,
> Hock, Claret, and Mosell,
> But Moët's Vintage only
> Satisfies this Champagne swell;
> What matter if to bed I go
> Dull head and muddled thick,
> A bottle in the morning
> Sets me right then very quick.[11]

His arch-rival Alfred Peck Stephens, known as 'the Great Vance', was soon belting out 'Cliquot! Cliquot! That's the Wine for Me!'

The advertisements now carried on street-mounted video screens had a Victorian forebear in the 'exhibition of dissolving views' which illuminated a second-floor window on the north side of the Strand at the end of 1875. Aimed at commuters to and from Charing Cross Station, these magic lantern incarnations of posters familiar from street hoardings – notices for hatters, newspapers, restaurants and sewing machines – had the power to bring the traffic to a halt. They were quickly dwarfed by a rival enterprise. Each night in January 1876, a team of men would unroll an enormous curtain and suspend it from the side of a house adjoining the western entrance of Charing Cross; upon this curtain a series of slides would then be projected from a powerful lantern mounted on a kiosk by the station gates. This initiative by the Metropolitan and District Railway company threw up scenes of London's most popular tourist attractions – the Albert Memorial, the Serpentine, the shops of Regent Street – accompanied by notices of the nearest tube stop. Soon, Pears' Soap were commandeering other locations to cast moving magic lantern slides depicting a child being scrubbed clean by its mother, and music hall managements were using projectors to turn the safety curtain into a lucent advertisement space.

Another innovation was formulated in November 1859 by William Smith, acting manager of the New Adelphi, to publicise the theatre's production of Watts Phillips's three-act French Revolution drama *The Dead Heart*. One of the most popular plays of the decade, it ran for eighty performances, was pronounced a 'distinguished success' by *The Times* and enjoyed numerous revivals over the next ten years. It was also buoyed by Smith's extravagant advertising campaign, which sent out five million handbills, one million cards and ten million adhesive labels, despatched sandwich men in heart-shaped billboards on to the streets of the capital, and employed touts to hurl armfuls of fliers through the windows of omnibuses and carriages. The labels, however, were the true novelty – a form of unofficial advertising currently practised by snow-boarding stores, club promoters, political parties, film publicists and sex workers. Today, anti-capitalist organisations slap labels on top of large billboard posters, sometimes placing them in ostentatiously inappropriate places. In 1859, Smith's minions ensured that his stickers were discovered in omnibuses, cabs, steamboats, vans, railway carriages, refreshment rooms, Windsor Castle, the Old Bailey and upon the glassware of London's restaurants and public houses.

Victorian capitalism transformed British cities into surfaces upon which advertising could be pasted, paraded and yelled. Like us, the Victorians were not even insulated from such messages in their own homes: in 1874, a group of investors attempting to float an ironworks in Leeds as a limited liability company sent out twelve tons of junk mail to prospective investors. In 1892, Henry Court patented a design for pre-paid envelopes with space reserved for printed puffs for goods and services, 'a medium for successfully reaching the homes and fireside circle – not of one class only, but of all classes of the subjects of Her Majesty the Queen.'[12] By the time Court had taken out his patent, the ubiquity of commercial images had become a source of public concern, and the first legal moves were being made to regulate their display. In November 1894,

Alfred Waterhouse, the architect of the Town Hall, Manchester, and the Natural History Museum in South Kensington, protested that 'Brobding-nag lettering and colossal sky-signs have almost ruined our street architecture. The walls and neighbourhoods of our railway stations are so overlaid with a mass of ridiculous iteration that the bewildered traveller has difficulty in identifying his destination.' Waterhouse's letter provoked controversy. Detractors complained that the mountains of North Wales, the estuaries of south Devon and the countryside around Malvern were becoming cluttered with advertising billboards and signs mounted on kites and balloons. (Notices for a brand of table sauce apparently filled hundreds of fields alongside the railway tracks of Herefordshire.) In a furious correspondence initiated by Waterhouse's letter, other readers wrote in to second his protests. John Evans of Nash Mills described how, on returning from a trip, he found his allotment surrounded by huge advertising hoardings. Two disciples of William Morris, W. B. Richmond and Heywood Sumner, declared that 'Advertisements are turning England into a sordid and disorderly spectacle from sea to sea ... Untruth is accepted as a mere mannerism of advertising style ... Fields and hillsides are being covered with unwonted crops of hoardings. The sky is defaced by unheavenly signs. Night succeeds day only to be utilized for the electrical announcement that "Messrs. So-and-so's soap is the best".' Charles Lawson wrote from Brighton to observe that foreigners visiting England for the first time might be forgiven for believing it to be a nation of soap-obsessives. Benjamin Brooke, the chairman of the company who made the popular Monkey Brand soap, wrote in to point out that newspapers such as the one in which the correspondence was running depended on advertising for essential revenue. W. P. Treloar, a carpet manufacturer and future Lord Mayor of London, reminded *Times* readers that 'the late P. T. Barnum once said that one who had goods to sell and did not advertise the fact was like a man winking at a pretty girl in the dark. Now, to wink at a pretty girl, either in the dark or in the light, may be wrong, but many pretty girls like it probably, and many old women will think it improper.'[13]

Whether these reactions were representative or not, it is certainly true that nineteenth-century advertising had a much more visible and aggressive presence on the streets than it does today. By William Smith's estimate, an astonishing 1,150 million advertising handbills were dis-tributed in London in an average mid-Victorian year. There were, by 1877, two hundred men working as bill-posters. The sandwich man was a familiar sight on the streets of London before Victoria's accession. The 'advertising van', a vehicle supporting two giant placards, appeared in the early 1840s; the first noted example depicted seven uniformed field marshals extolling the virtues of a dinner service. Tailors trundled vanloads of wax mannequins about town; one enterprising milliner converted a coach into a giant bowler hat, and trotted it around London. In 1862, a Brighton dyer dipped a poodle in mauve, and walked it up and down the Steine to advertise his services. It was from parades like this that more peculiar and extravagant publicity stunts developed. When his client Jenny Lind made her first appearance in New York, P. T. Barnum held an auction of the best stalls tickets. A well-known milliner paid $200 for the right to occupy one of the most prominent seats in the house – in which he placed his assistant, who, between the acts, modelled some must-have headgear bearing the name and address of his employer. Even the waters around the British coast were colonised by advertisers: the Beecham's pharmaceutical company supplied boat owners at popular resorts with free sails which were painted with details of its powders and pills. Slogans were stencilled on the sides of bathing machines, and, when the skipper of a Beecham-sponsored boat rescued a drowning pair of holidaymakers near the beach at Southsea, the company exploited the event in its advertising print.

Some of these activities would now be classified under the faux-martial title of 'guerrilla marketing', a term popularised by Jay Conrad Levinson's business self-help book of the same name, first published in 1984. On his khaki-clad website, a loyal army of entrepreneurs tell 'Tales from the Front Line', stirring stories of how they won their colours: a motorbike salesman in Gloversville, NY, tells how he publicised an in-store cat-shooting competition, and basked in the media attention, until it became clear that the animals were made of cardboard; a private investigator relates how he slipped his business card into books at his local law library; the head of a private school confesses that she pretended that she was forced to close her premises during a spell of bad weather, and found herself on the local TV news. In Britain, a number of guerrilla-style PR agencies have sprung up, the Hizbollah to Saatchi and Saatchi's Mossad. 'Guerrilla advertising', wrote one journalist on a visit to Cake, one of Britain's sharpest practitioners in this field, 'is a business of immaculate modernity and street credibility. It is targeted at that most elusive – and lucrative – group of consumers, the young. Guerrilla tactics include using stunts, events, music, flyposting, leafleting, festivals, e-mail, the Internet.

The idea is to sweep aside all the ropy old ad-grandads with ponytails and big red glasses, boring old posters and stupid TV slots, and give ver kids wot they want, yeah!'[14] So, a firm named Cunning Stunts projected a hundred-foot image of a naked – but otherwise undistinguished – children's television presenter on to the Houses of Parliament and assembled a forty-foot Maryland cookie in Trafalgar Square. Mark Borkowski PR persuaded a man to live in an enclosure in Regent's Park Zoo and staged the world's largest custard pie fight. Cake, which operates from a converted Victorian mission hall in west London, painted a street in Salford shocking pink to celebrate the thirty-eighth anniversary of the Barbie doll, filled a swimming pool with what they claimed was Evian mineral water (the Mersey was its real source) and put trousers on the chalk giant of Cerne Abbas. All this to sidestep the boredom and suspicion with which more traditional forms of advertising are now regarded.

Victorian advertisers experienced a similar crisis, and negotiated it with many of the same strategies. In the Darwinian struggle for market share, firms were making increasingly unlikely claims for their products. The formulators of Allan's Anti-Fat insisted that their product 'acts on the food in the stomach, preventing its conversion into fat'.[15] The makers of A. K. Balsam exhorted their potential customers to hammer a nail through the skull of a ram or hen, so that it pierced the brain, skull and tongue. If Balsam was then applied to the maimed creature, the advert claimed, this would 'directly stop the blood and cure the wound in eight or nine minutes, and the creature will eat as before'.[16] Fraudulent assertions like this turned many against advertising: some firms profited by refusing to involve themselves with the system, others found their advertisements refused under certain circumstances. In the 1860s, for example, the directors of *Blackwood's Magazine* exchanged anxious memos about the wisdom of placing ads for Dr Martin's Homeopathic Pills on pages facing an article by the actress Helena Faucit, the wife of a noted lawyer and a member of Queen Victoria's inner circle, lest it appear she was endorsing the product. The would-be business guru George Gentle reasoned in *Hints on Advertising, Adapted to the Times* (1870) that 'there are some persons who entertain the idea that Advertising has seen its best days, that the public are tired of it and do not appreciate it. If ever Advertising earns for itself a bad name, Tradesmen will have themselves in a great measure to blame for it. Let Tradesmen only keep good faith with the public, and follow out the inducements put forth in their advertisements by giving their Customers good value for their money, and a permanent increasing connection must undoubtedly be the result.'[17] However, purveyors of pharmaceutical brands, who were the most culpable, seem to have dealt with this problem by simply spending more money on increasingly saturated campaigns. After Thomas Barratt became a partner in the Pears Soap company in 1865, he raised its yearly expenditure on advertising to £126,000. Thomas and Joseph Beecham's outlay increased from £22,000 in 1884 to £95,000 in 1889 and £120,000 in 1891.

These campaigns were not simply for local constituencies of con-sumers: there were bigger prizes to be won. Between 1870 and 1901, foreign trade and capital flows, the best indicators of global economic integration, accounted for a greater proportion of Gross Domestic Product than they do today. The politics of Empire explains much of this commerce, but the inheritors of the imperial nation states, the giant multinationals, were mobilising during the period, forming the commer-cial networks through which they operate today. By the end of the nineteenth century, many of the world's biggest brands were already established: Philadelphia Cream Cheese first went on sale in 1880; Maxwell House coffee and Del Monte canned fruit in 1892; Cadbury's milk chocolate in 1897; Nabisco cereals in 1898; and Quaker Oats in 1901. The Beechams opened the world's first pharmaceuticals factory in St Helens, Merseyside, in 1859. Campbell began canning soup in 1869, the same year that Henry John Heinz went into preserves. Heinz sold his first bottle of tomato ketchup in 1876, and publicised his products by distributing brooches in the form of pickles, inscribing the number 57 on cliffs and conspicuous walls, and sponsoring the Heinz Ocean Pier at Atlantic City. By 1900, his company owned the largest electric sign on Broadway and their products were available on every continent in the world. This expansion had been planned for two decades: in 1886, Heinz had declared 'Our field is the world.'

Many advertisers smaller than Heinz, Beecham or Pears were, however, much more interested in using the media to pursue hit-and-run tactics with potential customers – and that included bribing editors to run advertorial copy on useless medical treatments. A provincial newspaper editor, writing to *The Times* in 1894, drew attention to the attempts of ad-vertising agents to place flattering stories relating to their clients' products:

A resident in a small village in Loamshire suddenly discovered that Blank's Universal Pills had banished his 'rheumatics' and made a new man of him. The news reaches headquarters, and presently a communication is received from a London advertising agency by the editor of a local newspaper, requesting him to send a reporter to interview the villager aforesaid, ascertain the facts of the case, and prepare a full statement of them with a view to publication in his paper at an early date. Expenses, of course, are guaranteed, instructions and suggestions are contained in a sheaf of newspaper cuttings of a similar character, and liberal terms are offered for a column of 'suitable matter'. The clever editor at once grasps the situation, and in due course the Loamshire Eagle comes out with a sensational account of a 'Miracle in Loamshire,' the pills being skilfully led up to by glimpses of Hodge's surroundings, his kitchen garden, his hobnailed boots, the sticks wherewith he wearily bore himself till he swallowed a box or two of Blank's wonderful specific, a long talk with the honest man himself and all so cunningly set out that you would really suppose the enterprising editor had taken up the whole matter on his own notion, and given to the world the history of the miracle wrought by Blank's Universal Pills as a public duty.[18]

Advertising agents were regarded as the engines of this process. Such agencies had been running since the end of the eighteenth century, but with the massive expansion in periodical publishing that took place in the 1850s and 1860s, many more sprang up, and were not always the most legitimate of businesses. A commentator who wrote under the pseudonym 'an Adept' described how:

Broken-down gentlemen, or even ladies, are sometimes employed as canvassers for advertisements; their appearance sustains the characters assumed, and clerks or servants are induced to take in cards on matters of importance, stated to occupy your time for a few moments only. Sometimes they write some fashionable address upon their cards, or describe themselves as representing a powerful journal, and desirous of giving an editorial notice of the merits of your specialty or invention. Of course they will tell you that if you would consent to appear in their advertising columns it would be more natural for the notice (or puff) subsequently to be printed.[19]

Advertising's criminal possibilities were exploited enthusiastically by more baldly dishonest operators. The simplest schemes were run by fake finance companies that advertised stakes in non-existent investment schemes. William Pearson of Liverpool found himself under scrutiny in 1889 for defrauding his clients of thousands of pounds. His plan was to bank the initial sums, dole out a few small payments of 'interest' from this fund and then abscond with the balance. The case of a woman who had lost her capital on the Stock Exchange, and sold her jewellery to sink a last £200 into Pearson's business, was noted by the court. In 1888, William Hastings Toone was tried for conning three thousand applicants out of agency fees for jobs which didn't exist. So-called 'baby-farmers' – women who took in unwanted children and disposed of them by adoption or murder – ran notices in journals whose advertising departments charged them premium rates, in full knowledge of their illegal activities. In August 1866, the Marlborough Street magistrates heard the story of a young woman who applied to an advertisement stating that a married couple required a travelling companion for a jaunt to the Continent; the successful applicant was raped, and on her expulsion from the house, soon saw that her employer was advertising for another victim. In May 1873, a young woman named Ellen Hurst took a Marguerite Spoeven and her mother to court for defrauding her family of £36, with an advertisement that promised instruction in 'the art and science of millinery' in their smart shop at 61 New Bond Street. (Instead, she found herself lodged in a dingy house on the Edgware Road with nine other 'apprentices', no discernible training and a starvation diet.) A pair of sharks named the Chrimes Brothers, sellers of abortion pills titled Lady Montrose's Miracle Female Tabules, attempted to double their money by sending out, on the morning of 8 October 1898, somewhere between eight and ten thousand letters to their female customers, threatening to expose their attempts to rid themselves of their unwanted pregnancy, if the recipient did not immediately send £2 2s.

In 1859, a writer for *All the Year Round* answered a series of newspaper advertisements which offered to improve the applicant's financial situation, health and sex life. One announced, 'If you wish to Marry, send a stamped-addressed envelope to the Advertiser, who will put you in possession of a *Secret* by means of which you can win the affections of as many of the opposite sex as your heart desires.' Instead, he received a printed slip requesting two shillings worth of postage stamps. The fee sent, the Secret was posted back to him on another printed paper: 'To the Male Sex – *If a woman is clean and neat in her dress, respects the Sabbath, and is dutiful towards her parents, happy will be the man who*

makes her his wife.'[20] The success of this scam relied on the embarrassment that would be caused by the public exposure of the applicant,
should they try to complain – the same guiding principle as today's
premium telephone lines offering sex and dating tips, or newspaper small
ads which exploit the aspirations of unemployed single parents with
offers such as 'Work from home. Earn £££££s.' A reader of Dickens's
magazine, the wife of a cash-strapped Assistant Surgeon, wrote in to
explain how she had been swindled in her attempts to earn enough to
maintain the appearance of prosperity necessary for attracting wealthy
clients to their practice. Three small ads promised to let her in on money-
making schemes. The first advertiser returned a betting slip, advising her
to increase her income by gambling; the second contained details of a
new method for staining glass; the third requested a brace of postage
stamps in return for an 'employment which has nothing to do with
photography, betting, papier maché, flower-making, &c ... It can be
practised by any one in any station of life, at their own homes.' The reply,
she explained, advised the respondent to 'keep a registry-office for
servants, and to have a black board outside the house, on which I am
to copy advertisements from the local papers.' For a couple requiring a
discreet way of earning extra cash, the information was next to useless.
'Many persons would say to me, you are rightly served, and deserve no
pity. But I think we are all prone to believe what we much wish for,
particularly in times of difficulty or distress.'[21]

In the last thirty years of the nineteenth century, a new kind of advertising
strategy was formulated to address the distrust and disgust that many
consumers felt towards the claims made for products and services. The
publicity stunt had a simple premise: it was a kind of street theatre, a
performance worth witnessing as an event in itself, irrespective of
whether a purchase was made, or whether the claims made for the
products on sale were true. In 1880, David Lewis, founder of the Lewis's
chain of department stores, opened a branch in Manchester by releasing a
huge swarm of helium balloons, upon which was printed a list of the
shop's stock: one of the balloons made landfall in Italy. Jesse Boot, the
man behind the chain of chemist shops, and, in 1883, installer of Britain's
first in-store lift, opened each new outlet with the help of a brass band.
Samuel H. Benson, the celebrated advertising agent of 100 Fleet Street,
concocted several landmark schemes for his clients. In 1897, he set up an
offer by which shoppers could exchange their copies of the *Daily*

Telegraph for a sample of Rowntree's Elect Cocoa. He followed it up by decking a fleet of London omnibuses with flags and cocoa pods, and enlisting their drivers to distribute free samples. Benson was also the brains behind the Bovril War Cable Scheme, a branded news service which brought details of the latest despatches from the Boer conflict by uniformed courier to a thousand participating grocery stores. As each new report came in, the cycle fleet would scoot out and pin up copies to a 'Bovril Board' placed in the window of the shop. In exchange for a small fee and a handful of Bovril labels, customers could have the despatches delivered directly to their door. With this scheme, and a special offer through which Bovril consumers could collect tokens for a free gravure print of the Relief of Ladysmith, the name of the product achieved a new prominence.

If the Boer conflict was the first media war – it was certainly the first for which newsreel footage was shot, even if much of it was faked on Hampstead Heath with blacked-up actors – then Bovril was its official sponsor. The company took out full-page advertisements in the *Daily Mail*, proclaiming 'Bovril's part in the South African War', boasting that '85,000 lbs. of Bovril, besides hundreds of thousands of Emergency Rations, have been supplied for use in South Africa' and depicting the beverage being fed to battle-weary troops. 'Doctors, nurses, officers, soldiers and newspaper correspondents,' gushed Rudyard Kipling, 'unite in bearing testimony to the great popularity of Bovril at the Front as an Invigorating and Nourishing Food, preparing the soldier for battle and aiding him to recovery when weakened by wounds and disease.' It was even suggested that, if traced out on a map, General Roberts's march across South Africa spelt out the name of the beef extract.[22]

The Bovril War Cable Scheme was a successful public relations exercise, one which did not convey any information about a branded product, yet pushed the public in its direction all the same. Many of these stunts were variations on those accomplished by Barnum to publicise his shows: 'the bigger the humbug, the better the people will like it', he maintained, signalling the separation of the pleasures of the ballyhoo from the reality of what was actually on sale. One Scottish PR pioneer, however, did more than any other to develop the grammar of the publicity stunt. In Britain, the name of Sir Thomas Lipton is now associated with the tea-importing business: some of the firm's blends still use his image, products with tasteful Heritage names such as Royal Ceylan [*sic*] and Orange Windsor. Globally, however, the multinational corporation that bears his name still flows along the lines of commerce he established in the late nineteenth century. The supermarket shelves of the world are stacked with his pasta sauces, salad dressings, soups, taco shells and noodles. Mention his name at a tea auction in Colombo, and you soon begin to sense the power that it still wields.[23]

On 9 July 1878, Lipton brought the traffic of his home city of Glasgow to a halt with three pigs, dolled up in bright fabric, emblazoned with the words, 'The Orphans, Home-fed, Bound for Liptons'. Chivvying them through the streets with a shillelagh was a man dressed up as a stage Irishman, who persuaded his charges to hunker down in the mud of Glasgow Cross, occluding the city's main artery of communication. The Orphans were materialisations of a print campaign Lipton had used successfully in his shops, which depicted a cohort of happy porkers scuttering to the grocer's, clearly content to lay down their lives in order to be incorporated into such a high-quality range of products. Another print campaign featured a group of scrawny human specimens entering a branch of Lipton's to emerge later as rosy-cheeked, well-fed individuals. Lipton experimented with all kinds of variations on this theme. He fitted mirrors above the doorways of his shops, one convex, the other concave. On entering the premises, the customer would see his or her image stretched and skinny; on exiting, rounded and huge. He hired gangs of the most emaciated men he could find, and marched them up a street bearing the legend 'Going to Liptons'. Down the other side of the street came an identically dressed parade of pleasantly corpulent males, ticketed 'Coming from Liptons'. He printed fake pound notes, redeemable against goods from his stores – many of which found their way into the safes of businesses, banks and building societies. He engaged a balloonist to shower a hundred thousand 'sky telegrams' over Glasgow, each one extolling the virtues of Lipton's bacon. He placed a gigantic butter sculpture of an Atlantic liner in the window of his store in Liverpool. He hired a gang of medical students to dissect hams and cheeses in his Edinburgh branch. He paid a pair of newlyweds to spend two days in the window of his Dublin outlet, making pots of tea in their glad rags. He sent a procession of men in oriental costume to the opening of his Oldham branch, which caused a horse pulling a carriage to bolt, nearly killing its occupant – Herbert Gladstone MP, the son of the Liberal Prime Minister. He staged a peculiar stunt in which he presided over the first attempt to hypnotise a subject down a telephone line. Most audaciously, perhaps, his response to being stranded on board the SS *Orotava* when it ran aground on a sandbank in the Red Sea was to pay a crewman to make a stencil reading 'Drink Lipton's Tea' and use it to transfer the legend to the crates and barrels that were being jettisoned -to raise the ship's position in the water.

1881 was a golden year for Lipton's enterprises. In January, laconic adverts began to appear in the *Leeds Express*, simply stating 'Lipton is Coming'. This mystification was not Lipton's innovation: enigmatic slogans such as 'Where's Eliza?', 'WHO'S COMING?', 'Have you seen it?' and 'Somebody's Luggage' were pasted over the brickwork of London in the 1850s. This latter inspired a *Times* editorial reflecting on the interest generated by such mysterious graffiti, and was revealed a few weeks later to be a teaser for the Christmas number of Dickens's periodical *All the Year Round*. Lipton's announcement – assumed to be advance publicity for some kind of theatrical event – heralded the expansion of his chain of grocery stores from his Scottish base and into English territory. From this point onwards, his stunts began to gain wide coverage in the national press.

On 12 December 1881, the steamship SS *Surania* docked at Glasgow with Lipton's most audacious publicity weapons stowed safely in its hold. Two cheeses, each weighing 3,472 pounds, churned and set by Dr L. L. Wright of Whitesboro, head of America's largest dairy. The press were sent all the sexiest statistics well in advance. Two hundred dairymaids, Lipton claimed, had milked eight hundred cows for six days to produce the four thousand gallons of milk necessary to make the eleven-foot wide, two-foot thick monsters. At Broomielaw, where a crowd numbering hundreds had assembled to greet these new arrivals, the giants parted company. One was despatched by rail to the Universal Cookery and Food Exhibition at the Royal Aquarium, Westminster, for a week-long stint. The other – christened Jumbo, after an elephant used by Barnum to attract publicity by ploughing up fields near towns where his entourage was due to perform – was conveyed by traction engine to the Lipton's flagship branch on the High Street in Glasgow, but turned out to be too big to fit through the front door. Fortunately, the Jamaica Street branch possessed a wider entrance, and the cheese was hoisted into position in the front window. Pleased with the attention garnered from this stunt, Lipton returned home and boasted about his success to his mother, who replied, 'It will be a better advertisement still, Tom, if the cheese is a good cheese.'[24]

'Fortunately,' he recalled, in *Leaves from the Lipton Logs*, his notoriously unreliable memoirs, 'I was able to assure my mother that "Jumbo" was a cheese of unassailable reputation, for I had already tested it myself with every possible satisfaction.' Just in case anyone disagreed, however, Lipton had an insurance policy. 'Why not make the Giant Cheese "a better advertisement still" by turning it into a Golden Cheese by the simple method of hiding a large quantity of sovereigns or half-sovereigns in its vast interior? By carrying this into effect I scored a big hit. Indeed, I never expected anything like the public excitement it created.'[25] To generate more excitement, Lipton requested the assistance of a dozen police officers to keep order at the Christmas Eve carve-up of the coin-stuffed Jumbo. However, the crowds who turned up at Jamaica Street eager for a slice created enough clamour and chaos for the grocer to be grateful for the police presence. He stood atop the cheese, clad in his trademark white suit and apron, paring off hunks, which customers ripped from the wrapping there and then to discover if they had been lucky enough to receive a coin. One policeman found a sovereign in his portion and was so overjoyed that he started dancing a fandango, during the course of which he lost his helmet. 'The newspaper reporters,' reflected Lipton, 'came along in force and next morning I had columns of free publicity.'[26] Which, of course, had been the object of the exercise. He repeated the cheese stunt many times, until Christmas 1886, when the police confronted him in the act of pressing sovereigns into a two-ton cheese in the window of his store on Clayton Street, Newcastle, with a warrant to prevent its sale on the grounds that it constituted an illegal lottery. His attempt to import a twelve-ton Canadian cheese from the Chicago World's Fair ended in malodorous disaster: the six-foot-tall specimen was rotten when it landed at Liverpool in November 1893. The bad smell, reports alleged, was perceptible when the SS *Laurentian* was still miles from port. Lipton dumped the rancid cargo, and consoled himself with the large number of articles written about the incident. As his bulging scrapbooks in Glasgow's Mitchell Library show, he was content with publicity on any terms.

Lipton's relationship with the press adumbrates that sleazy interdependence which exists today between business, the PR industry and the media. His method of getting the name of his stores into the newspapers was an improvement on the system that allowed quack pharmaceuticals companies to give backhanders to editors in exchange for flattering copy, but it fuelled the addiction of the press to stories supplied ready-made by commercial organisations. Once Lipton and his fellow entrepreneurs had deduced which sorts of stories would appeal, they circumvented the need for bribery: the press came running of their own accord.

Securing 'advertising space without paying for it' is, according to the public relations expert Mark Borkowski, 'the very essence of great PR'.[27] He made this remark in the book that accompanied *Improperganda*, an exhibition he staged in London in the summer of 2000, celebrating history's greatest publicity stunts – many of which, of course, turned out to be the work of his own agency. Visiting the exhibition, in a gallery in a backstreet off the Strand, it was impossible not be impressed by its evidence of the gargantuan efforts exerted by publicists on behalf of their clients. The walls were lined with images of flocks of sheep herded through Edinburgh city centre, cars chainsawed in half, a field planted with Cabbage Patch dolls – pictures that would make a Barnum or a Lipton weep with delight. But it was also impossible not to suspect that the Messrs Gabriel had already worked out the fundamentals of this philosophy in 1864. Did this sharp pair of tooth-pullers really expect to find a string of Members of Parliament waiting outside their Harley Street surgery on Monday morning, desperate to be fitted with indestructible mineral teeth and gums? Probably not. It is much more likely that they desired only to see the name of their firm in the paper, for the price of a few telegrams. As it turned out, the indignation of their victims ensured that the Gabriels' names, address and opening hours were printed in italics on the editorial pages of *The Times*, firmly separated from the gaggle of indistinguishable practitioners jostling in the small ads.

CHAPTER FOUR

The Gutter and the Stars

Parliament has attained its utmost development. There is need of a new representative method, not to supersede but to supplement that which exists — a system which will be more elastic, more simple, more direct, and more closely in contact with the mind of the people.

W. T. Stead, 'The Future of Journalism' (1886)

Monica Lewinsky and I shared a precious moment on 3 March 1999. It was in Borders bookshop on Oxford Street – which, if you've never been to a branch before, is the kind of place where they pile self-help manuals and unauthorised film star biographies high and sell them cheap, like the literary equivalent of a discount frozen food store. She owed her lawyers a million dollars, so with the help of Andrew Morton – the former *News of the World* hack well known for having penned an exposé of the miserable married life of Diana, Princess of Wales – she knocked together a book and began a promotional tour of the world. I went along to see if I could pull off a cheap little stunt for a newspaper column. I would write her a cheque for a couple of hundred quid, offer it as a contribution to the repayment of her legal debts, and then sit back and wait for her to cash it. Would she be too proud to take money from a complete stranger? Or would she thank me on bended knee?

Waiting in line, I soon realised that not everybody had turned up for such altruistic motives. Nobody admitted to buying the book because they liked or admired Monica. My fellow queue-members fell into three categories: journalists like me foraging for copy, hare-eyed men with whom no sensible person would like to be alone in a lift, and American college girls who had come to bitch and have their photographs taken standing next to her. 'I don't really know why I came,' said one of the latter. 'She sucked off the president of the United States. She's famous.' What other reason could there be? I tried to read the book: 'It was the smell of the eucalyptus wafting along the powder-blue corridors that first seduced Monica.' I stopped trying to read the book. After an hour or so

6 *Carte de visite*, autographed by W. T. Stead (courtesy the Salvation Army)

of shuffling, my part of the line neared the finishing post. 'You can go down now,' said the shop assistant, without a flicker of irony. And suddenly I was standing in front of Monica herself.

She was cheerful. She had a kind of big-boned, slapped-up glamour. She was more composed than most people would be if they were making a public appearance as the world's most famous exponent of fellatio. 'Hello there,' I said, rather weakly, feeling pretty stupid for being there at all. 'How are you?' she beamed, as if some invisible drama coach was whispering *eyes and teeth, eyes and teeth.* 'Listen,' I ventured, 'I've brought you this because I wanted to make a small contribution to your legal costs. I think you've had a pretty bad deal from all this.' I held out the envelope, which was immediately whipped out of my hand by a well-manicured man standing by her right shoulder. Andrew Morton. 'Well, thank you, that is *soooo* kind of you,' Monica exclaimed, genuinely surprised. And I was ushered away from the table by another shop assistant, robbed of the opportunity to tell her that I believed she represented the confluence of two phenomenally important nineteenth-century cultural discourses: the cult of celebrity and the newspaper sex scandal.

As examples from the history of advertising have already demonstrated, the jittery symbiosis that exists today between public figures and the media had been firmly established by the middle of the Victorian era. The in-depth press interview was born during the period: by 1900 most magazines and newspapers carried profiles of the famous, often conducted in the subject's domestic environment, in order that telling details of décor and furnishing might be conveyed to their readers. The photographic *carte de visite* brought public personalities into the domestic sphere in a more corporeal form than ever before. For the first time, figures whose names were well known were also instantly recognisable on the street. Public personalities recognised photography as a medium through which they could amplify their prestige. Buckingham Palace gave permission for the release of dozens of casual portraits of the royals, in cute domestic scenes that would still sit easily on the pages of *Hello!* magazine. A new kind of public figure, the 'professional beauty', whose fame devolved from less obvious sources, also made her first appearance. Lillie Langtry, for instance, could not go shopping without crowds turning up to gawp at her. When she stepped off a train, she was inevitably confronted by a brass band, a red carpet and an effusive mayor.

When she arrived in America for the first time, she was met by an army of reporters and Oscar Wilde, waving a bunch of lilies in the air. Langtry has somehow succeeded in getting herself remembered as a great Victorian actress, but she only took up acting as a last resort during a financially sticky moment in 1881, and by all accounts she was pretty mediocre. (A crushing notice in an American periodical dismissed her as a pointless novelty, comparing her unfavourably to Jumbo, Barnum's performing elephant.) Her fame was formed from the air of genteel scandal that surrounded her, and circulated in little cardboard photographic pin-ups. She had a long-running affair with the Prince of Wales (swiftly broken off after she stuck a glob of strawberry ice cream down his back at a ball thrown by Randolph Churchill). She sat for John Millais and James Whistler, was worshipped by Oscar Wilde, collected rich paramours, amassed a great fortune and ended her days gambling it away in Monte Carlo, but perhaps the only really fascinating thing about her was that lots of people thought she was really fascinating.

Like other celebrities of her day, Langtry used the newspapers to facilitate a profitable iconisation. As we have already seen, the endorsement of products in newspaper and magazine advertisements provided a new medium for the amplification of celebrity. Gossip columns carried stories about such figures that intensified their exotic separation from reality. Sarah Bernhardt was rumoured to travel with a menagerie of pet cheetahs and pythons and to sleep in a coffin lined with pink silk. Oscar Wilde let it be known that he was considering rebranding himself as 'The Oscar' or 'The Wilde', reasoning that the more famous one became, the less one needed nominal ballast like Fingal O'Flahertie Wills. 'My name has two 'O's', two 'F's' and two 'W's',' he reflected. 'A name which is destined to be in everybody's mouth must not be too long. It comes so expensive in the advertisements.'[1] As Wilde discovered, well-placed publicity could be used to shape a public persona for mass consumption. He also discovered that when a name became associated with scandal, it took on a different kind of commercial value – in shifting copies of the *Police Gazette*.

The Victorians did not invent the sex scandal, but as the critic William A. Cohen has argued, 'nineteenth-century scandals establish the terms for, and supply the history of, the manifest absorption of contemporary Anglo-American culture in sensational stories of sexual exposure.' And, he notes, 'Our own press tends to ignore the fact that scandal even *has* a history, treating each new case as if it sprang up sui generis.'[2] This history is compendious: long before Monica Lewinsky produced a frock bearing evidence of presidential infidelity, nineteenth-century American politics was already generating a large and stinky assortment of dirty linen. In 1828, Andrew Jackson's wife Rachel Donelson Robards was denounced in the press as an adulteress by John Quincy Adams, who alleged that she had failed to divorce her former husband before marrying the President (the scandal may explain Jackson's presence upon the body of Lydia the Tattooed Lady). The shock of these revelations killed Robards, but did not prevent Jackson acceding to the White House. The 1884 election campaign was one of the filthiest on record, dominated by two parallel sensations. The first involved the Republican candidate James Blaine, who failed to make a convincing refutation of allegations in the *New York Times* and *Indiana Sentinel* that he had been forced to marry his six-months-pregnant wife at the end of a shotgun. To even matters out, a report in the pro-Republican *Buffalo Evening Telegraph* claimed that, in 1874, the Democratic candidate Grover Cleveland had fathered an illegitimate child by a widow named Maria Halpin, who sold cloaks in a department store in Niagara Falls. Worse still, the report – published under the banner headline 'Terrible Tale – Dark Chapter in Public Man's History' – alleged that Cleveland had abandoned his mistress and little Oscar, and connived to place Halpin in an insane asylum and the child in an orphanage. As Cleveland's campaign team had determined upon presenting their man as a morally scrupulous alternative to Blaine, this was a serious setback. Cleveland conceded that he had indeed had sexual relations with that woman, but insisted that he was not the father of the child. He claimed that he had chosen to support the pair financially, knowing that the real father would not offer any assistance. Halpin's developing alcoholism, however, had forced him to place her in an institution, and her son in an orphanage – from which he was soon adopted by a wealthy couple. During the election campaign, Cleveland's sexual history became public property, but he managed to spin the story enough in his favour for the electorate to judge that he had acted honourably, and vote him into office. Republicans who chanted, 'Ma, Ma, where's my Pa?' were forced to listen to the retort, 'Gone to the White House, ha! ha! ha!'[3]

One of Cleveland's most vocal supporters – and enthusiastic enumerators of Blaine's shortcomings – was Joseph Pulitzer's newspaper, the *New York World*. Pulitzer assumed editorship of the ailing title in 1883, repositioning it as a vehicle of entertainment as well as information. He filled its pages with investigative reporting, sensational exposé stories, celebrity gossip, cartoons and sports coverage, under the attractive tagline 'Spicy, Pithy, Pictorial'. In two years he had pushed the circulation up from fifteen thousand to a hundred thousand. It was just the kind of editorial strategy for which Matthew Arnold was then castigating the American press. 'I should say', Arnold asserted, 'that if one were searching for the best means to efface and kill in a whole nation the discipline of respect, the feeling for what is elevated, one could not do better than take the American newspapers. The absence of truth and soberness in them, the poverty in serious interest, the personality and sensation-mongering, are beyond belief.'[4] Arnold was one of the first great theorists of popular culture, and his dislike of the American media had a personal dimension. Disembarking at Boston in the early 1880s, he was disappointed to find his arrival briefly noted along with an item of gossip concerning the Prince of Wales's interest in the Californian actress Mary Anderson. The report also got his age wrong. When he reached Chicago, Arnold had even more cause for dismay. 'An evening paper was given me soon after I arrived; I opened it, and found under a large-type heading, "*We have seen him arrive,*" the following picture of myself: "He has harsh features, supercilious manners, parts his hair down the middle, wears a single eyeglass and ill-fitting clothes." '[5] Arnold also noted that this editorial thinking was exerting influence upon the British press, and, in 1887, he coined a phrase – 'the new journalism' – to describe it. 'It is full of ability, novelty, variety, sensation, sympathy, generous instinct; its one great failure is that it is feather-brained. It throws out assertions at a venture, because it wishes them true . . . and to get at the state of things as they truly are, seems to have no concern whatever.'[6] One editor in particular, whom he dubbed 'the inventor of the new journalism', was the object of this criticism. His name was William Thomas Stead.

Stead – journalist, spiritualist and one of the more distinguished victims of the *Titanic* disaster – is the father of modern British popular journalism. By the time he was twenty-two years old, he was editor of the *Northern Echo*, a Darlington-based paper which, thanks to the city's excellent railway connections, enjoyed national circulation. He popularised the use of banner headlines, short, punchy paragraphs, human interest stories, gossip columns, celebrity interviews and pictures. He was also the first journalist to interview a Tsar. Order up an archived copy of the *Pall Mall Gazette,* the newspaper he edited between 1883 and 1890 (and which eventually merged with the London *Evening Standard)* and you can immediately see what it is: a modern tabloid newspaper, conveniently sized for reading on a tube crammed with commuters, and offering a familiar mix of moral outrage and titillation. The edition of Saturday 4 July 1885 carried a particularly juicy teaser for the following Monday's paper. 'We say quite frankly', warned a front-page notice, 'that all those who are squeamish, and all those who are prudish, and all those who prefer to live in a fool's paradise of imaginary innocence and purity, selfishly oblivious of the horrible realities which torment those whose lives are passed in the London Inferno, <u>will do well not to read the *Pall Mall Gazette*</u> on <u>Monday and the three following days</u>.' It was a terrific marketing ploy. The Monday issue sold so quickly that one and a half million pirate copies were rushed into print. It contained a story so sensational that it set the pattern for journalistic exposure to which the British press still adheres. It also caused a riot outside the *Gazette*'s office on Northumberland Street, inspired a quarter-million-strong demonstration in Hyde Park, bounced Parliament into approving the controversial Criminal Law Amendment Act and propelled Stead into Holloway Prison.

The story behind the story begins in the winter of 1879, when a cell of campaigners led by Alfred Dyer, a publisher of religious tracts, decided to investigate claims emerging from Brussels that English girls were being kidnapped and forced into sexual slavery in Belgium. Dyer was a member of a circle that included Josephine Butler, Benjamin Scott and James Stansfeld, political activists working for the repeal of the Contagious Diseases Acts, introduced in the 1860s to give the authorities the right to subject suspected prostitutes to compulsory medical examination. The results of these inquiries were inconclusive. Dyer and his band claimed that the girls they interviewed were kidnap victims eager to be released, the Brussels police and the British consul insisted they were old hands who knew exactly what they were doing. Stonewalled by both British and Belgian officials, Dyer established the snappily-titled London Committee for the Purposes of Exposure and Suppression of the Traffic in English Girls for the Purposes of Continental Prostitution. Josephine Butler pitched into the argument in May 1880, declaring – with scant evidence to support the claim – that 'in certain of the infamous houses in Brussels there are immured little children, English girls of from ten to fourteen years of age who have been stolen, kidnapped, betrayed, carried off from

English country villages by every artifice, and sold to these human shambles.' Held prisoner in disreputable lodging houses, 'the presence of these children is unknown to the ordinary visitors; it is secretly known only to the wealthy men who are able to pay large sums of money for the sacrifice of these innocents.'[7] Butler's article implied the existence of a clandestine Continental economy of child prostitution, for which foreign agents supplied abducted English virgins. She petitioned the foreign secretary, Earl Granville, a Liberal peer sympathetic to her views: he instituted a select committee to investigate what was soon known as the 'white slavery' issue, which reported in July 1882. The committee found extensive evidence of fraud – brothel employees were routinely charged at inflated rates for their lodgings, and for expenses incurred when entertaining their clients – but uncovered no convincing evidence of abduction. Even so, it recommended that the age of consent be raised to sixteen, and that police be empowered to enter houses where it was suspected that under-sixteens were employed for sexual purposes. Broader political events, however, prevented these recommendations from reaching the statute books. A Criminal Law Amendment Bill was drafted, but Gladstone's weak and Irish Home Rule-fixated second administration did not regard it as a priority. There was also widespread scepticism about the legislation's origins in the campaigning of a small but vocal pressure group. Had Parliament any mandate to revise the age of consent from fourteen to sixteen when, as Lord Oranmore and Brown pointed out during a debate in the upper chamber, there were very few of their lordships who had not, at some point in their lives, had sex with a partner of an age below the proposed new limit? The Bill tottered backwards and forwards between both houses, becoming weaker on each progress. By May 1885, an inconclusive Commons debate, which only forty members bothered to attend, saw the Bill shelved once again. On 9 June 1885, Gladstone's government tumbled; an interim Conservative administration was installed. Butler and her colleague Benjamin Scott had only a matter of weeks to generate enough publicity to get white slavery back on the agenda before the balance of power in the Commons altered, and made the Bill even less likely to become law. To that end, they went to see W. T. Stead.

Stead sympathised with Butler and Scott's agitations against the Contagious Diseases Acts and the consent laws. He also sensed an opportunity to intensify his own celebrity and personal influence. He enlisted the help of contacts in the Salvation Army and police force to compile a dossier on the kidnapping of English virgins. They worked throughout the summer, interviewing brothel-keepers and prostitutes, and assembling a collection of testimonies. They also reviewed evidence that had been collected the previous summer, which related to the aristocratic patronage of a number of brothels on what is now Old Church Street, Chelsea, which were run by a madam named Mary Jeffries. Disappointingly, they could find no conclusive proof that girls were being trafficked between Britain and the Continent. A much-needed breakthrough came, however, when Josephine Butler introduced Stead to Rebecca Jarrett, a former procuress she had encountered in a women's refuge in Winchester, where her husband, the Rev George Butler, was canon of the Cathedral. Stead formulated a plan that would give him a sensational exclusive, preclude the need for strong evidence and advance Butler's cause. If Jarrett could procure a child, and help him spirit her away to France, that might prove that such outrages were possible. She agreed to the plan only after severe bullying: 'Jarrett consented most reluctantly,' admitted Stead, 'and under moral pressure of the most imperious kind.'[8] Through the offices of a go-between, Nancy Brought-on, Jarrett found a thirteen-year-old girl who would suit their purposes, paid off the mother with a sovereign, and took young Eliza Armstrong to rooms in Albany Street, where she was interviewed by Stead and a representative of the Salvation Army. The party then moved on to Milton Street, where the girl's virginity was established by medical examination. Jarrett and Armstrong then went to lodgings over a butcher's shop in Poland Street, where they prepared the girl for bed, and attempted to drug her with chloroform. At an appointed time, Stead entered the bedroom. Armstrong screamed. Jarrett rushed in and made a show of saving her from the intruder. The stunt over, the group then took a cab to Harley Street, where Dr Heywood Smith – the inventor of haemorrhoidal forceps – certified that Armstrong was still a virgin. The next morning, Jarrett and her charge took the boat train from Charing Cross, from which they travelled to Paris. A few days later, they returned, Jarrett resuming her place in the Winchester refuge, and Armstrong remaining in the care of the Salvation Army. Stead had his story. A series of articles with the lurid title of 'The Maiden Tribute of Modern Babylon' began their run on 6 July.

The following year, Stead wrote a piece for the *Contemporary Review* that defended his methods: 'It would not be difficult to maintain that nothing can ever get itself accomplished nowadays without sensationalism.'[9] The 'Maiden Tribute' articles put that theory into action. They were instalments of quasi-pornographic Gothic melodrama which transmitted the details of the affair with sensational precision.[10] Stead depicted London as a sinister hunting ground for men who desired to 'enjoy to the full the exclusive luxury of revelling in the cries of an immature child'. To these monsters, he insisted, 'the shriek of torture [is] the essence of their delight, and they would not silence by a single note the cry of agony over which they gloat.' He did not shirk the use of outrageous hyperbole: 'Thousands of women', he claimed, were being 'literally killed and made away with.' The first instalment relates the perils of Lily, his fictionalised version of Eliza Armstrong: 'And then there rose a wild and piteous cry – not a loud shriek, but a helpless, startled scream like the bleat of a frightened lamb. And the child's voice was heard crying, in accents of terror. "There's a man in the room! Take me home; oh, take me home!"'[11] Exposé stories in the tabloids may no longer be so keen to replicate the register of the penny dreadful, but they tread a similar path between pornography and moral indignation.

'I have not a word to say in favour of any method of journalism that can fairly be called exaggerated or untrue,' Stead wrote the following year. 'Mere froth-whipping or piling up the agony, solely for the purposes of harrowing the feelings of the reader ... I have nothing to say about that kind of work. That is not the sensationalism which I am prepared to defend. The sensationalism which is indispensable is the sensationalism which is justifiable. Sensationalism in journalism is justifiable up to the point that it is necessary to arrest the eye of the public and compel them to admit the necessity of action.'[12] Unfortunately, there were many details in Stead's story that were exaggerated and untrue – principally his assertions that his heroine's parents, Charles and Elizabeth Armstrong, were hopeless drunkards, that Elizabeth had knowingly sold her daughter into prostitution, and that Nancy Broughton's home was a brothel. Rival newspapers gave their support to the libelled couple, hoping to undermine Stead's position. Opponents declared him a hypocrite who had served up 'a wonderfully cheap two-pennyworth of vice, filth, and exaggeration' in the form of a moral crusade; and offered sarcastic praise for his underlined warning to readers as a ploy that 'Mr Pears "must have admired, and may, perhaps, have envied"'.[13]

The Cabinet, however, had been stirred into action. Not simply by Stead's stunt with Eliza Armstrong, but by a threat he issued to the government from the front page of the *Gazette*'s edition of 8 July. If the

Criminal Law Amendment Bill was not passed swiftly, he warned, he would release the names of the 'noble and Royal patrons' of Mary Jeffries' brothels – which, according to his police contacts, included the King of the Belgians and Edward, the Prince of Wales. 'We await the commencement of those talked-of proceedings with a composure that most certainly is not shared by those whom . . . we should be compelled to expose in the witness box,' he rumbled.[14] Miraculously, on the following day, the Home Secretary, Sir Richard Cross, proposed a motion to debate the Bill at the earliest convenience; it had become law by August. Although Stead was charged and found guilty under the Offences Against the Person Act for his actions regarding Eliza Armstrong, he had secured his victory: he had used his newspaper to transform the agitations of a peripheral pressure group into legislation. His three months in Holloway only amplified his self-belief. Indeed, he revelled in the martyrdom conferred by the sentence. Every 10 November, the date of his committal, he would parade through London in his prison uniform: more publicity for the *Pall Mall Gazette*, and proof that the media could shape opinion and exert power over the legislature, even in the absence of a groundswell of public support.

Although he proved to be the nineteenth century's greatest exponent of the art, using Eliza Armstrong to sell newspapers in much the same way that Lipton had employed pigs to sell bacon, British sensationalism did not begin with Stead. Reforms in the tax system and technological innovation had just as much effect upon the development of the more colourful wing of the popular print media. In 1836 the newspaper stamp duty was reduced to one penny, allowing a number of new titles to emerge and operate profitably – notably the *News of the World*, which began producing its familiar mixture of titillating crime and sex stories in 1843. The first edition led with an 'Extraordinary Case of Drugging and Violation', the tale of a female pharmacist who was doped, raped and dumped in the Thames. (As the next chapter will show, accounts of violence and murder were a huge hit with Victorian readerships.) In 1851, John Julius Reuter established a telegraphic news agency in London, which allowed tasty titbits of news – the 'ticker' items which Matthew Arnold read with disgust in Boston – to be disseminated across continents.

The abolition of duty on advertisements in 1853, and on paper in 1861, further boosted the newspapers' potential incomes and allowed titles to be sold at lower prices. Between 1861 and 1877, the circulation of the penny *Daily Telegraph* rose from 130,000 to 240,000, beating the more expensive *Times* by an enormous margin. In 1888, following Stead's example at the *Pall Mall Gazette*, the Irish nationalist politician and former *Telegraph* journalist Thomas Power O'Connor launched the *Star*, a paper aimed at the new readers created by the 1870 Education Act. 'We live in an age of hurry and multitudinous newspapers,' he reflected, in an article in the *New Review* warming readers up for the launch of the new title. 'The newspaper is not read in the secrecy and silence of the closet as is the book. It is picked up at a railway station, hurried over in a railway carriage, dropped incontinently when read.' This mode of consumption, he argued, had to be reflected in the stories on its pages. 'To get your ideas through the hurried eye into the whirling brains that are employed in the reading of a newspaper there must be no mistake about your meaning ... you must strike your reader right between the eyes.'[15] The *Star* offered a mixture of brisk human interest stories, bold typography, political cartoons and racing tips. It introduced the stop press and the football report to British newspaper readers. O'Connor's wife, a Texan divorcee named Elizabeth Paschal, contributed a gossip column, 'Mainly About People', which opened with the revelation that 'Lady Colin Campbell is the only woman in London who has her feet manicured.'[16] Like its sister paper *The Sun* (launched 1893), it had a radical political agenda. The right-wing bias of today's British newspaper market has its origins in the last significant development in nineteenth-century journalism: in 1896, Alfred Harmsworth inaugurated the *Daily Mail*, a middlebrow, mid-market newspaper which rode the wave of anti-South African populism that broke during the Boer War, and became the first newspaper to achieve a circulation of a million a day.

By the end of the Victorian era, journalism was no longer a profession conducted by anonymous hacks, but had generated a star system of its own. Figures such as William Howard Russell, who reported for *The Times* from the Crimean War and is generally regarded as the first war correspondent, became well-known public figures. (His despatches were celebrated for having inspired Florence Nightingale to take herself to the front.) Other writers became identified with particular issues: Ida Wells Barnet, for instance, was an African American journalist who bought an interest in the *Memphis Free Speech* newspaper, and made a long career out of tackling issues of racial inequality, often putting herself in danger to do so. Winifred Sweet Black was a hard-boiled political reporter who hid under a table in President Benjamin Harrison's railroad car in order to obtain an interview. Elizabeth Cochrane Seaman of the *New York World* was an undercover investigative journalist who wrote under the pen name Nelly Bly, and often conducted her enquiries in disguise. She investigated sweat-shops, tenements and the mental health system, assuming madness in order to get herself committed to the asylum on Blackwell's Island – whose abuses she then exposed.

Stead delighted in such methods, and as the Eliza Armstrong case demonstrated, he did not worry excessively about concomitant matters of ethics. He saw the professionalisation of journalism as part of a broader movement which would transform the mass media into a parallel form of government, offering a moral authority strong enough to shape the decisions of those in elected office. 'I have not yet lost faith', he wrote in 1886, 'in the possibility of some of our great newspaper proprietors who will content himself [*sic*] with a reasonable fortune, and devote the surplus of his gigantic profits to the development of his newspaper as an engine of social reform and as a means of government. And if it be impossible for those already in the purple to display such public spirit, then it may be that the same spirit which led pious founders in medieval times to build cathedrals and establish colleges, may lead some man or woman of fortune to devote half a million to found a newspaper for the service, for the education, and for the guidance of the people.'[17] In July 1929, the Empire Crusade, a campaign for imperial economic protectionism, was launched by Lord Beaverbrook, proprietor of the *Daily Express*, who attempted to put Stead's ideas into practice. By 1931, it had gained the support of Lord Rothermere, proprietor of the *Daily Mail*. When they fielded their own candidate in the by-election at St George's Westminster, the two newspapers nearly succeeded in toppling Stanley Baldwin's Conservative administration.

Rupert Murdoch, the Australian media tycoon, proprietor of *The Times*, the *Sun* and the *News of the World*, endower of a professorship at Oxford University, would recognise the aspiration. He might also recognise Stead's unrepentant attitude to Eliza Armstrong's ordeal. In 1964, Murdoch's Australian tabloid, the Sydney *Daily Mirror*, published extracts from the diary of a fourteen-year-old school pupil under the banner 'WE HAVE SCHOOLGIRL'S ORGY DIARY'. A thirteen-year-old classmate was identified from this journal, and expelled from the school. At home, he hanged himself from the garden clothes line. When the girl was examined by a doctor from the Child Welfare Department, she was found to be a virgin. The diary was an elaborate piece of fantasy. When the journalist Richard Neville confronted Murdoch about the case, he replied, 'Everybody makes mistakes.'[18] He made another one, perhaps, in November 2000, when he offered Monica Lewinsky an enormous fee to appear on an Australian chat show during the week of the American presidential election. She cancelled her appearance days before transmission, prompting the producer of the show to offer this shrill riposte via the pages of the Sydney *Telegraph:* 'I suppose that's the sort of behaviour you can expect from soiled goods. This behaviour should bury any perception that she is a naïve victim.'[19] Sometimes, as Stead discovered, the objects of sensational journalistic interest turn out to be less passive than the reporter can anticipate. Monica Lewinsky never appeared on Murdoch's Foxtel channel. She didn't cash my cheque, either. But she may have looked at it for a moment, guessed my game and murmured, 'Nice try, but no cigar.'

CHAPTER FIVE

I Knew My Doctor Was a Serial Killer Because ...

The villain then cut off her head, and burnt it in the fire;
And likewise cut off all her limbs, to satisfy his ire.
The trunk alone remained to tell her lamentable fate,
'Twas chopped and cut; the entrails gone;
How awful to relate!
    The Edgware Tragedy (184?)

A general practitioner in an unremarkable English town kills at least fifteen of his patients with prescription drugs. He is tried for murder and forgery, and found guilty. Newspapers fill up with accounts of his crimes and hastily written biographies are rushed into print. Readers reflect uncomfortably on the unquestioned authority of doctors; remind themselves to double-check the label next time they're given medication; wonder, vaguely, if their local GP might have snuffed out the life of the odd irritating patient, confident that the crime would never be detected.

For the people of Hyde, Greater Manchester, this is the painful legacy forced upon them by the activities of Dr Harold Frederick Shipman, the most prolific serial murderer in British history. On the last day of January 2000, Shipman was found guilty of taking the lives of fifteen women with overdoses of morphine. It is certain, however, that Hyde's cemeteries contain more of his victims. Nobody will ever know how many patients Dr Shipman sent gently to their deaths; still less why he pursued his lethal hobby so tenaciously. There are few people in Hyde whose lives have not been touched by his crimes: it will probably take a generation for the town's sense of outrage and horror to fade. Fifty miles further south, however, in Rugeley, Staffordshire, the trial induced a strange sense of *déjà vu*. It was here, in 1856, that the police finally caught up with Dr William Palmer, Victorian England's most notorious poisoner.

The pattern of similarity between these two cases is remarkable. Study the details, look over the texts that accrued around these killers, and you

[71]

THE ONLY AUTHENTIC LIKENESS OF WILLIAM PALMER.

7 William Palmer, the Rugeley poisoner, from *The Illustrated Life and Career of William Palmer*, 1856

can almost feel the past and present meshing together. Like Dr Shipman, Dr Palmer preyed on his patients, using their faith in his professional authority to kill them with drugs from his little black bag. As in the Shipman trial, the defendant was found guilty, even when forensic evidence was questioned and motive was not fully established. Palmer's trial attracted so much media coverage that the inhabitants of Rugeley thought very seriously about renaming their infamous town. Their descendants, however, as I discovered on a visit to Rugeley the day after the Shipman trial concluded at Preston Crown Court, are quietly pleased with their murderous heritage.

William Palmer's house still stands on Market Street, directly opposite the pub where his final victim was poisoned with a bowl of strychnine-laced beef broth. It has been split down the middle into two shops: Thrifty, a discount boutique pitched firmly at the giro market; and Videoworld, the town's most compendious VHS rental outfit. Close by the spot where Dr Palmer stirred the soup pan on his kitchen range, I found Videoworld's manager Kerry Spink sorting through last night's returned tapes. 'People are quite proud of Dr Palmer,' she told me. 'Let's face it, nothing much else has ever happened in Rugeley.'

After he qualified at St Bartholomew's Hospital, London, in 1846, Palmer rented a house in his home town, set up in general practice and married a local girl named Annie Brookes.[1] But his predilection for the racecourse meant that he was usually short of cash: so short, in fact, that he often complained of the burdensome expense of having young children to look after. Conveniently, four of the five little Palmers died within a month of being born – and a sixth child, by a mistress named Jane Mumford, expired unexpectedly after a visit to its biological father. From this point, Palmer's biography becomes a series of pressing debts and suspicious deaths: sixteen lethal poisonings, if the rumours are to be believed. He invited his moneyed mother-in-law to move into his home, but she declined, declaring, 'I know I shall not live a fortnight'. Sure enough, she dropped dead of an 'apoplexy' several days later. A Mr Bladon of Ashby-de-la-Zouch fell suddenly sick while visiting the Palmer household, and was soon lying lifeless on the carpet. A Mr Bly of Beccles suffered the same fate. An uncle of Palmer's, an eccentric fop reported to have fathered a child by his own illegitimate daughter, was the next to croak, after a friendly chat with his nephew over a glass of brandy. Then an aunt was suddenly taken ill on a visit to her Rugeley relations: Palmer supplied her with medication, but when she got home, she threw the pills out of the window – and found herself with a yard full of deceased chickens.

As Palmer's gambling debts increased, he got into the habit of forging his mother's signature on bills of acceptance. In 1854, he took out an extravagant life insurance policy on his wife. A few days after her husband had paid the first £700 premium, Annie Palmer unexpectedly expired in a firework display of vomiting and diarrhoea ('English cholera' wrote her husband on the death certificate.) The same pattern of extravagant insurance and sudden demise occurred in the case of Palmer's brother Walter. This time, the insurance company refused to pay up, and an inquest into brother Walter's death proved inconclusive – mainly because his body exploded when its lead-lined sarcophagus was prised open. The victim for whose murder Palmer was eventually hanged was John Parsons Cook, a racing acquaintance whom he had been treating for syphilis. At the end of a successful day on the turf, Cook became violently sick after taking a glass of brandy-and-water with Palmer. The doctor moved Cook into a room at the Talbot Arms, where he dosed his patient with morphine and fed him beef broth. In the early hours of 20 November 1855, Cook thrashed his life away in a series of violent convulsive fits.

Though the evidence against Palmer was purely circumstantial – like Shipman, nobody actually saw him administer any lethal drugs – an Old Bailey court found him guilty after a twelve-day trial. While his friends and surviving family members protested that he had little to gain from Cook's death, twenty thousand people made the journey to Stafford to see the doctor swing. As Palmer stepped tentatively up to the scaffold, he is supposed to have enquired of the hangman, 'Are you sure it is safe?', after which he shook his executioner by the hand, exclaimed 'God bless you!' and was soon gurgling his last on the end of the rope.[2]

Our attitude to Victorian murder is paradoxical. A repertoire of familiar images – swirling fog, hansom cabs, a top-hatted figure with a knife glinting in the gaslight – has imbued nineteenth-century killing with a seasonal charm, a cuteness that we would be unwilling to extend to the activities of more recent murderers such as Jeffrey Dahmer or Peter Sutcliffe. Arthur Conan Doyle's Sherlock Holmes stories – set principally in the 1880s and 1890s, but produced by their author until 1927 – helped to foster this murderous nostalgia. George Orwell's essay *Decline of the English Murder* (1946) offered a witty take on the tendency, by suggesting that killing was a genteel art form at which the English had once excelled but which had been lost along with the Empire. Murder was something the Victorians did with style.

In this important article, Orwell compared the canonical cases of British homicide (Crippen, Palmer, Jack the Ripper) with a recent incident, a thrill-seeking murder spree involving a GI and a teenage stripper, known as The Cleft Chin Murder.[3] The details of this case are easily summarised. Elizabeth Jones and Karl Hulten met in a teashop and went joyriding in a stolen car. Hulten ran over a girl on a bicycle – 'to show how tough he was,' according to Orwell.[4] They killed a taxi driver, George Heath – the owner of the physical feature which gave the killing its moniker – and spent the contents of his wallet at the dog track. They stole a truck, in which they picked up Violet Jones, a teenage hitcher who had just discovered that her American fiancé was already a married man. Somewhere near Windsor, Hulten knocked the passenger unconscious, swiped her handbag and hoicked her into the river. For Orwell, the deterioration in the quality of the murders committed in his homeland was the work of cultural imperialism. The post-war killer had become less distinguished, the product of 'the anonymous life of the dance halls and the false values of the American film.'[5] The killer was now a gangster (or a gangster wannabe) rather than a gentleman or lady amateur.

But there is more to the story than this. The figure of the Victorian murderer has also been employed in Whiggish accounts of the period with which this book takes issue. The male killer embodies that stereotype of hypocrisy habitually associated with nineteenth-century society. His activities suggest a dark underworld which we suppose lurked just underneath the surface of 'respectable' Victorian society. This is the prejudice that produced the Tod Slaughter villain, who killed by night and attended polite tea parties by day, and the popular – but ludicrous – theory that the Jack the Ripper murders were committed by the Duke of Clarence, in an attempt to silence prostitutes who threatened to damage his chances of accession. It is a stereotype found in Victorian crime writing, particularly Stead's 'Maiden Tribute' articles, as Judith Walkowitz has demonstrated in *City of Dreadful Delight* (1992). It is also found, in a mutant form, in recent academic attempts to reclaim female killers of the nineteenth century as proto-feminist figures whose poisonings and shootings were, in some sense, anti-patriarchal acts – responses to intolerably over-regulated lives and social hypocrisies.

Neither model of Victorian murder – the nostalgic or the repressive –

sits comfortably with the uncanny parallels between the careers of Doctors Palmer and Shipman, and the way in which their stories circulated through British culture. In the weeks following Palmer's execution, a souvenir industry developed around the dead felon. Sermons were preached and printed on the moral lessons to be drawn from the case. Off-cuts of the hangman's rope were sold for a shilling an inch. The doctor's facsimile became the star attraction at Madame Tussaud's Chamber of Horrors. Illustrated biographies and engraved portraits were published in Britain and on the Continent. An *Illustrated Life of William Palmer* was published in weekly parts in 1856. A clue to the identity of its readers comes from the books and journals advertised on the wrapper: *The Practical Housewife, Treasures in Needlework, The Wife's Own Book of Cookery* and *Elegant Arts for Ladies*, 'including Ornamental Rice Shell-work; Painting on Velvet; Etiquette, Politeness and Good Breeding.'

When Dr Shipman went down, columnists and religious broadcasters drew moral lessons from his crimes. Newspapers rushed out their souvenir editions. The *Manchester Evening News* produced a 'Dr Death Supplement' and its dedicated Harold Shipman website offered 'photos of him at school, as a medical student, and at a friend's wedding ... pictures of all but three of the alleged victims, including exclusive pictures of Marie Quinn, pictures of the relatives, scenes of the exhumations and the cemetery where his patients are buried, including an aerial shot. Also a death certificate, his surgery, his homes, property involved in the will of a patient etc ...' Two hack-written biographies, Mikaela Sitford's *Addicted to Murder: The True Story of Dr Harold Shipman* and Brian Whittle and Jean Ritchie's *Prescription for Murder: The True Story of Mass Murderer Dr Harold Frederick Shipman*, materialised in bookshops a few days after the verdict was given. Both books made an instinctive recourse to nineteenth-century analogues. ('They all read like Victorian melodrama,' said one review.) Sitford's account likens Shipman to Dr Jekyll and Mr Hyde and suggests he had 'a Florence Nightingale-cum-Hannibal Lecter persona'. Whittle and Ritchie describe the exhumation of Shipman's victims in purplish, penny dreadful terms: 'The night was so black and the rain so unremitting that [the officiating policeman] could imagine at any moment lightning forking across the sky, illuminating a black carriage with plumed horses and bats fluttering overhead, like a scene from a Denis [*sic*] Wheatley novel or a Hammer horror film.' And 'Walking around Hyde Cemetery on a sunny afternoon it is, to quote Emily Brontë, impossible to imagine unquiet slumbers for the sleepers in that quiet earth.'[6]

In the fortnight following the verdict, a slew of other serial killer-related events took place in London, from which any future researcher could draw gruesome conclusions about twenty-first-century attitudes to such crimes. Spike Lee's film *Summer of Sam* – which dramatised the events surrounding the murders committed by David Berkowitz in New York during the hot months of 1977 – was on general release in British cinemas. A black comedy, *So I Killed a Few People*, ran at the Riverside Studios in Hammersmith, west London. On the south side of the Thames, the Royal Vauxhall Tavern held a serial killer theme night, at which patrons were invited to take part in a pub quiz about gay mass murderers, and complete the sentence 'I could tell my doctor was a serial-killer because ...' in as witty a way as possible. The Poet Laureate, Andrew Motion, published a fictional autobiography of the nineteenth-century Romantic and murderer Thomas Wainewright. Anyone who logged on to the Internet could watch as Dr Shipman's crimes were tabulated on serial killer-themed websites: Serial Killer Central, for instance, placed him as a new entry at number five. The site also presented the opportunity to buy serial killer trading cards, tee-shirts and postcards, items autographed by Patrick Kearney (an electronic engineer who killed thirty-two gay men in 1970s California) and offered an invitation to join the Ed Gein Fan Club. (Gein, the killer on whom Norman Bates was based, used the skulls of his victims as kitchen utensils. Catalogue of Carnage, a mail order company in Arizona with links to this site, has replicas for sale.)

Along with religious and pornographic works, accounts of true crime have always been one of the pillars of the publishing industry. In the early nineteenth century, before the abolition of the Newspaper Stamp Tax made the *News of the World* viable, crime broadsides were hawked on street corners. Semi-literate, unauthoritative, prurient and decorated with stock illustrations, these were close cultural cousins of today's serial killer webpages. For your penny or ha'penny you would get a single sheet bearing a bloodthirsty woodcut, an account of some dreadful outrage, and a sententious little poem, often purporting to be the final apostrophe of the guilty. Their publishers established a repertoire of atrocity to which today's newspapers still adhere. *Shocking Tragedy at Penge!*: 'A fearful crime was committed at Melbourne Terrace, Dulwich Road, near

London, on the 28th of March, by an Accountant named Frederick Hunt, who murdered his WIFE and CHILD and attempted to poison his other children, and tried to take his own life!'[7] *A Particular Account of the Cruel Murder of Mrs. Thompson*: 'Only 19 years of age, in the city of Liverpool, at mid-day, by a woman with a red-hot poker, who afterwards robbed the house of property of great value, on Wednesday, the 5th of February, 1825.'[8] *Horrible Case of Starvation of a Child*: 'who was starved by its parents, till it actually ate its finger-ends as well as the skin off its feet.'[9] *Another Case of Unnatural Cruelty*: 'Being an account of the sufferings of a girl ten years of age who was barbarously treated and fastened with iron hoops to the wall of a damp and dark cellar in which state she was found by some persons who searched the house.'[10]

Most of these crimes are long forgotten. Others live on in unusual ways. If somebody asks, when pouring you a drink, 'What's your poison?', they are making unconscious reference to the Palmer case. And if they use the expression 'sweet FA', they are alluding to little Fanny Adams, an eight-year-old girl who was dismembered in a Hampshire hop garden on 24 August 1867. Fanny Adams's name soon became naval slang for regulation tinned mutton, which was introduced at around the time of her death. Gradually, however, the phrase became used for anything inconsequential or small.

Execution broadsides were sold as souvenirs of hangings, so that the face which was blackening and bloating on the scaffold was also being circulated in facsimile through the crowd. Hawkers would move through the audience like usherettes with choc ices, sheaves of biography slung over their arms. These publications were popular. One and a half million copies of *The Trial and Execution of William Corder, Murderer of Maria Marten* were shifted by James Catnach, a Seven Dials publisher who specialised in this material. Over two and a half million punters stumped up for his broadside on *The Execution of F. G. Manning and Maria, His Wife*, which told how a suburban couple murdered Maria's lover Patrick O'Connor and buried his body in quicklime under the kitchen floor of their Bermondsey home. ('Are you looking for a goose?' asked Maria Manning, as the police yanked up her hearthstone and found a human mulch identifiable only from dental records.) Charles Dickens attended their executions at Horsemonger Lane Gaol in November 1849, renting a ten-guinea room that overlooked proceedings. He took a picnic hamper and several bottles of wine, and later complained about the hangman's 'unseemly briskness'. The executioner on this occasion was William

Calcraft, a man notorious for his professional slackness: rather than making a clean break of it, his clients often expired in slow, sputtering fits of agony. His successor, William Marwood, always referred to Calcraft as 'the short-drop man.' 'He throttled them,' he once remarked. 'I execute them.'[11]

When public executions were outlawed in 1868, Britons had to go elsewhere to satisfy their curiosity about violent death and those who perpetrated it. We can do it through cinema and the Internet: the Victorians did it with waxworks. Although Dickens had written against public execution in *The Times*, he was one of the most enthusiastic visitors to what Madame Tussaud euphemistically referred to as her 'Chamber of Comparative Physiognomy'. (The name suggesting that you could gaze upon the figures of Frederick and Maria Manning and decide whether you had the earlobes of a killer.) The relationship with the gallows-show was very explicit. When the Chamber opened, the company declared that the 'sensation caused by the crimes of Rush, the Mannings, etc. was so great that thousands were unable to satisfy their curiosity. It therefore induced Madame Tussaud and Sons to expend a large sum in building a suitable room for the purpose.' Those concerned that close inspection of these felons might prove an unhealthy pastime were placated with this assurance: '[Tussaud's] need scarcely assure the public that so far from the exhibition of the likenesses of criminals creating a desire to imitate them, experience teaches that it has a direct tendency to the contrary.'[12] Which, presumably, was good enough for Dickens. His children, however, don't seem to have shared his passion for dead cons. Charles Dickens junior described the Tussaud's experience in a London guidebook in 1893:

> Very grim and a trifle horrible is the Chamber of Horrors, which contains counterfeit presentments of some of the most desperate criminals of late years, with a gallows to suggest the means by which the world got quit of them. There are also some particularly blood-curdling casts of heads dating from the first French Revolution, and the original Guillotine, bought by Madame Tussaud from Samson, grandson to the 'Monsieur of Paris' of the time of the Terror. There is no better place in London for children than Madame Tussaud's, but parents and guardians will do well to remember the contents of the Chamber of Horrors are strong meat for babes.[13]

The *Spectator* decided that the Chamber was 'a disgrace to our civilization', but other writers were more ironic about the strange titillation experienced when coming face to face with the duplicate of a killer.[14] In Mary Elizabeth Braddon's novel *Three Times Dead!!!; or The Secret of the Heath* (1860), the villain of the story is executed for his crimes, and immediately reconstructed as a dubious sexual icon:

> The agents from an exhibition of waxworks, and several phrenologists, came to look at, and to take casts of his head, and masks of his handsome and aristocratic face ... Young ladies fell in love with him, and vowed that a being – they called him a being – with such dear blue glass eyes, with beautiful curly eyelashes, and specks of lovely vermilion in each corner, could never have committed a horrid murder, but was no doubt the innocent victim of that cruel circumstantial evidence.[15]

The Chamber of Horrors was completely refurbished in 1996. 'Kids said it wasn't frightening enough, so we made it a bit more scary,' the Tussaud's PR officer told me when I rang for a ticket. On a previous visit in 1995, I can remember feeling strangely impressed by the indecency of the place. I recall a brightly-lit, white-tiled room in which Dennis Nilsen rubbed shoulders with Charles Manson and his crew. The chill effect must have been just the same for those nineteenth-century people who filed through these passages, and caught their breath as they came face to face with the Mannings and Palmer. These were killers of recent vintage, at which you could peer under a white, clinical light. There was a brutal honesty at work in it.

Making a return visit, I was quite prepared to see waxworks of the Wests skulking in a mocked-up cellar with a bag of Blue Circle and a roll of gaffer tape, or Jeffrey Dahmer hunched by the refrigerator, Polaroid in hand – especially as I had been assured that the nastiness had been amplified. But walking around the Chamber, I was surprised by how tasteful, how heritagey an experience it has become. The place has been reformulated to counter the threat of the London Dungeon, the high-tech horror show under London Bridge station, and the emphasis is on ghost-train whoopdedoo: stereophonic screams ring out above your head; mouldering corpses twitch on gibbets; an animatronic Christie, the Rillington Place killer, drops from the scaffold. For those unnerved by such hi-tech horror, the amount of fright on offer is more impressive. But the feeling of perversity, of a taboo broken, is quite gone. The Manson family have moved out, leaving Dennis Nilsen to represent killers of contemporary history. I imagine that he has remained here – unaccompanied by more recent serial killers like the Wests – because of the matter of identification. Many of Nilsen's fifteen or so victims were never named. Difficult, I suppose, to extract identities from the material that was glugging through the plumbing of his home. We all know, however, those mournful Photo-Me images of the student girls abused and butchered by the Wests. Nilsen's victims were homeless gay men, most of whom were estranged from their families: families who may have visited Tussaud's and gazed into the glassy eyes of Nilsen's waxwork, not guessing that their runaway boys had been boiled down on his stove in Muswell Hill.

Dr Crippen is still present in the Chamber, as mild and respectable as ever, but his medicine box, from which he served the dose of hydrobromide of hyoscine which killed his wife, has been put into storage. George Joseph Smith, the Brides in the Bath murderer, stands beside him. This counts, I think, as a demotion. I remember from a childhood visit the disturbing tableau in which Smith was depicted in the act of killing his wife Margaret Lofty. She was a clergyman's daughter who, at thirty-eight, had thought her chances of dying married were highly unlikely. Smith proposed to her. She accepted, and was persuaded to withdraw her £19 savings from the post office. Later that night, he drowned her in the bath at their lodgings by yanking her under the water by her ankles. After the struggle was over, he sauntered into the sitting room and began to play *Nearer, My God, to Thee* on the harmonium: the hymn that was supposed to have comforted the drowning passengers on board the *Titanic*. The little scene at Tussaud's included the actual bath from the case, made all the more gruesome by the air pipe that bubbled the waxwork Margaret Lofty's last few breaths up through the soapy water. The house where he committed his crimes – 14 Waterlow Road, Highgate, according to *Crime and Scandal: The Black Plaque Guide to London* (1987) – still stands, and I'm sorry to say that I once strolled down there and attempted to peer surreptitiously through the window.

Other murderers from what George Orwell identified as the 'great period in murder ... between roughly 1850 and 1925' have been permanently retired.[16] The Mannings are nowhere to be seen. Neither is Mary Eleanor Pearcey, the baby-suffocator of Kentish Town, who in October 1890 bludgeoned Phoebe Hogg, her lover's wife, to death with a poker, spattering the kitchen wall with blood. She then did for little Hogg by stuffing her mother's body into the pram on top of her, covered both with an antimacassar, and trundled them westwards towards Hampstead. She dumped her bloody cargo at two locations: Mrs Phoebe Hogg and the perambulator in Crossfield Road, Hampstead, and baby Phoebe Hogg on a stretch of waste ground off the Finchley Road. When the police attempted to interview Pearcey at the Hogg's family home, she sang loudly and played the piano. When they asked her where all the blood had come from, she replied, 'Killing mice.' In his grief, Frank Hogg was comforted by a cheque from Madame Tussaud, who bought the pram and put it on display with a figure of Mrs Pearcey and a boiled sweet recovered from the baby's mouth. As for William Palmer, his decapitated head has been relegated to the trophy room of has-beens in a display illustrating the history of the waxworks. Stowed awkwardly on a shelf, in close proximity to Bjorn Borg and Margaret Thatcher, Palmer surveys the crowds – who have no idea who he is – with a look of chubby-cheeked indulgence playing across his face.

Does this demotion signal a move away from the barbarism of the past? Not exactly. Modern killers are better served by other media: murder is quickly recycled into true-life TV movies. A British TV channel bought the rights to screen the videos Fred and Rosemary West made of their victims. Self-confessed killers such as the British mobsters Dave Courtney and Freddie Foreman appear at literary festivals touting their autobiographies, in which they exploit a legal loophole by confessing to crimes for which they have been acquitted. Victorian murder, meanwhile, has become the object of academic interest, in studies such as Mary S. Hartman's *Victorian Murderesses* (1977) and Virginia Morris's *Double Jeopardy: Women Who Kill in Victorian Fiction* (1990). In 1999, one cheery subscriber to the Victoria Research Web Internet discussion group solicited members' advice on hosting a Jack the Ripper theme party. These days, you can take a guided tour of the East End alleys where Jolly Jack sliced up his victims. Women's groups occasionally protest, but the tour organisers show no sign of giving in to such pressure.

One short part of this walk will demonstrate how the Victorians viewed these crimes. Take the tube to Whitechapel, and you emerge from the station to find yourself staring at the front of the Royal London Hospital. It was here, in the winter of 1886, that Joseph Carey Merrick, the Elephant Man, arrived penniless from Brussels, having been robbed by his manager, to seek the mercy of the surgeon Frederick Treves. Turn right, and you soon come to Woods Buildings, a dank little passage in which the scrofulous stench of the Elephant Man's skin still seems to hang. Pass through here, and you cross a footbridge over the railway track that leads you to what was once Swanlea Secondary School, a sturdy Victorian building that has now been converted into an apartment block. Turn left and walk around the old school and you'll find yourself on Durward Street, formerly Buck's Row. Smart new flats now occupy what was, a century ago, an area dominated by slum housing and Harrison and Barber Ltd, a horse-slaughtering firm. Here, where the long red brick wall of the schoolyard terminates, was a row of terraces outside which, at 3.30 am on 31 August 1888, an odd bundle was discovered by Charles Cross, a cabman on his way to work. This was the mutilated body of Mary Anne Nichols, a forty-four-year-old prostitute who had wandered down the ill-lit back street, hoping to turn a trick that would secure her a bed for the night at her lodging house on Thrawl Street.

In his notebook, Inspector John Spratling of J Division recorded what he saw: 'Her throat had been cut from left to right, two dist[inct] cuts being on left side. The wind[pipe] gullet and spinal cord being cut through, a bruise apparently of a th[umb] being on right lower jaw, also one o[n] left cheek, the abdomen had been [cut] open from centre of bottom ribs a[long] right side, under pelvis to left of the stomach, there the wound was jag[ged], the omentium, or coating of the stomach, was also cut in several places, and tw[o] small stabs on private parts, apparently done with a strong-bladed knife.'[17] The brutality of the killing had soon earned its perpetrator the nickname of Jack the Ripper. W. T. Stead had another chance to increase the circulation of the *Pall Mall Gazette*.

Retrace your steps, turn right when you emerge from the entrance to Wood's Buildings and stop at number 259. It was once a glass ware-house, the front of which was hired out to passing showmen. In November 1884, it was the temporary home of Joseph Merrick, and the façade was draped with a huge banner depicting a strange bipedal pachyderm running amok through the palm trees. By September 1888, it was home to a waxwork exhibition themed around the Ripper murderers. A *Daily News* journalist who ventured inside reported: '. . . there is a waxwork show with some horrible pictorial representations of the recent murders, and all the dreadful details are being bleated out into the night, and women with children in their arms are pushing their way to the front with their pennies to see the ghastly objects within.'[18] The killer was still active in the very streets on which this display was being offered. One hundred and thirty suspects have been suggested since 1888, but whoever Jack the Ripper was, it's hard to believe that he would have turned down the opportunity to look upon his works in effigy. You can imagine him, loitering at the back of the audience, staring coolly down at the counterfeit corpses, his Gladstone bag of knives gripped firmly in his gloved hand.

The *Daily News* report mentioning the waxworks appeared at the close of September 1888. On 9 November, the body of Mary Jane Kelly was discovered in an upstairs room on Miller's Court, Dorset Street. It was a killing of appalling ferocity: Kelly was reduced to a misshapen mass of meat, barely recognisable as human. Look at the photographs of her remains which have been endlessly reproduced in a hundred tacky Jack the Ripper souvenir books, and the case soon loses the fog-bound, Christmassy charm that a century of mythologising has generated around it. The Ripper murders were a campaign of the most dreadful slaughter. But, as the evidence of the waxwork show demonstrates, the Victorians were as keen as us to convert atrocity into recreational pleasure. The similarities between the Palmer and Shipman cases, and the ways in which they were disseminated through culture, demonstrate that process. In another 150 years or so, will the people of Hyde feel a proud and cosy glow when the name of Dr Harold Shipman is mentioned? Will local children do school projects on his crimes? Will the deaths of Kathleen Grundy, Winifred Mellor, Joan Melia, Irene Turner, Jean Lilley, Muriel Grimshaw, Maria West, Lizzie Adams, Kathleen Wagstaff, Norah Nuttall, Pamela Hillier, Maureen Ward and dozens of others take on that jokey *Kind Hearts and Coronets* quality which surrounds our accounts of Victorian murder?

A taxi driver, who moved to Rugeley in 1993, told me how reports of the Shipman trial had been received in the town. 'When we heard about the Dr Shipman case in our office,' she said, 'we said it was like Dr Palmer all over again. A Dr Palmer job. He's like an icon round here. Nobody agrees with what Dr Palmer did, but it was a very modern crime. He was ahead of his time, Dr Palmer.'

At William Palmer's parish church, St Augustine's, most of the nineteenth-century graves have been cleared away, laid flat on their backs around the perimeter of the churchyard. The tomb of John Parsons Cook, however, remains. Just to the right of the door, it lies in full view of what was once the house of Dr Palmer's mother, where, for years after, she would stand at the gate declaring, 'The judges hanged my saintly

Billy', to anyone who would listen.[19] Just before I left Rugeley, I wandered into the church, and found myself sitting at the back of an overwhelmingly female, overwhelmingly elderly congregation. Just the sort of sprightly old ladies who might have got Dr Shipman's syringe-finger twitching. The Rev Michael Newman opened his address with a gag: 'What's the difference between a doctor and God?' There was a small pause as we tried to guess the punch line, but nobody managed it. 'God', said the Rev Newman, 'knows he's not a doctor'. There was an audible 'Ah!' as his parishioners absorbed the truth of this observation, and fifty-odd snow-white perms nodded away in rueful agreement.

CHAPTER SIX

Last Exit to Shadwell

The Black Drop: Take 1/2 a pound of opium, sliced; 3 pints of good verjuice; 1 1/2 ounces of nutmeg; and 1/2 an ounce of saffron; boil them to a proper thickness, then add a 1/4 of a pound of sugar and 2 spoonsful of yeast. Set the whole in a warm place near the fire for 6 or 8 weeks, then place it in the open air until it becomes of the consistence of a syrup; lastly, decant, filter, and bottle it up, adding a little sugar to each bottle. Dose, 5 to 15 drops. The above ought to yield about two pints of the strained liquor.

The Household Cyclopedia (1881)

Three days after Christmas 1889, a sixty-four-year-old man coughed his last in a lodging house under the arches of the London and Blackwall Railway. He was taken to Ratcliff mortuary, a low building behind the graveyard of St George's-in-the-East, Shadwell, where he lay on the slab for a week. The coroner poked about inside him, and concluded that the cause of death was a ruptured blood vessel, exacerbated by the effects of poverty. The following Sunday, the cadaver was transported to Bow Cemetery, where the registrar wrote the name 'George Harsing' in the burial book. It was the wrong name. But the mistake was understandable. Over the years, the dead man had been known by several. The enumerators of the 1871 census put him down as John Johnston. His wife, Hannah Johnston, a tailoress from Bath, knew him as George. George Ah Sing. (A less attentive listener, Joseph Vatcher, the curate of St George's, recorded him as 'Ah Ching' in the marriage register.) Most other English people who encountered him – the hacks hunting colour, the novelists after dirty realism, the West Enders randy for a gawp – probably didn't bother asking his name. On this quiet immigrant from Amoy, however, was founded one of the most enduring myths of Victorian London.

Ah Sing's funeral was a modest event. The officiating clergyman had already put two corpses in the earth that day. The mourners – Hannah Johnston, her neighbour Mrs Godfrey and Mrs Godfrey's three daughters – left their home in Cornwall Street at two o'clock in the afternoon, and were back home within the hour. At the funeral tea, they concluded that thanks to Arthur Bradford, the young head of a long-established family of undertakers on Cannon Street Road, Ah Sing had been 'buried most comfortable'. Naturally enough, the conversation took a spiritual turn. Mrs Godfrey, more garrulous than her bereaved friend, asserted that he 'must have known the third chapter of John by heart'. The widow recalled how she 'had often seen him clasp his hands and heard him beg his Heavenly Father to "take 'im 'ome" '. They discussed how his debtors had contributed to his woes. Hannah waved a piece of paper, which listed, in Chinese script, the names of the Lascar sailors who owed him some £700 in unpaid rent. One of the guests, however, a reporter from the *East London Observer*, was keen to push the conversation in another direction. What did Hannah Johnston recall about the night Charles Dickens visited her late husband's opium den?[1]

In the summer of 1869, Dickens, his American publisher James T. Fields and an obliging lodging-house inspector took a nocturnal tour of Shadwell. They peered into lock-up houses, watch-houses and slum kitchens. They surveyed squalid yards and alleyways. But don't think of them as adventurers or explorers. Dickens and his cosy little posse took a well-trodden path through a well-documented quarter of London, whose picturesque decay, unruly nightlife and obvious cosmopolitanism made it a magnet for writers in search of easy copy. Think of them instead as shock tourists visiting an attraction that, only a decade later, would be listed in the guidebook along with Regent's Park Zoo and Madame Tussaud's. This jaunt, however, was not without important consequences. In New Court, a shabby little habitation in the East End, the novelist found the opening chapter of his last, and unfinished, work *The Mystery of Edwin Drood* (1870).

It begins with narcosis. John Jasper, the choirmaster of Cloisterham, fuddled with opium in some frowsy den, hallucinates a vision of Oriental psychedelia in which the spire of his own cathedral is transmuted into the architecture of a sultan's palace. He emerges from this state to find himself staring at an iron bed-post, sharing a broken-down divan with a haggard woman – the proprietor of the joint – and two wasted Oriental customers. The woman offers him another pipe. 'Ye've smoked as many as five since ye come in at midnight,' she observes, before trying to elicit his further patronage with a spot of professional self-pity: 'Ah, poor me, the business is slack, is slack! Few Chinamen about the Docks, and fewer

8 The marriage of Ah Sing and Hannah Johnston, from Joseph Salter,
The Asiatic in England, 1873

Lascars, and no ships coming in, these say! Here's another ready for ye, deary. Ye'll remember like a good soul, won't ye, that the market price is dreffle high just now? More nor three shillings and sixpence for a thimbleful! And ye'll remember that nobody but me (and Jack Chinaman t'other side of the court; but he can't do it as well as me) has the true secret of mixing it?'[2]

From this little scene, textual opium dens blossomed: most subsequent journalistic and literary accounts of such places – even those by Oscar Wilde and Arthur Conan Doyle – owe more to Dickens than any genuine field-work. Novelists, wrote the Sinophile and ghost-story writer James Platt in an 1895 article for the *Gentleman's Magazine*, exploited their exoticism 'without taking the trouble to inspect the dens themselves'.[3] The veracity of Dickens's own research was contested as soon as the first shilling number of *Edwin Drood* went on sale in W. H. Smith's. Sir John Bowring – a former Governor of Hong Kong who, in October 1856, had initiated the Second Opium War by responding to the boarding of a British schooner by despatching a naval force to bombard Canton – took issue with Dickens's depiction of the woman's smoking kit, 'made from an old penny ink bottle', and sent him a sketch of a traditional Chinese opium pipe, illustrating how it should be properly used. Dickens replied, rather sniffily, that he had only described what he saw with his own eyes. Graciously, Bowring conceded, 'No doubt the Chinaman whom he described had accommodated himself to English usage, and that our great and faithful dramatist here as elsewhere most correctly pourtrayed [*sic*] a piece of actual life.'[4] Six years later, James Fields described the visit to the den in his memoir of the author. 'In a miserable court', he wrote, 'we found the haggard old woman blowing at a kind of pipe made of an old penny ink-bottle. The identical words which Dickens puts into the mouth of this wretched creature in 'Edwin Drood' we heard her croon as we leaned over the tattered bed on which she was lying. There was something hideous in the way this woman kept repeating 'Ye'll pay up according, deary, won't ye?' and the Chinamen and Lascars made never-to-be-forgotten pictures in the scene.'[5]

So where did this scene take place? Certainly not in Limehouse, that region of East London whose name, for many years, was synonymous with Chinese criminality and drug use. The district – or more accurately, two streets in the district, Limehouse Causeway and Pennyfields – was not settled by Chinese immigrants until the 1890s, twenty years after Dickens suffered a fatal apoplexy in his Kentish garden. That, however, didn't stop later authors naturalising the Limehouse link: Peter Ackroyd's *Dan Leno and the Limehouse Golem* (1994) locates the dens of Drood and Dorian Gray in the area of its title; Daniel Farson's *Limehouse Days* (1991) even speculates that John Jasper got his fix in a house on Narrow Street belonging to the author. But it was the Edwardian popular press and a novelist named Arthur Henry Ward who flooded Limehouse with a narcotic atmosphere. In 1911, Ward – who wrote under the pen name Sax Rohmer – was commissioned by a magazine to cover a police investigation into a crime syndicate based in Limehouse. The owner of a Chinese gambling establishment was under suspicion, though the police never charged him with any crime. Not wanting to waste his material, Rohmer turned his notes into *The Mystery of Fu-Manchu* (1913), a sensational detective story about an opium-bibbing Chinese master criminal operating out of the East End. Fu-Manchu is a fanatical patriot working to restore the primacy of the Oriental races: 'Imagine a person', rumbles the villain's nemesis Sir Denis Nayland-Smith, 'tall, lean and feline, high-shouldered, with a brow like Shakespeare and a face like Satan, a close-shaven skull, and long, magnetic eyes of the true cat-green. Invest him with all the cruel cunning of an entire Eastern race, accumulated in one giant intellect, with all the resources of science past and present, with all the resources, if you will, of a wealthy government – which, however, already has denied all knowledge of his existence. Imagine that awful being, and you have a mental picture of Dr Fu-Manchu, the yellow peril incarnate in one man.'[6]

Fu-Manchu's principal role, however, was as an embodiment of the powerful anti-Oriental racism that flourished in Britain in the first few decades of the twentieth century, nurtured by the violence of the Boxer Rebellion in 1900 and the unexpected victory of the Japanese in their war against Russia in 1904–5. It was a racism which argued that Chinese men benefited from the Great War by stealing the women and jobs of men fighting at the Western Front. A racism that assumed when, in November 1918, the showgirl Billie Carleton was found dead of a cocaine overdose in her West End flat, that the Limehouse Chinese had administered the drug. The following year, Rohmer's fictional account of the case, *Dope: A Story of Chinatown and the Drug Traffic* (1919), helped consolidate the belief that Chinese Londoners were using narcotics to keep young white women in sexual servitude.

In the chunky file of newspaper cuttings in the Tower Hamlets Local History Library relating to the presence of the Chinese in the borough, the stories have a monotonously Rohmerian theme. 'YELLOW PERIL IN LONDON. VAST SYNDICATE OF VICE WITH ITS CRIMINAL MASTER. WOMEN AND CHILD VICTIMS,' shrieks a clipping from the *Daily Express* of 1 October 1920. 'Patient police work carried on against tremendous odds has resulted in establishing the fact that scattered throughout the world are thousands of the agents of [a] secret Chinese syndicate, which promotes the pernicious opium trade.' (This secret syndicate is, of course, headed by a 'Chinese Moriarty'.) The Chinese, these cuttings argue, have transformed East London into a place of exotic danger, where subterranean tunnels link gambling dens and brothels, and electric buttons hidden under the linoleum are used to communicate early warnings of police raids. There is a comic desperation in the extent to which the writers of such copy attempted to invest ordinary Chinese lodging houses and businesses with a weird, recondite atmosphere. After a drugs raid on Limehouse premises in 1930, an Inspector Lawrence told the *Star* newspaper that this was 'rather a mysterious shop'. This quality, he affirmed, was embodied in its 'antique vases in the window and in the shop many show cases, boxes of soap and washing powder'.[7]

There were dissenters from such attitudes. Even Thomas Burke – on whose story 'The Chink and the Child' (1917) D.W. Griffith based his lurid melodrama *Broken Blossoms* (1919) – felt that Oriental villainy had been exaggerated: 'One has read, in periodicals, of the well-to-do people from the western end, who hire rooms here [in Limehouse] and come down, from time to time, for an orgy. That is another story for the nursery.'[8] His disavowal didn't stop pornographers concocting opium den scenes in which white Billie Carleton types were ravished by Chinese smokers – or at least European actors wearing eye-shadow and flesh-coloured stockings on their heads. Nor did it prevent these sinister visions being projected back on to the nineteenth century, to generate retrospectively – in sources as various as academic work on *Edwin Drood*, film adaptations of Conan Doyle and episodes of *Doctor Who* – a Victorian East End populated by divan-sprawled dope-fiends.

The Victorians have only themselves to blame for this misapprehension of their culture. Nineteenth-century writings on opium dens, by novelists, evangelists, journalists and activists, rarely let the facts impede the flow of Gothic extravagance. Read through Victorian accounts of such places, and you soon begin to notice their common formulae: the navigation of a feculent East End labyrinth; the prospect of a squalid court; the murky opium room, with its tumbledown divan and dazed patrons; the courteous and affable opium master, cooking up his raw material; his smoke-dried Cockney wife; the suggestion that the place has received distinguished visitors. There is a very simple reason for this shared repertoire. Nearly every account of an opium den in nineteenth-century journalism is a description of one of two establishments in New Court, Shadwell, and the shifting cast of characters that occupied their beds and floors. Two small businesses run by a handful of Chinese immigrants and their English wives and girlfriends: this is the reality obscured by clouds of textual smoke.

Mid-Victorian Shadwell was a thoroughly multicultural district. Jewish immigrants – among them Karl Marx's family – had settled the western end of Cable Street, clustered at the junction with Cannon Street Road. A community of Scandinavians had established themselves in the area around Prince's Square and built themselves a Swedish church. A more transient population of Malaysians, Chinese and Indians – many of whom were employed by the Blue Funnel shipping line, which offered the first direct routes to the Far East – occupied boarding houses in the vicinity of Victoria Street, at the back of St George's-in-the-East. Those not employed on the docks found work in the sugar refineries, until this industry was sent into decline in the 1860s by a burst of French economic protectionism. The trade in exotic animals, however, flourished throughout the period. Charles Jamrach – an animal dealer responsible for introducing budgerigars into British homes – kept a commercial menagerie on Ratcliff Highway, where in the 1870s a lion went for £70, an orang-utan for £20. The Brighton Aquarium stocked itself from Jamrach. Dante Gabriel Rossetti found him an excellent source of wombats. The naturalist Francis Buckland – whose simian enthusiasms will be further explored in Chapter 9 – bought a monkey from his shop, a creature which once tried to steal the umbrella of the Rev Harry Jones, Rector of St George's-in-the-East.

Harry Jones is a significant figure in the history of the Shadwell dens. He lobbied for the demolition of the streets which bordered New Court (an objective eventually secured by the destabilising excavations of the East London underground line and the redevelopment initiatives of the Peabody Trust), but unlike the evangelical missionaries who loitered in the region, exhorting its heathen inhabitants to embrace the Lord, he had no moral objection to the presence of opium-smoking rooms behind his church. Joseph Salter, 'Missionary to the Asiatics in England', characterised them as 'pest-houses of sin and death', but Jones reflected that 'in this court of evil fame we have been ever welcome when paying a kindly visit or attending the sick'.[9]

New Court was a dilapidated square of twelve three-roomed houses at the heart of Jones's parish. To its north was Cable Street and the stately span of the railway viaduct. To the south, Ratcliff Highway, renamed St George's Street in an attempt to break its proverbial association with murder and villainy – in much the same way that today's inner city regenerators rechristen sink estates whose names have become synonymous with crime. To the west lay the Portland limestone tower of Nicholas Hawksmoor's St George's, and the vine-tangled Wesleyan burial ground, long disused, which the Rev Jones enjoyed as a private garden. To the east was Victoria Street (known as Bluegate Fields before another effort of diplomatic redesignation), a rowdy thoroughfare which housed several dancing joints and gin saloons, a Ragged School, a meeting house and a small music hall named Quashie's. Those who wished to pay a visit to the inhabitants of New Court reached their destination not through the 'extraordinary tangle of dark alleys' described by Blanchard Jerrold in *London: A Pilgrimage* (1872) or the 'devious way' noted by Charles Dickens Jnr in his *Dictionary of London* (1888), but – as the less excitable account of the Ordnance Survey reveals – through an arched passageway by the Royal Sovereign public house, which in one short, straight line brought the sightseer to the opening scene of *Edwin Drood*.

Census records, parish registers and personal accounts of variable reliability offer a fragmentary history of the New Court opium dens. Piecing them together is confusing work: some of the names in these accounts may have been used by more than one individual; some individuals may have gone by more than one name; many of these names may have been the inventions of the authors of the texts which describe them. Joseph Salter's published work is the source for many of these details, and this is clearly full of factual errors and religiose wishful thinking. As W. T. Stead's treatment of Eliza Armstrong and her family demonstrates, descriptions of the lives of the poor were often sensationalised for the satisfaction of the middle classes, and journalistic accounts of opium smokers were strongly influenced by the wild-eyed style of the *Pall Mall Gazette*. James Greenwood, a celebrated 'roving correspondent' for the *Gazette* and the *Daily News*, wrote several articles about the New Court opium dens, and on one occasion was upbraided by a policeman for their exaggerations: ' "Pish! the newspapers!" returned Mr Policeman in tones of such profound contempt as naturally grated harshly on my sensibilities, "what's the newspapers? There's a precious lot that appears *in* 'em that never appears *out* of 'em." '[10]

This much, however, can be deduced with reasonable certainty. The older of the two opium-smoking establishments was presided over by a man called Latou, a Chinese immigrant of advanced years. Latou shared his home with two Englishwomen, Sarah Graham (known as Lascar Sal) and Chinese Emma, women who became minor institutions in the journalism of Darkest London. (' "Chinese Emma" has no successor to-day,' observed one East End commentator in 1925, without having to explain who she was.)[11] In the early 1870s, Emma emigrated to New York in the company of her Oriental husband, the couple taking jobs as stewards on a transatlantic steamer. The older of the two women, Lascar Sal – who learned Hindustani and the secrets of opium preparation, and was the original for the haggard dope-peddler encountered by Dickens – remained faithful to Latou until his death. There were other, more minor players too. Joseph Salter, on one of his periodic visits to New Court on soul-saving duties, also recorded the presence of an Indian opium-dealer named Abdool Rhemon, whom he describes as having worked as a crossing-sweeper in St Paul's churchyard before he elected to return to Bombay at some point before 1873. Other figures associated with the court – Canton Kitty, Achee, Ching Chee, Chi Ki, Chang Wao and Old Yahee – are invoked less often, and may be variant names for figures already mentioned. Many unrecorded figures also passed this way: the Royal Sovereign was run as a boarding house for Chinese crewmen who could not stomach the clean-living regimen of the Limehouse Strangers' Home, a charitable sailors' hostel endowed in the 1850s by the Maharaja Duleep Singh. In New Court, these men could smoke and gamble as they pleased.

Latou and Lascar Sal stayed put in New Court, but their partnership did not last for long. In 1877, the *London City Mission Magazine* reported that 'the proprietor is gradually breathing out his last – a living skeleton – merely animated skin and bone, scarcely able to stand; and, as he lies curled up on his dirty coil of rags, smoking his pipe over a fitful flame with Lascar Sally, his companion, also smoking over the same lamp, he looks unearthly – a waif from another world – and yet he marshals his expiring strength in favour of Mohammed, and to protest against Christ, and the salvation wrought out on the Cross . . .'[12] Latou was dead before the end of the year. Sal, however, before she ended her days in a workhouse, continued his work alone for more than a decade – with Ah Sing as her principal rival in business.

A number of sources, including the memoirs of his neighbour the Rev Jones, identify Ah Sing positively as the 'John Chinaman' of *Edwin Drood*. He arrived in London in the 1860s, and appears on the 1871 census under the name of John Johnston, an identity he seems to have adopted for professional purposes. His den was known variously as Johnstone's, Johnston's and Johnson's to a generation of curious sightseers, whose number included Prince Charles Bonaparte, the Marquis of Bassano, the novelist and critic Augustin Filon, the artist Gustave Doré, the Prince of Wales, Charles Dickens Jnr and a small army of journalists. Reading through the blotched pages of the census, even on a fuzzy microfilm print, gives you a shivery connection with the lives of people long dead, long disregarded. You can see that when the census officials move from a well-to-do row of houses to New Court, there is a visible deterioration in their handwriting, that they refill their pens less diligently. Were they nervous, as they entered the passageway by the Royal Sovereign? Or just bored with their work – tired of trying to verify names and dates with respondents with a limited command of English? Whatever the case, they did their work. At number nine, they recorded the presence of a pair of Hong Kong-born sailors, and attempted to render their names in some Anglicised form, before giving up and resorting to an exasperated 'NK' = Not Known. At number seven, they logged a single mother of two, Eliza Jowell. At number six, they discovered the Johnstons, and entered their names in the return book.

One more official document registers the presence of Ah Sing. In 1878, he walked up to the altar of St George's with a woman named Emma Day – in spite of the jeers of a small crowd of protestors and his obvious inability to follow the service. As Chinese Emma had emigrated by this date, and no record survives of a separation or falling-out between Ah Sing and his wife, this woman must surely be Hannah, whose illiteracy would have prevented her from spotting the error in the register.

Married life for the Johnstons was not comfortable. At a date between 1879 and 1881, debt forced them out of New Court. They auctioned their few possessions to a group of sentimental bidders, who included at least one of the journalists who had used them to fill space during a slow news week. A picture of an English church executed by a Chinese sailor was sold to a friend of the writer James Platt. Other buyers picked up Ah

9 'Opium Smoking – The Lascar's Room in Edwin Drood', from Gustave Doré
and Blanchard Jerrold, *London: A Pilgrimage*, 1872

Sing's scales for weighing opium, his opium-lamp, his box of dominoes, two photographs and a small library of Cantonese books. From this point, however, their troubles only multiplied. New lodgings in Angel Gardens were condemned almost as soon as they moved in, obliging a final relocation to Cornwall Street, where Ah Sing fell ill, declined and died. Hannah's fate is less clear. 'I traced his widow from one address to another,' recalled Platt in 1895, 'until she was taken in charge by some charitable ladies. Since then I have heard nothing further of her, and know not whether she is living or dead.'[13] The day Ah Sing and his wife moved out of New Court, their life in the opium business ended, as did the association of New Court with the smoking of the drug. By the time Oscar Wilde and Conan Doyle sent their protagonists to the divan, the East End's principal supplier had gone to meet his ancestors. Not that this worried anybody but sightseers and journalists. Why would ordinary Victorians have gone to all the trouble of visiting some rat-ridden den to get their fix, when the stuff was available on demand in any chemist's shop?

For the Victorians, opium was the opium of the people. Agricultural workers popped pills as they worked in the fields. Teething babies were dosed with a mixture of opium and black treacle, in preparations sold under proprietary names such as Godfrey's Cordial and Mother Bailey's Quieting Syrup. Some brewers and publicans spiked their beer with opium; many more of their patrons whooped up their pints with a pennyworth of poppy-powder bought from the chemist. Bored suburbanites inhaled a cocktail of opium and alcohol from their handkerchiefs. The chronically ill used it as a palliative pain-killer, the hungry as an appetite-suppressant and Mrs Isabella Beeton advised all sensible householders to keep their kitchen cupboards well stocked with the drug in both powdered and liquid form. Even after the Pharmacy Act of 1868, which attempted to outlaw opium peddling from handcarts and street vendors and to limit its sale to licensed pharmacists, it remained as widely available as tobacco is today.

Thanks to the precedents of Coleridge and De Quincey, there was already a tradition of drug use in literary and artistic circles before the Victorian age began, a practice which occupied that uncertain territory between therapy and recreation. Jane Morris, Jane Carlyle and Florence Nightingale were enthusiastic users of opium-based narcotics. Elizabeth Barrett Browning knocked back laudanum, a cocktail of opium and alcohol, to help her sleep; William Gladstone used laudanum to settle his nerves before making parliamentary speeches, and once glugged down so much that he was forced to go to Baden Baden to recuperate. Elizabeth Siddal took a fatal dose. Dickens treated himself with laudanum after being injured in a train crash in 1865. Wilkie Collins became a laudanum drinker to check the excruciating pain of 'rheumatic gout', a condition which, according to one observer, turned his eyes into 'literally *enormous bags of blood!*'[14] Although he was subject to hideous hallucinations (notably of a green-skinned woman with tusks, and a murderous *Doppelgänger*), Collins continued to use the drug until his death in 1889 – even after he was told by the surgeon Sir William Ferguson that he was taking enough to kill twelve people. Leonard Smithers, publisher to decadent poets such as Ernest Dowson and Arthur Symons – men who preferred absinthe and alcohol to opiates – became addicted to Dr Collis Browne's Chlorodyne, an opium-based patent medicine which claimed to act 'like a charm in diarrhoea, dysentery and cholera', after taking it for lung disease. It didn't help him. In 1907, on his forty-sixth birthday, Smithers's naked body was discovered in a house near Parson's Green, London. The property was empty except for a wicker hamper and fifty empty bottles of Dr Browne's remedy.

Then as now, this drug culture inspired a steady output of half-baked literary work. An anonymous poet in Lewisham waxed chemical in *Sleep Scenes: Or, Dreams of a Laudanum Drinker* (1868), reflecting that 'Within one tiny phial, what hidden joy/ Is adumbrated to my eager mind!'[15] Owen Howell, a verse-maker who knocked off periphrastic doggerel on the subject of Westminster Abbey and the Penny Post, took a Romantic view of the subject in *The Dream of the Opium Eater* (c.1850). A drug-fuelled anticipation of *The Time Machine*, its speaker is propelled by opium – 'Mightiest of drugs' – from Creation to Ancient Egypt to Thebes to Victorian England to Judgement Day in fifty-two whacked-out stanzas. Here, opium inspires a vision of the modern nation state reduced to ivy-shrouded desolation:

> The serpent crawled where once were streets and squares;
> Owls and dull birds sat on the mouldering walls
> Of crumbling buildings, that marked the spot
> Where England, France, had stood – to utter ruin gone.[16]

An ironic suggestion, as state-sponsored drug-dealing was actually helping to sustain the prosperity of Britain and her Empire. True, the majority of the opium consumed in the United Kingdom was imported from Turkey, whose crop was regarded as a product of better quality than that farmed in great quantities in colonial India – but the Victorians' disinclination to buy British didn't prevent this becoming one of their most furiously lucrative businesses. Between 1840 and 1878, the opium trade netted £375 million for the colonial Indian government. Indeed, critics of the relaxed British attitude towards this sector of the imperial economy suspected that opium was being used to keep indigenous populations docile and co-operative. Dr George Smith, an anti-opium campaigner, observed that before the British arrived in Burma, its inhabitants were 'hard-working, sober and simple-minded'. After this date, he argued, the officially-sanctioned opium trade brought about their 'utter ruin, physically and morally'.[17] Small wonder that the Empire's constituent governments were so keen to use military force to prevent China, their biggest and juiciest market, from closing its borders to narcotic commerce.

Not all opium products were harvested from such distant plots. The white poppies you can still see growing on the skirts of Sedgemoor in Somerset, and in the fields around Bridport, Dorset, are descended from flowers cultivated during the nineteenth century for use in the domestic manufacture of narcotic brews. Poppy production was pursued most intensively in Mitcham, Surrey, then Britain's main centre for the cultivation of pharmaceutically useful plants. Under the patios of this strait laced commuter town, under the dwarf conifers and rows of lobelias, under the carports and faux-Regency conservatories, lie the roots of Victorian drug culture. Hemp and wormwood – the hallucino-genic ingredient of absinthe – were also cultivated here, sowed next to strips of lavender and liquorice. 'They grew about 5 or 6 feet high, bearing large heads as large as your fist,' recalled an elderly resident of Mitcham in 1923. 'Their stalks were thick and strong, standing on the ground until they were quite dry, then they were gathered and stored for sale.'[18]

In one area of Britain, opium use was so widespread and enthusiastic that it began to attract official attention. As Virginia Berridge has demonstrated in her book *Opium and the People* (1999), the Fens – an area covering parts of Cambridgeshire, Lincolnshire, Norfolk and Huntingdonshire – was 'the opium-taking area par excellence' in a country that was already extremely unselfconscious about the consump-tion of the drug.[19] In the early 1860s, Dr Henry Julian Hunter was despatched to the area by Sir John Simon, Medical Officer to the Privy Council, reporting that: 'A man in South Lincolnshire complained that his wife had spent a hundred pounds on opium since he married. A man may be seen occasionally asleep in a field leaning on his hoe. He starts when approached, and works vigorously for a while. A man who is setting about a hard job takes his pill as a preliminary, and many never take their beer without dropping a piece of opium into it.'[20] Snap a penny piece on to the counter of any chemist in Wisbech, and a small stick of opium would be immediately forthcoming. So common was the practice that the purchaser did not even need to name his poison. One druggist in Ely – a settlement dubbed 'the opium-eating city of Ely' by the *Morning Chronicle* in 1850 – was reported to shift three hundredweight of opium a year.[21] 'The chemists of those districts sell immense quantities of opium in its crude state every market day, rolled into little sticks, in pennyworths and twopennyworths,' reported a Dr Bayes. 'I have seen fen-farmers who were in the habit of buying laudanum by the half-pint, or even more, on every visit to their market town.'[22]

These images of an entire region of England in a state of narcotic dilation were seized upon by anti-opium campaigners, who argued that the trade was an immoral form of profiteering which had generated millions of chemical dependents across the world, particularly in China. In the process, they invented the pathological figure of the dope fiend, who, according to the anonymous author of *The Celestial Empire* (1863), 'in addition to the lank and shrivelled limb, besides the weak voice and sallow visage, has a fierce and foreboding expression, a hollow-eyed vacant solemnity, as though death had set a mark upon his victim, dooming him to an untimely grave'.[23] For most of the nineteenth century, however, the argument was evenly balanced. Supporters compared the drug favourably to alcohol. 'If we examine the parallel addictions of European nations,' argued E. Impey, the Indian government's Examiner of Opium, 'we shall find them quite as injurious and demoralizing when carried to excess.'[24] When detractors such as Cardinal Manning compared the effects of opium addiction to slavery, apologists could point out that, unlike sugar, the poppy crop was harvested by paid workers, and that William Wilberforce himself had been an habitual user.

Beyond opium, other substances which have now been prohibited were then notably less controversial. A brand of hashish-centred chocolate was marketed for some time in the United States.[25] In 1863, Pope Leo XII awarded a medal to Angelo Mariani, the formulator of Vin

Mariani, a wine fortified with cocaine, which was used by millions across the world. (Celebrity consumers included Thomas Edison, Sarah Bernhardt, Jules Verne and Henrik Ibsen.) Non-alcoholic versions marketed under brand names such as Coca-Cola and Dope were also popular, particularly in American cities where the consumption of alcohol was prohibited. Indeed, for most of the nineteenth century, there was less concern about the perils of taking cocaine than there was about the negative side effects of drinking green tea. Today, when green tea is often claimed to guard against cancer and reduce high blood pressure, this Victorian suspicion seems rather eccentric. The beverage is made from leaves that have been spared the firing process which blackens tea, and therefore has a much less aggressive flavour than the Assam and Darjeeling blends consumed more commonly in nineteenth-century drawing rooms. And yet, readers of Victorian fiction and journalism were used to seeing green tea evoked as a stomach-churning, nerve-jangling threat to health. A writer in *Temple Bar* magazine, for instance, compared the sickening chaos of the 1863 Lord Mayor's Parade with 'the phantasmagoric vision of a raving maniac with superadded *delirium tremens*, who has been supping on raw pork chops with Mr Home the medium, and reading Hoffmann's Tales and *The Woman in White* to the accompaniment of cavendish tobacco and strong green tea'.[26] Collins, Gaskell and Hardy alluded to its deleterious effect upon the body, and the idea was resonant enough with Sheridan Le Fanu's readers for him to suggest, in *In a Glass Darkly* (1872), that the beverage might be capable of breaking the barriers between our own universe and one populated by hideous Swedenborgian demons.

When, in 1924, the German pharmacologist Louis Lewin considered the toxicity of tea, he concluded: 'There is no doubt that the abusive application of concentrated infusions of tea is liable to call forth physical disorders of a general nature in persons susceptible to its action, if only on account of the theophylline which, medicinally applied, is apt to give rise to symptoms of convulsions.' Five cups a day, Lewin suggests, are enough to propel tea-drinking into the pathological zone: 'A man who from youth had become accustomed to drinking exaggerated quantities of tea and had reached a daily consumption of 30 cups suffered from symptoms of anæmia, suffocation, and hallucinations.'[27] Theophylline – the caffeine-like component of tea which stimulates the heart, relaxes the muscles and dilates the veins – could not in itself be the cause of such symptoms. It was the substances with which green tea was frequently adulterated that pushed the drink on to the danger list. Unless you were a connoisseur, it was impossible to tell whether gunpowder tea – a Chinese variety in which the leaf is rolled up into a tiny ball – was not actually gunpowder combined with gum, pale Prussian blue dye, turmeric and sulphate of lime. Other fake teas might be composed of leaves plucked from English hedgerows and heated on copper plates until browned and curled. Chinese tea that reached England was not always of the best quality. 'There is a legend, I hope without foundation, that the tea sent to Europe has already been used in China for cleaning carpets,' muttered Platt. 'But this cannot be true, because carpets in China are never cleaned.'[28] Five cups of such stuff would be enough to make anyone hallucinate the black imps.

For the entirety of Victoria's reign, the narcotic substances that are criminalised in our society remained easily obtainable through legal channels. Organisations such as the Society for the Suppression of the Opium Trade did not begin to win their argument until the final years of the nineteenth century – by which time opium had gone out of fashion as both a medical and recreational drug. By the time Britain felt ready to involve herself in international efforts to outlaw the habitual use of the substance, and participate in events such as the International Opium Conference in Shanghai in 1909, the crop had also lost its importance to the colonial economy. It took the First World War to produce the prohibitions upon opium and cocaine around which current narcotics legislation was formed, and a series of scare stories about the extent of opiate use at the Western Front, and by soldiers on leave in London, which bounced the wartime government into designating opium and cocaine prescription-only drugs. The effects were far-reaching: Harrods was forced to stop selling packets of heroin for sweethearts and mothers to send to their boys in the trenches; international criminal cartels were formed to traffic freshly-outlawed substances to their habituates; Fu-Manchu emerged from the fog of Limehouse; the opium den became amplified as a symbol of exotic degradation and vice; tour companies began to offer discerning clients nights out in the Chinese East End; the story of George Ah Sing, Hannah Johnston and their royal clientele was quietly forgotten.

A few traces of Ah Sing's London still remain, however. The narrow courts between Victoria and Albert Streets were demolished in the late 1880s to make way for the playground of a new Board School. This too has now disappeared, and in its place has risen one of those vertical equivalents of the nineteenth-century slum – still providing housing to the capital's most recent arrivals. Victoria Street has been renamed Dellow Street (after one of the school's governors), but it is easily detected by the row of ventilation towers that run along its length – brick-built lungs for the East London line, whose trains must have rattled Ah Sing's bedstead as they passed below his feet. If you follow the towers to the main road, you'll find yourself standing on what was once Ratcliff Highway. When Ah Sing stood here, he could have followed the path past a rum warehouse and a sugar warehouse, down to the water of the East Dock. Turn right at the end of Dellow Street, make your way behind the swimming baths and through the gates on your right, and you'll discover the former Wesleyan cemetery which, in the 1880s, Harry Jones had cleared, planted with rose bushes and thrown open for public use. Just within the gates, the mortuary where Ah Sing's body lay still stands, though the structure is crumbling and the doorways sealed with corrugated iron. The arrow-slit windows, elaborate air bricks and lantern ventilator betray the history of the building, though the legend inscribed above the door, 'Metropolitan Borough of Stepney Nature Study Museum', advertises its later conversion to a different kind of civic amenity. Mrs Godfrey's daughters, perhaps, brought their children here to gaze at the exotica of its aquarium, constructed in the chamber that had once housed the corpse of their neighbour.

As for Ah Sing's physical remains, he was buried in a public grave, so there is no precise record of where he is interred. You could spend a lifetime hunting for it among the creepers and brambles and toppled tombstones of Bow Cemetery. I spent a rainy September morning trying to locate it for myself, dragging back armfuls of ivy and scraping at the mossy carapaces of headstones, before the sight of a scraggy brown rat scuttering over the path persuaded me I was better off at home. Ah Sing is lost in a dark warren once again. But he's somewhere down there in this dark tangle, sleeping a deeper sleep than his poppy pipe could ever have provided.

CHAPTER SEVEN

The Archaeology of Good Behaviour

The name 'Mrs Beeton' conjures up the best and worst of the
Victorians: cosy, solid, certain, if not a little smug.
　　Kathryn Hughes, introduction, *Mrs Beeton's Book of Household
Management* (2000)

Every August since 1981, the inhabitants of Llandrindod Wells, a spa
town in Powys, have put on their corsets and bonnets and epaulettes and
wing-collars, and tottered around town pretending to be Victorians.
Neckerchiefed urchins crouch in doorways, offering a shoeshine for
twenty pence. Shop assistants climb into starched aprons, and slip on
plain-glass *pince-nez* spectacles. The main shopping street is blocked by
two handcarts brimming with lobelias. The bandstand is transformed
into a venue for events such as the 'Best Victorian Child Competition' –
in which a mob of ragamuffins and Little Lords Fauntleroy sashay about
under the eye of a stout lady dragged up as Queen Victoria. Everywhere
you look, there are people cramming themselves with sponge cake,
scones, pastries, roast beef and pork pies, and bowing to each other.

When I visited the Llandrindod Wells Victorian Festival in the
summer of 2000, I felt as if I was walking around in a theme park
dedicated to British parochialism. The event was not a celebration of the
nineteenth century: historical specificity had been policed to an absolute
minimum. Instead, the event appeared to be an attempt to materialise that
sunny fantasy of complacent provincialism recognisable from the rhetoric
of Conservative politicians: a world of red-faced, smiling butchers,
respectful shop-boys, impeccable social etiquette, warm beer and bitty
lemonade. Walking around town, it was clear that anything that fitted this
basic pattern of nostalgic comfort – even if it had nothing to do with the
nineteenth century – could be accommodated within the Llandrindod
Wells definition of 'Victorian': a rank of arcade games from the 1930s and
1940s; hamburger and hot dog stalls; bouncy castles; a milk-shake stand;
inflatable Tiggers; actors got up as eighteenth-century pirates; the Usk
Valley Jazz band; the Llandrindod Wells Theatre Company performing

extracts from *Show Boat* and *South Pacific*. The same permeability was reflected in the fancy dress. Although some participants had clearly spent all year hemming and ruching and brocading to create convincing costumes, most of the men opted for that dickie bow and waistcoat combination familiar from the fish-counters of modern hypermarkets – a uniform that whispers phonily of individual attention in an era of self-service and mass-consumption.

So what was the appeal? 'They had such good manners,' a woman in a well-upholstered black frock told me, as we listened to two black-faced chimney sweeps bashing out *My Baby Has Gone Down the Plughole*, with accordion accompaniment. 'They knew how to behave. They treated each other with respect.' However, non-participants in these events – those who watched from the sidelines, bemused in their twenty-first-century trousers – cited Victorian over-reliance on etiquette as one reason why the era was best left unresurrected. 'Look at that wanker over there,' muttered one detractor, directing my attention to a mutton-chopped man with a voluminous belly straining inside a Union Jack waistcoat, nodding graciously to customers emerging from the refreshment tent. 'Stodgy people, stodgy behaviour, stodgy food.'

The first few chapters of this book have concentrated upon the sensational and permissive aspects of Victorian culture that an interpretative tradition shaped by Strachey and Freud has tended to obscure. For the next few chapters, I want to concentrate upon several aspects of Victorian living which figure highly in conservative, sentimental depictions of the period – etiquette, food, home furnishings – and to attempt to undermine their fussy, staid and parochial associations; to demonstrate that Victorian etiquette could be both practical and radical, that there was more to nineteenth-century food than is suggested by the grim menus of twenty-first-century Victorian-style carveries, and that nineteenth-century interior design ideas did not revolve around the accumulation of frills and clutter.

Let's deal first with the question of stodginess. It's one of the adjectives most commonly applied to the Victorians. And it is an epithet with muscle, adding sinew to pronouncements on Victorian culture, attitudes, social behaviour and food – as if the whole period was, in some fundamental way, irremediably bunged up with suet. Examples are not hard to find. The *Encyclopaedia Britannica* refers to the 'dull, stodgy, moralistic Victorian novel'. A recent BBC programme described how

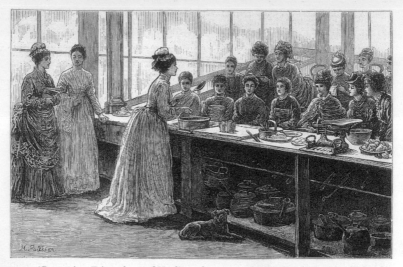

10 'Seasoning Fricandeau of Veal' – a lecture at the National Training-School of Cookery at South Kensington (*The Graphic*, 1871)

audiences at 'Victorian music hall entertainment ... guzzled beer and pies to a stodgy diet of ... music hall classics.'[1] A writer in *Equity* magazine suggested: 'If the Monica Lewinsky case seems shocking today, consider how similarly scandalous circumstances played out in the stodgy Victorian Era.'[2]

The negative image of Victorian social events – dinner parties, afternoon teas, luncheons – is of occasions at which guests, their natural behaviour constipated by elaborate etiquette, consumed unfeasible amounts of cabinet pudding, spotted dick, Pumblechookian pie and other lard-filled confections designed more for combating the cold than pleasing the palate. Go to a Victorian-styled restaurant, and you'll find yourself being offered a number of variations on the Sunday roast, bookended by starters and puddings that owe more to the 1960s than the 1860s. Real Victorian food, however, wasn't nearly so boring. The nineteenth century saw the first major incursion of French cuisine into British life, thanks to the PR work done by celebrity chefs such as Louis Eustache Ude, Charles Elmé Francatelli and Alexis Soyer. Soyer, *chef de cuisine* at the Reform Club, educated the palates of club members beyond their dependence on pork chops, set up a model soup kitchen in Dublin during the potato famine and encouraged charity workers to serve more nutritious and interesting food to their dependants. Vegetarianism also grew in popularity, thanks to the work of the Vegetarian Society (founded in Ramsgate in September 1847) and celebrity advocates such as Isaac Pitman (originator of the shorthand system), Dr Thomas Allinson (whose wholemeal bread company still flourishes today) and Dr Anna Kingsford (a women's rights and anti-vivisection campaigner). The first vegetarian restaurant opened in London in 1849. By the 1890s, Britain had fifty-two similar dining establishments.

Victorian recipe books also reveal the variety of the nineteenth-century diet. Even those aimed at cooks of modest means are not paeans to the pleasures of lard. Charles Selby's *The Dinner Question, or How to Dine Well and Economically* (1860) – written under the stage-name of his popular drag act, Tabitha Tickletooth – contains instructions on how to make spinach purée, omelette soufflé and a lobster sauce with anchovies and soy. R. K. Philip's *The Practical Housewife* (1860) offers recipes for cranberry juice, buttered chervil and artichoke ragout. The great heavy-weight of the period, Isabella Beeton's *Book of Household Management* (1861), instructs its readers how to prepare coconut soup, sea kale and salmon curry.

The popularity of curry is worth savouring – particularly as not so much as a poppadom was on offer at the food stalls of Llandrindod Wells. By the time Beeton published her magnum opus, Indian food was a mass-market favourite. In fact, Britain's first Indian restaurant was pre-Victorian: the Hindostanee Coffee House opened in 1809 at 34 George Street, Portman Square (over fifty years before the first fish and chip shop began trading in the market square at Mossley, Lancashire, in 1863). Like its modern descendants, the Coffee House was not aimed at Indian expatriates. It catered for a clientele of enthusiasts who had acquired a taste for Indian food while on duty on the subcontinent: the real-life equivalents of Jos Sedley, the chilli-fixated colonial of *Vanity Fair* (1848). The manager, Dean Mahomed, was a former subaltern in the East India Company's Bengal Army, and the first published Indian writer in English. When the business collapsed in 1812, he and his Anglo-Irish wife downshifted to Brighton, where he established himself as a masseur (or 'shampooing surgeon to the English royal family and sundry gentry') at Mahomed's Baths on the Steine, a short walk from Brighton Pavilion. (The building is now part of the Queen's Hotel.) By the time of his death in 1851 – at the age of ninety-two – curry had become an immovable fixture of the British diet.

Although many of the nineteenth century's favourite dishes are our favourite dishes, the body of social rules that appears to have structured their consumption is one of the most alienating aspects of Victorian culture: baffling rituals with celery, *cartes de visite*, cutlery and crinolines, now so peculiar that facsimiles of nineteenth-century etiquette books are sold for their comedy value. Their very oddness has given them a new set of admirers. In Llandrindod Wells, I attended a lecture on Victorian etiquette that was held in the basement of the Glen Usk Hotel. Four-fifths of the audience came in costume: the dingy conference room, still spotted with the remains of last year's Christmas decorations, was a riot of fob watches and flowery hats and white kid gloves. The speaker read from a number of advice books, describing in some detail the thoughts of a handful of etiquette writers on how to eat fish, how to serve cheese, and how to leave a *carte de visite*. The audience listened appreciatively, enjoying these titillating snippets as other denominations of fetishists might have enjoyed the public reading of a rubber goods catalogue. There was the occasional titter of delight, suggesting that despite the complexity and apparent pointlessness of the acts being described, many members of the audience found the strictness of the rules to be curiously attractive.

Having examined these rituals, however, I am convinced that many of the most arcane usually contain some excavatable logic. For instance, the time-consuming process of calling upon friends to leave a visiting card (even when the caller knew that there was nobody at home to receive him) was an essential tool for the weekend. As *Manners of Modern Society* (1879) argued – in the same year that the first telephone exchange opened, thus condemning the card-leaving ritual to a long, slow death – 'in towns, and more particularly that vast Babylon, London, people cannot be aware of the movements and arrivals of their friends, as is the case in the country; so that unless an intimation of this kind reached them, the town friend would be quite ignorant of the proximity of his country friend.'[3] Opt out of this process, and you might find yourself sitting in every night, staring at the dado.

Other social codes are more difficult to crack. Take this little exhortation, for example: 'Ladies seldom eat cheese at dinner parties.'[4] It was the counsel of Madame Marie Bayard, a beauty, fashion and etiquette guru who peddled her own range of branded advice books from her boutique between the Strand and Covent Garden. Should we take this injunction seriously? Could anything practical underlie her advice?

The first thing to be noted is that this cheesy disinclination was not universal. J. H. Walsh's *A Manual of Domestic Economy* (1857), for instance, devotes several pages to the buying and storing of cheese, and although Isabella Beeton pronounced that 'cheese in its commonest shape is fit only for sedentary people, as an after-dinner stimulant, and in very small quantity', she conceded that 'a celebrated gourmand remarked that a dinner without cheese is like a woman with one eye'.[5] Moreover, consumption of the foodstuff rose dramatically during the century: Britain's first commercial cheese factory opened in 1871, and the following twelve years saw a 30 per cent rise in cheese-eating from 4.25 lbs to 5.51 lbs per head of population. Despite these figures, Victorian cheese had an image problem. The varieties which had emerged as market leaders by the end of the eighteenth century – Cheddar, Cheshire, Stilton and Double and Single Gloucester – were, by the mid-Victorian period, considered unattractively rustic. It would have been as unacceptable to serve these at a nineteenth-century dinner party as spaghetti hoops at a twenty-first century equivalent. Soft cheeses were the only varieties considered suitable for presentation at a social event.

Fiction provides jokey evidence that cheese was anathema to a certain type of over-refined lady. 'I shall take the children and go to an hotel until those cheeses are eaten. I decline to live any longer in the same house with them,' declares the wife of an inveterate lactophile in Jerome K. Jerome's *Three Men in a Boat* (1889).[6] In Elizabeth Gaskell's *Wives and Daughters* (1866), the newly-wed Hyacinth Clare denounces cheese as 'a strong-smelling coarse kind of thing . . . only fit for the kitchen.'[7] These are comic exaggerations, which might be discounted were it not that many nineteenth-century cookery books exhibit a puzzling lack of interest in the ingredient. There is scarcely any mention of cheese in Eliza Warren's *How I Managed My House on Two Hundred Pounds a Year* (1864), R. K. Philip's *The Practical Housewife* (c.1860) or Lady Judith Montefiore's *The Jewish Manual* (1846). Francatelli's *The Modern Cook* (1864) offers no cheese recipes, and *Plain Cookery Book for the Working Classes*, the celebrity chef's no-frills domestic management text (a book with no interest in the rituals of the genteel dinner party), suggests only two little snacks – Welsh Rarebit and Eggs Stewed with Cheese – and one main course: Italian Cheese, which turns out to be a concoction of baked pig fat and chitterlings. And, as with Jerome K. Jerome's abandoned husband, cheese-bibbing was usually characterised as a particularly male pleasure. An article in *Cassell's Magazine*, 'A Family Chat on Cheese,' is narrated by a Mrs Thompson, who professes that 'I never buy the cheese, I leave that to my husband. He always says I can do a great many things, but I cannot choose cheese.'[8]

What was driving a wedge between Victorian women and cheese? The answer, I think, lies in the development of nineteenth-century microbiology. Although the cholera epidemics of the mid-century had made waterborne bacteria a priority for researchers, other scientists were considering the microbial life of the larder. In 1872, Ferdinand Cohn identified a bacterium which he named Tyrothrix (literally 'threads from cheese'). His experiments with thoroughly boiled flasks of cheese, hay and turnip helped undermine the popular theory of spontaneous generation. This work, according to one nineteenth-century American bacteriologist, 'reopened the cheese problem' for further exploration by bacteriologists such as Emile Duclaux, Leopold Adametz (who counted 140,000 organisms in a gram of fresh cheese) and Edward von Freudenreich (who totted up 1,800,000). By 1895, the agronomist C. M. Aikman was reflecting, rather nervously, that 'to bacterial life is also due the poisonous properties which, unfortunately, cheese has been found not infrequently to develop.'[9]

Today, it is widely known that soft cheeses can harbour the harmful bacteria *Listeria monocytogenes*, and standard medical advice warns pregnant women not to eat these foods. Although the organism is named after Joseph Lister, the Victorian pioneer of antiseptic surgery, Listeria was not identified as a pathogen until 1911. It has only been a reportable disease since 1985, when fifteen Mexican women succumbed to its effects. But if soft cheeses such as Brie, Roquefort and Camembert were the only ones likely to be served at one of Madame Bayard's dinner-parties, then her injunction to young women may not have been some pointless lurch of snobbery. Given the unreliability of Victorian contraceptive methods, she probably saved hundreds of women from infection.

Here's another puzzling movement from this quadrille of manners. Most etiquette books of the period insist that diners abandon their knives during the fish course. 'Fish should be eaten with a fork, aided by a crust of bread, except in the most elite circles where silver knives are used for the purpose,' pronounced the author of *The Ladies' Guide to Etiquette* (1855). 'Fish, I repeat, must never be touched with a knife,' counselled the 'Man in the Club Window', author of *The Habits of Good Society*

(1859). In *Jack in the Green* (1850), a stage comedy by Mark Lemon, editor of *Punch*, an etiquette teacher upbraids his pupil, a socially aspirant small coal dealer, for not abiding by this rule: 'My dear fellow, you really must not eat your fish with a knife. The earl would disinherit you if you were twenty times his son.' A slew of mid-Victorian advice books, from *The Gentleman's Manual of Modern Etiquette* (1864) to *How to Dine* (1876), make the same point, but by the end of the 1870s, the custom seems to have waned. *Manners and Tone of Good Society* (1879) decrees: 'Fish should be eaten with a silver fish knife and fork. Two forks are not used for eating fish, and one fork and a crust of bread is now an unheard-of way of eating fish in polite society.' The prohibition is not even considered worth mentioning by the 1907 reissue, though the preposterous Lady Agnes Grove, author of *Seventy-One Days' Camping in Morocco* (1902), declared in 1907 that 'there are actual possessions which are reserved solely for the use of middle-classdom. Napkin-rings, fish-knives, tea-cosies and oh! I shudder as I write the word, "tidies" and nightgown-cases.' One of these bourgeois knick-knacks, however, Lady Agnes was willing to countenance: 'It is true that fish-knives are creeping up,' she concedes. 'And if it were not for one's prejudice against them they really are more serviceable and cleaner than the quondam piece of bread.'[10]

Grove's distaste was doubtless founded on the certainty that anybody who owned an item as new-fangled as a fish-knife could not possibly have inherited it from an illustrious ancestor. (One wonders if she'd inspected the cutlery drawer of her friend Thomas Hardy, to whom she dedicated the book, before speaking her mind.) The business with the bread, however, did have a practical basis. The mid-century spread of this habit was a consequence of Emperor Napoleon III's desire to win the Crimean War with long-range artillery shells, and a chance meeting at a house party on the Rue Balzac, Paris, in the winter of 1854.

The hostess, Mme Gudin, the daughter of the Waterloo veteran Lord James Hay, was giving a farewell dinner in honour of General Hamlin, and a number of other French officers, who were due to depart for the war. The highest-ranking guest was Napoleon Joseph Charles Paul Bonaparte, cousin and heir to the Emperor, an amoral character whose conduct in the Crimea earned him the ironical nickname Plon-plon (a corruption of *Craint-plon*, 'Fear-bullet'). At some point during the evening, His Royal Highness was introduced to Henry Bessemer, an entrepreneurial engineer from Hertfordshire, who had made a strong impression on crowds at the Great Exhibition of 1851 with a machine for separating molasses from crystallised sugar with a combination of steam and centrifugal force. Bessemer told the prince about the trouble he was having with the British War Office, who had recently rejected his design for a new kind of war machine – an artillery barrel which could launch steel projectiles spinning into the air at an enormous speed, and hit targets with revolutionary accuracy. It just so happened that he had the little mahogany model of the device in his luggage. The Prince was pleased with the demonstration, and a few days later Bessemer was invited to the Tuileries to explain his idea to the Emperor – who gave his blessing to the project. After concluding that the facilities at the palace of Vincennes were inadequate for these purposes, Bessemer returned to England to begin his work – with leave to draw as much cash as he needed from the Bonaparte account at Baring's Bank.

Bessemer's problem was this. No traditional cast-iron cannon was tough enough to fire his projectile. In 1854, wrought iron was used for all large structural projects, hammered into shape for use in ships, bridges and railway systems. To make a gun barrel, however, Bessemer needed a material which could be moulded. Cast iron, with its high carbon content, was too brittle for the purpose. Steel – which had first been cast by the Sheffield clockmaker Benjamin Huntsman in the 1750s – was precluded by its laborious and expensive manufacturing process, and the physical limitations of the end result. Casting steel involved heating bars of Swedish wrought iron on a bed of charcoal for six weeks, breaking up the result and melting it down in crucibles with a capacity of only 50 lb – far too small for moulding anything capable of firing an artillery shell.

Later in life, Bessemer reflected upon this dilemma:

I well remember how, on my lonely journey back to Paris that cold December night, I inwardly resolved, if possible, to complete the work so satisfactorily begun, by producing a superior description of cast-iron that would stand the heavy strains which the increased weight of the projectiles rendered necessary. At that moment I had no idea whatever in which way I could attack this new and important problem, but the mere fact that there was something to discover, something of great importance to achieve, was sufficient to spur me on. It was indeed to me like the first cry of the hounds in the hunting field, or the last uncertain miles of the chase to the eager sportsman. It was a clear run that I had before me – a fortune and a name to win – and only so much time and labour lost if I failed in the attempt.[11]

During an experiment that nearly set fire to the buildings surrounding his laboratory at St Pancras, Bessemer cracked the problem. By venting air into the furnace, he burnt off the excess carbon from a bath of molten pig iron, which forced a large volume of red-hot slag out on to the roofs of nearby houses, and left Bessemer with a new material that could be poured and moulded like cast iron, but which had the strength of the wrought variety. The Bessemer Converter, as it was patented, had produced mild steel – and was capable of spewing out thirty tons of the stuff in half an hour. Mindful of his commission from the Emperor, Bessemer cast a miniature cannon from this new metal, and took it back to Paris. Napoleon III, however, seems to have lost his enthusiasm for the research project. 'His Majesty,' recalled Bessemer, 'who had desired me to report progress, accepted this experimental gun, remarking that some day it might have an historical interest.'

Bessemer, however, was forced to endure a more serious setback than the cooling of a patron's interest. Commercial trials of the process were a failure, and it took two years to iron out its flaws, by which time Bessemer's reputation had suffered greatly. He was forced to set up his own works in Sheffield, the heart of the British steel industry, and in doing so, ushered in a new era of construction technology. By the 1870s, Bessemer steel was forming the skeletons of ships, bridges and railway engines. Steel provided the suspension cables of the Brooklyn Bridge and the metal beams of America's first skyscrapers. In the England of the 1850s, however, the most obvious application of Bessemer's technique was for accelerating the industrial processes in which steel was already being used – principally, the manufacture of cutlery. The Bessemer converter facilitated an enormous increase in output at the cutlery works, and a subsequent drop in the price of knives, forks and spoons which allowed large swathes of the public to possess, for the first time, elaborate canteens of eating implements. However, it also exaggerated a negative attribute of the steel cutlery that Sheffield factories were producing: a tendency to react with acidic solutions.

A quick glance through Isabella Beeton's fish recipes illustrates the trouble that this would have given mid-Victorian diners. Vinegar is an essential ingredient for boiled flounders, lobster salad, boiled pike, collared salmon and skate with caper sauce. For baked white herrings,

Beeton writes, you will need 'sufficient vinegar to fill up the dish'. Her standard fish sauce requires a quart of vinegar. To make her Epicurean sauce, you shake up a 'pint of vinegar with a base of walnut and mushroom ketchup'. And where vinegar is not demanded, another acidic ingredient is often substituted: a properly stewed plaice, for instance, requires a whole pint of lemon juice. Bring modern steel knives into contact with any such dishes, and, she warns, 'these are liable to impart to it a very disagreeable flavour'. The solution? 'Where silver fish-carvers are considered too dear to be bought, good electroplated ones answer very well, and are inexpensive.' Beeton recommends purchasing these implements from Messrs Slack of the Strand, where they can be had 'from a guinea upwards'. When the *Book of Household Management* was first published in 1861, the lowest annual income upon which a middle-class couple could contemplate setting up house was £150. No wonder most people eschewed Mr Slack and stuck to the routine with the crust of bread.[12]

It is difficult to judge how assiduously the Victorians adhered to these rules. It is certain, however, that the practices of the etiquette book were not simple potato-prints of events in people's lives – any more than pronouncements in the style sections of Sunday newspapers offer an uncomplicated reflection of fashionable life today. Most of these volumes sold for a shilling or just a few pennies (at a time when the average price for a novel was over a guinea), which suggests that some of the social events they described were well beyond the means of their readers. These books were offered as a cure for social anxiety, but they may well have been read for pleasure – or with amused scepticism.

Their prefaces and introductions acknowledge this possibility. *Etiquette for All* (1861) concedes that 'some captious critics may question the necessity of such books as this, and sneer at the seeming shams which people practice in society'. *How to Behave* (1865) admits that many of the customs of 'what is called fashionable society' are 'simply absurd'. *The Gentleman's Guide to Etiquette* (1855) suggests that 'the multitude of treatises that have already been issued on the Art of Politeness ... are written in a style so pedantic, that it is impossible to peruse them without exciting a feeling of disgust in the mind of any sensible person.' With manuals themselves discoursing on the silliness of the genre, it wasn't long before spoof volumes were being produced. *Always: A manual of Etiquette for the guidance of either sex into the Empurpled Penetralia of*

Fashionable Life (1884) insists that 'if you damage your partner's skirt while dancing, engineer her into obscurity as inconspicuously as may be. To go on your knees, and undertake to repair the rent with a tooth-pick in the centre of a crowded floor, will evince more sympathy than tact.'[13]

Advice columns in periodicals also afforded the same mixture of instruction and cruel amusement. *The Young Ladies' Journal* ran a weekly column, 'Etiquette of Good Society', which considered the usual repertoire of social situations. Direct enquiries from readers were answered on the back inside page, under suggestive pseudonyms such as 'Saucy Annie', 'Vampire Bat' and 'Lady Raven'. As the questions were not supplied, the clusters of mysterious – and incongruous – replies must have seemed as funny to the *Journal*'s subscribers as they do today.

> THERESE.— (1) It is not polite to give attention to correspondence in the presence of friends. If, however, you receive anything of great importance, to be attended to at once, you can ask permission to read your letter. (2) All kinds of fish. (3) You would say, 'I shall be happy to do so,' or merely bow, according to the proximity of the gentleman. (4) They are a drawback; but not to the extent that you estimate. (5) You can procure very pretty stove ornaments from Mr Bedford, whose address you will find in our journal. (6) You do not say what sort you require. The Japanese fans sold by many drapers and some grocers, for less than 2d. each, are some of them very pretty. (7) We have not heard of an instance since George III.[14]

Ironic enjoyment, however, could not have supported such a substantial industry. Just as modern mind-body-spirit manuals prey on the insecurities of our self-absorbed age, these books answered – or exploited – the social anxieties which accompanied the rapid realignment of the class system which took place in the Victorian period. 'There are few amongst us who have not at times been in the painful situation of doubt and uncertainty regarding the method of procedure in some particular circumstances either in public or private,' reflects the author of *Etiquette for All* (1861), a tiny volume that would fit discreetly into the pocket of any member of – as etiquette writers FWR and Lord Charles X identified – 'an exceedingly large class of folk who, far from being boorish by nature, are as yet so unfortunate as to lack, from various causes, the cultivation which alone will bring the gentle spirit into such training as will fit it practically for exhibition in society.' Snobbery, agrees *The*

Gentleman's Manual of Modern Etiquette (1864), has nothing to do with it. The alleviation of unnecessary suffering is the aim; the enumeration of 'those laws, whose adoption in the highest circles has entailed their acceptance as fixed laws by all classes claiming a respectable position, would supply a want long keenly felt by multitudes, who through fear of exposing their lack of knowledge on these points by requesting information of those more enlightened than themselves, have continually experienced an uncertainty as to the proper course to be pursued when placed in particular situations.'[15]

Annotations by a reader named Ira Careti in the British Library's copy of *Etiquette for Gentlemen* (1856) suggest that such books may also have functioned as primers in British customs for the many immigrants who came to Britain during the period – in the same way that manuals such as the Calcutta-published *A Few Hints on English Etiquette* (1887) attempted to initiate Indians into the social mysteries of the Raj. Advice books for colonial subjects continued to be produced until the middle of the twentieth century. Harold Hardless's *The Indian Gentleman's Guide to English Etiquette* (1920), advised, 'To give a person a loan of money and then ask him as a favour to get your son a job, or yourself an increase of pay, or the grant of leave, is entirely outside the bounds of English friendship or etiquette.'[16]

What makes reading these books such a puzzling experience today is that much of the advice they contain seems forehead-smackingly obvious. Don't pour tea or coffee in the saucer to cool. Don't eat peas off your knife. Don't crack nuts with your teeth. Don't use your fork as a tooth-pick. Don't pad your underwear, if you want to avoid inspiring disappointment: 'A little may be judiciously used to round off the more salient points of an angular figure,' advises *All About Etiquette* (1879), 'but when it is used for the purpose of creating an egregiously false impression of superior form, it is simply snobbish.'[17] Don't repeat malicious gossip: 'What is more absurd, for instance,' asked Henry P. Willis, 'than if one lady should say to another – "well, Jane, what do you think Lucretia Smith says of you? She says you have the thickest ankles and the thinnest arms of any girl in town – that your shape is like an alligator's, and your head resembles that of a bison!" '[18] Did people really need to be told these things?

Perhaps their authors were trying to instil a sense of confidence in their readers, in the manner of Benjamin Spock's assurance on the first page of his *Common Sense Book of Baby and Child Care* (1946): 'Trust Yourself: You know more than you think you do.' Many Victorian commentators clearly found their contents facile. 'It is sometimes asked,' reflected the Lounger in Society, narrator of *The Glass of Fashion* (1881), 'For whom are manuals of etiquette intended? And when we find their pages filled with such instructions in the minutiae of behaviour as one is wont to supply to children, we can scarcely wonder at the question.'[19] Perhaps the Lounger is too blasé: there is some evidence that the elementary rules of politeness which are now so thoroughly inculturated are relatively recent arrivals. American advice manuals published in the 1830s and 1840s saw nothing wrong in eating off your knife – 'provided you do it neatly, and do not put in large mouthfuls, or close your lips tightly over the blade'.[20] (Dickens commented on this shocking habit in *American Notes*, comparing US diners to circus sword-swallowers.) As late as the seventeenth century, forks were considered to be luxury items owned solely by the rich. For most of the eighteenth century, Europeans and North Americans customarily used their right hand for eating and their left for sanitary purposes. La Salle's *Les règles de la bienséance et de la civilité chrétienne* (1774), for instance, insists that in French aristocratic circles, all cutlery was set on the right hand side of the plate. Some Victorians may well have preferred to stick with this tradition. Toilet paper, after all, did not become widely available until the 1880s. If you've ever been digging in the garden and come across a cache of oyster and mussel shells, resist the temptation to coo over them too much: they may be nineteenth-century arse-wipers. If your left hand had been pinching an excrement-globbed sea shell, and it was before 1872 – when the first perfumed soap, Colgate's Cashmere Bouquet, went on sale – you'd be forgiven for only wanting to eat with the right.

If, however, such seemingly obvious advice was genuinely required by the readers of these books, then the etiquette project was hugely successful. By the end of the century, nobody – well, nobody worth talking about anyway – ate peas off the flat of their knife, or drank tea from their saucer. The widespread abandonment of such practices, however, and the adoption of new ones, ensured that the mystique of aristocratic living was partially dispelled. These were the Baedekers of the class system: manuals which aimed to facilitate the movement of aspirants between socio-economic groups. And like those tourist guides which eventually made their destinations seem stale and passé, etiquette books eventually undermined the very behavioural codes they sought to promulgate.

[117]

'The circles of good society', reflected the author of *The Habits of Good Society* (1859), 'are growing wider and wider, admitting repeatedly, and more than ever, men who have risen from the cottage or the workshop.' This process, the writer suggested, was exposing the aristocracy as a bunch of undignified frauds, cosying up to a new class of wealthy capitalists, and leaving the middle-classes, diligently applying themselves to their etiquette handbooks, as the true exponents of politeness. If the 'railway kings and mushroom millionaires had studied their grammars and manner-books in the respites from business,' she suggests, then the aristocracy might not have been 'sneered at by the middle classes for a worship of gold, which could induce them to put up with gross vulgarity.'[21]

Who were these boors whom the aristocracy was courting? The railway kings were a generation of speculators who got rich through the massive expansion in the rail transport system between 1844 and 1847. In the final year of this Railway Mania, 6.7 per cent of British national income was being invested in rail shares. Principal among these new entrepreneurs was George Hudson, a farmer's son who founded the York and North Midland Railway Company and made York a major hub of communication. At the height of his career, he controlled 1,106 miles of track, and was able to buy the Londesborough estate at Market Weighton from the Duke of Devonshire for half a million pounds. He was always self-conscious about his class background, however, and once persuaded the Duke of Wellington, to whom he dispensed lucrative broking advice, to pay a visit to his daughter's expensive private school in Hampstead, in order to impress his aristocratic connections upon the parents of the other pupils. They must have sniggered into their lapels when an investigative committee looked into Hudson's predilection for bribery and insider dealing, and he was imprisoned for debt in York gaol. The author of *The Habits of Good Society* must also have been quietly satisfied by this reversal. His fall came in 1865 – the same year that the railway reached Llandrindod Wells.

Llandrindod has good reason to be enthusiastic about the Victorians. Until the middle of the nineteenth century, the place was nothing more than a lake, a cluster of farmhouses and the Llanerch Inn (which still stands today). A brief flurry of activity began in 1749, when a far-sighted entrepreneur named Grosvenor established a waterside hotel, but this had sunk into disrepair by the end of the 1780s. It wasn't until the opening of the Central Wales Railway in 1865 that the settlement started to expand – a process which occurred at a breakneck, Milton Keynesian rate. By 1880, several large hotels, numerous apartments, two hydropathic institutions, two pavilions, a bowling green, a putting green and a fourteen-acre boating lake had been constructed to cater for an annual influx of eighty thousand tourists.

This period of prosperity, however, didn't last long into the twentieth century – by which time the holidaying public had switched their allegiance to the seaside. They were wooed away by attractions such as John William Outhwhaite's Blackpool Pleasure Beach – which first whitened British knuckles in 1896 – and by the growth in the popularity of sea bathing. When Llandrindod entered its boom time, swimming was a comparatively rare skill. Only one in ten of those who made their living on the sea were capable of keeping their heads above water, and, troubled by this statistic, the founder members of the London Swimming Club declared in 1859 that they would dedicate themselves to 'Raising the art of swimming from its comparative disuse, and placing it amongst the first of our national recreations'.[22] (Once you know that, the nineteenth-century predilection for bathing machines – wheeled huts that conveyed their occupants into the sea – looks less like an affected attempt to preserve modesty, and more like an eminently practical way for a non-swimmer to get into water deep enough to allow her to immerse herself.)

Unlike Blackpool, Llandrindod could only offer cold showers, mineral water and tea dances. The boating lake was unsuitable for swimming, and the authorities never considered building a roller-coaster. If the town had not been made the new administrative centre of Radnorshire in 1888, it might now be a forlorn and run-down sort of place. As depressed, perhaps, as the Carmarthenshire mining villages farther south, which suffered from the impact of the pit closure programme in 1984 – initiated by Margaret Thatcher's government just after she had won the 1983 General Election on a platform advocating a return to 'Victorian values'.[23]

If you arrive in Llandrindod by rail from Shrewsbury, the first thing you'll see is an eccentric acknowledgement of the town's debt to people like Hudson: a metal plaque which commemorates the 'Re-Victorianisation' of the station in 1990. In the nineteenth century, the Central Wales Railway Company ran trains all night, transporting coal and steel and metal ore between the industrial areas of south Wales and north-west England. Thanks to Mrs Thatcher, the railway is privately-owned once more, but the industry it was built to serve is dead, and the single-carriage trains rattle through unmanned stations just three times a day, depositing hill-walkers at the beauty spots along the line. It livens up at festival time, however. For a week or so of August afternoons and evenings, the trains bring tourists to Llandrindod to witness the strange spectacle of black-bonneted women scooting around in Volvos, men in scarlet hussar's tunics clutching digital camcorders, Florence Nightingale clones sipping Diet Coke. And to participate in the town's celebration of everything olde-worlde and parochial and uncosmopolitan.

CHAPTER EIGHT

Check Out Your Chintz

The Victorians have a lot to answer for. It was their embarrassment over their bodies that forced bathrooms into the darkest,
smallest room in the house, and us along with them. Now all
that's changing.

Ali Hanan, 'Come in, the water's lovely', *Independent on Sunday*
(5 March 2000)

St Luke's advertising agency occupies the carcass of a Victorian toffee
factory near Euston station. The waiting area is dominated by a beech-
veneered park bench. The metal staircase is wrapped with plastic ivy.
The desks are dotted with iMac computers in bright boiled-sweet orange
and purples. The conference rooms are a jumble of swivel chairs and
coffee tables and box files. It was in these offices that one of the most
seductive examples of late twentieth-century anti-Victorianism was
formulated: a high-profile advertising campaign for the IKEA home
furnishings store, in which the entire population of a suburban street
binned their thick curtains, threadbare armchairs and tasselled standard
lamps, singing and smiling like a chorus from one of those eastern
European musicals about a boy, a girl and a tractor. The slogan 'Chuck
out your chintz' was cute, memorable and effective. One of the team
responsible for the campaign, a bright-eyed strategic planner named
Mitchell Bates, is explaining the ideas around which the advertising was
formed. 'It wasn't just against Victoriana,' he tells me. 'It was a whole
group of associated ideas. One-nation Conservatism. The myth of Little
England. John Bull. An obsession with the aristocracy, the monarchy.
The chintz aesthetic is determined by upper middle-class aspirations –
people wanting to have a country house, even if they live in a semi.'

My visit to Mitchell Bates's office was prompted by the results of his
latest research project. Using focus groups and a survey of a thousand
households, he has completed the most thorough investigation into
English interior décor ever undertaken. Participants have been interviewed about their attitudes to parquet and pelmets, had their sideboards

11 Japanese-style wallpaper, from *The Practical Decorator and Ornamentist*, 1892

surveyed, their scatter cushions photographed. Using this tranche of data, Bates has generated a typology of English taste – six 'style groups' reflecting a spectrum of attitudes to home decoration – which IKEA hopes will enable it to determine who is buying their furniture, and who wouldn't have it in the house. The results have taken both agency and client by surprise. The nation's chintz, it seems, remains substantially unchucked. Ranks of polished knick-knacks are infinitely more common than Philippe Starck chairs. Fuzzy floral dados coexist unselfconsciously with squashy modern sofas in turmeric orange and Matisse blue. 'It's been something of a reality-check,' confesses Bates.

'Home is my Castle' is the name he has given one of the largest of his demographic clans. The most conservative   both socially and aesthetically – of all the categories, this group includes many retired people and a disproportionate number of dog-owners. These people hoard ornaments, they are very keen to 'materialise their lineage' with photographs of living and dead family members, and they are pessimistic about the future. In the photographs, their homes shriek with flowery Dralon, fake ormolu, Axminster whorls. In the fat report on the survey, one of their number, a Mrs D, says, 'A couple we know have just spent a fortune redoing their house. They've completely thrown everything out and brought new in. I couldn't do that. I was adopted, so I've got no family history other than that I've created myself. I think you have security in things, because you have none from people.' They are people entrenched, both aesthetically and ideologically. For them, Modernism is something that happened to other people.

On my way back home from this meeting, I stop off at W. H. Smith's in Euston to browse through the interiors magazines. Many of the titles on display reflect the tastes of the Home is my Castlers. One particular magazine catches my eye: *Period Living and Traditional Homes*, a publication to which Raphael Samuel makes reference in *Theatres of Memory* (1994), in his essay on the nostalgic 'retrofitting' of British homes in the 1980s. Samuel's study records a cycle of twentieth-century taste: the enthusiastic post-war destruction of Victorian buildings, furniture and architectural features, in order to accommodate the hygienic, formally pure innovations of Modernism; the subsequent retreat from this project in the 1970s and 1980s, and the upsurge in the popularity of reproductions of the very objects and buildings the previous generation had attempted to erase.

Samuel would have loved this issue. It has a free gift gummed to the cover. Three packets of seeds. And they're not just ordinary seeds. They're 'Heritage Seeds to Remember'. Asters, which the packet reminds us 'commanded a high price in the Victorian flower markets of Paris and London' – as if the old girl ruled France as well as the British Empire. Sweet Williams, the result of hybridisation by 'Victorian plants-men', some breed of silver-bearded rustics long vanished from the earth. Poppies, which will produce 'nostalgic fringed flowers'. Advertisements inside reflect the same confused yearnings. The Brontë furniture company in Northamptonshire offers to supply readers with pseudo-Victorian kitchen dressers in unvarnished beech-blond wood. Thomas Crapper and Company of Stratford-upon-Avon peddle restored antique bathroom fittings 'in addition to our *exclusive* range of NEW "Victorian" Sanitaryware'. The magazine's lead feature is a step-by-step guide to creating your very own Victorian parlour: how to be bold with gold damask wallpaper, add elegance with faded floral fabric and create a contrast with small blue repeats. Looking at these adverts, it's hard not to be persuaded by Mitchell Bates's definition of 'the chintz aesthetic'. Who could possibly want to submerge themselves in such curlicued frippery, apart from middle managers who have retired to the Cotswolds with nothing left to look forward to but death? And would these people be so enthusiastic if they knew that 'chintz' was a Hindi word used to describe brightly coloured fabrics, and that, far from conveying staid Englishness, the Victorians saw chintz as exciting, exotic and cosmopolitan?

What happens when you strip Victorian rooms – not these *My Fair Lady* pastiches, but real Victorian rooms – of their current association with the parochial anti-Modernists of the Barratt estate? Or, for that matter, the anti-Victorianism of their opponents: the design writers who decry 'dingy Victorian interiors [with] dark Victorian panelling and heavy drapery'; the scientists who bizarrely claim that 'the dark Victorian interiors still favoured in many Indian and especially Indonesian house-holds' are a contributory factor in the high incidence of childhood pneumonia in those countries; the editors of *A Guide to the Architecture of London* (2000), who confidently state that St Pancras railway station was built of red brick in order that it should be 'visible through the smoky atmosphere of nineteenth-century London' (nothing to do, apparently, with the fact that brick was the most flexible and economical building material of the age).[1]

Insulating the house from pollution was a problem with which many British householders had to engage until the 1950s, when the Clean Air

Act was introduced in response to five days of smog in December 1952 that resulted in the deaths of four thousand Londoners. 'Those whose work compels them to dwell in, or very near to, large centres of industry,' wrote George Faulkner Armitage in 1886, soon discovered that 'the soot, dust, and grime reduce all colours to a dull monotonous grey.'[2] Air pollution may go some way to explaining the bold palette with which style-conscious mid-Victorians decorated their new homes – rich crimsons, Christmassy scarlets, golds, magentas and holly greens – but those who decamped to the greener spaces of the new suburbs, which began to coalesce around British cities in the 1850s, were also keen on these intense tones. Wilkie Collins was one of the first authors to give serious consideration to these brash, new, fresh-painted territories. In his novel *Basil* (1852), the eponymous hero takes a sudden libidinous fancy to Margaret Sherwin, a teenage girl he spies on the omnibus on his way home from cashing his latest allowance cheque. Unable to resist her attractions, he follows her back to a half-built London suburb and secures an interview with her father, a successful draper and new recruit to the middle classes. The decor of the Sherwin household is an affront to the hero-narrator's self-consciously cultivated taste. 'Everything was oppressively new,' he writes. 'The brilliant-varnished door cracked with a report like a pistol when it was opened; the paper on the walls, with its gaudy pattern of birds, trellis-work, and flowers in gold, red and green on a white ground, looked hardly dry yet; the showy window-curtains of white and sky blue, and the still showier carpet of red and yellow, seemed as if they had come out of the shop yesterday ...' As Basil gazes around the room, the searing colours and busy patterns start to overpower him. 'The print of the Queen,' he notes, 'hanging lonely on the wall, in its heavy gilt frame, with a large crown on the top, glared at you.' Other objects make him wince inwardly: '... the chairs in flaring chintz covers ... the blue and pink glass vases and cups ranged on the chimney-piece, the over-ornamented chiffoniers ... The room would have given a nervous man the headache, before he had been in it a quarter of an hour.'[3] George Faulkner Armitage would have sympathised: he considered that decorating a sunny room in reddish hues might be enough to inspire a nervous breakdown.

The Sherwins' living space confounds the received image of Victorian interiors as drab and dark – principally because more muted colours only became fashionable in the last quarter of the nineteenth century. In the mid-century, bright colour schemes and strong patterns were advocated in the wake of Jakob-Ignatius Hittorff's *L'Architecture polychrome chez les* *Grecs* (1851), which asserted that the colourless restraint that appeared to be a feature of classical buildings was an archaeological illusion: time and the elements had simply stripped these structures of their pigmented and variegated decoration. The popularity of Owen Jones's *Grammar of Ornament* (1856), a book of colour lithographs illustrating decorative techniques from all over the globe, also contributed to the recolouring of British homes. It was technology, however, more than any radical realignment of sensibilities, that propelled the later shift back to darker colours. The loud tones of 1850s interiors were designed to be viewed under daylight, candlelight and firelight, all of which were flattering to these intense shades. In the subtle glow of the fire – the centrepiece of every room – or the tallowy luminosity of the beeswax candle, such colours were comforting and rich. When, in the 1870s and 1880s, the more focused glares of gas and electric lamps began to illuminate homes more brightly than ever before, those colours suddenly seemed garish and violent. From this point, both old-fashioned decorators and a new breed of professional interior designer began to favour a more under-stated palette: olive greens, russets, apricots, slate blues, teals and dark browns. And when new heating technologies such as hot air systems and gas-fired boilers arrived, rooms no longer had to be oriented around the hearth: a fitting which, for the whole of the nineteenth century, stood as a toasty-warm symbol of the very idea of home. (John Ruskin, for example, wrote of home as 'a temple of the hearth watched over by household Gods'.) As a consequence, windows became more important and, crucially, less heavily masked with the fabric layers that prevented the incursion of soot and airborne dirt, and the escape of precious heat. With electricity came the possibility of Le Corbusier.

It is the aesthetic density of some nineteenth-century rooms that makes them appear so alien to a generation for whom blond woods and stainless steel are the *ne plus ultra* of domestic style. The tendency towards clutter, however, that is now so widely despised, arrived comparatively late in the period, was not approved by any of the nineteenth century's leading design writers, and was not even a native custom. The fashion was imported from France, where, according to Frances Trollope, 'the tenth part of what would be considered necessary to dress up a common lodging in Paris, would set the fine London Lady in this respect upon an enviable elevation above her neighbours.'[4] By the 1880s, this habit had established itself in Britain, and had interacted with other developments – the invention in the 1840s of mass-production systems for printing wallpaper, for instance – to turn some nineteenth-century homes into showcases of plush materials, patterned surfaces, elaborate woodwork, dados and knick-knacks and cabinets of curiosities. Affluent Victorians knew they were affluent Victorians by casting an eye over the volume of material objects with which they shared their homes. Poor Victorians knew they were poor because they didn't own these collections of things. Modern interiors are organised around the opposite principle. Today, it is the provincial and unfashionable who surround themselves with stuff, and the rich and metropolitan who occupy environments that telegraph their emptiness with loud insistence. My most affluent friends live in a house which is dazzlingly white, gloriously spacious and contains scarcely anything but a dining table and an Aga. My auntie, conversely, lived in a council house surrounded by a small army of Capodimonte figurines – until she was burgled, that is. In the Victorian period, their situations would have been precisely reversed. My auntie would have lived in a more sparse environment, my friends with the Aga would have lived amid the most extraordinary clutter, their Capodimonte figurines heavily insured. Over the last one hundred years, absence has become plenitude.

The enthusiasm of the Victorians for collating elaborate assemblages of objects is one of the reasons why most twentieth-century designers have rejected the nineteenth-century aesthetic so firmly. In *Orlando* (1928), Virginia Woolf proposed that this habit was a consequence of the damp, chilly nature of the Victorian mind: 'Rugs appeared, beards were grown, trousers were fastened tight under the instep. The chill which he felt in his legs the country gentleman soon transferred to his house; furniture was muffled, walls and tables were covered; nothing was left bare.' As possessions were accumulated and swaddled, 'The sexes drew further and further apart. No open conversation was tolerated. Evasions and concealments were sedulously practised on both sides.'[5] There is a less fanciful explanation for the busy extravagance of these rooms. For most Victorians – and for most twentieth-century people without Virginia Woolf's income – furniture was for life. You bought it when you set up house, and you were stuck with it – like your spouse – for the rest of your natural. Or at least until the offending item fell to pieces. 'I suppose there are few greater delights to the feminine heart', reflected M. L. Frith, a columnist in the *Englishwoman* magazine in 1892, 'than to be able to furnish throughout new from top to toe, and without too rigid a regard for economies, but with the exception of an engaged girl about to enter the first home of her own this pleasure does not come to many people.'[6] This was true long after 1901. When my grandparents married, they did what everybody in Hull in the 1940s did – went down to Turners, a shop with the arch slogan of 'Everything but the Girl', and bought the contents of their new home on HP. A sofa, armchair, dining table, chairs, sideboard, bed. Like them, most Victorian couples had to get it right first time – and, once chosen, to look after what they had. They also had to live with the choices made for them by their family and friends. 'Most young folk start in life handicapped with a hundred of cushions, photograph screens, modern Dresden groups, and the like, in the worst possible taste,' wrote Frith, celebrating the joy of 'those happy ones who have broken or given away their wedding presents'.[7]

With fewer opportunities to jettison furniture once it had lost its appeal or become less than fashionable, even relatively well-off Victorian householders found it easier to assert the individuality of their tastes with add-ons, accessories and knick-knacks – which is one of the reasons why they loved to drape household objects in covers and embroidered mats. Pretty fabric could conceal regrettable purchases as well as protect treasured pieces from wear and tear. As Asa Briggs describes in his book *Victorian Things* (1998), nineteenth-century homeowners often had ambivalent attitudes to their furniture. Briggs records a bad relationship with a piano endured by Jane Ellen Panton, one of the period's most powerful domestic goddesses – daughter of the eminent painter William Powell Frith, a Fellow of the Zoological Society, a novelist and the author of a number of style manuals. In one of the latter, *From Kitchen to Garret* (1888), she confessed that she had never really learned to love the instrument, that she considered it a 'very ugly piece of furniture' and described how she set about trying to disguise its shortcomings. She thought about doing the job with 'a turquoise-blue material worked with pale green campanulas', but plumped in the end for 'a very pretty frame [made] out of sage-green silk worked with rosebuds'.[8] A rival columnist in the *Ladies' Home Journal* favoured 'crimson or peacock blue plush, with old-gold embroidery', and provided an illustration for her readers – in which every portion of the instrument is covered except the keyboard and the legs.[9]

This imperative to transform mass-produced objects with touches of individuality became more urgent as the suburban belts around British cities continued to swell. Time has added a sentimental charm to the streets of Jesmond, Tooting and Didsbury, but their first occupants found these areas brash, shiny and aggressively uniform. Separate gables and hedges, and the odd romantically allusive name or ostentatious Gothic turret might have done a little to dispel the suburb's atmosphere of sameness and ahistoricism, but it was through the contents of the home that the new generation of suburban residents asserted their differences most vigorously. W. Pett Ridge, in his collection of short fiction *Outside the Radius, Stories of a London Suburb* (1899), notes these 'attempts in the direction of individuality ... Bamboo stands with ferns in giant egg-shells. Webster's Dictionary. A stuffed cockatoo. St Paul's Cathedral in white wax. Bust of the late Mr Spurgeon. Photograph of Her Majesty. Three Graces under glass shade.'[10] Bell-jars containing displays of taxidermy or dried flowers might indicate the owner's scientific interests; Venetian glassware and busts of composers or artists, that connoisseurs lived within. Elaborate arrangements of cabinet photographs and *cartes de visite* articulated their social world. Autographed images of celebrities, whether politicians, aristocrats, writers or circus performers, were also commonly seen on mantelpieces and occasional tables. Photography was a driving force behind a new interest that middle-class Victorians developed in styling their living spaces. It allowed them – like Mitchell Bates's interviewees – to 'materialise their lineage'. It also enabled them to see into the drawing rooms of fashionable people, to whose houses they had no hope of being invited. And, once they had absorbed the details in front of them, out came the paint-tins and the carpentry sets.

The arrival of DIY was recorded in music-hall songs about fathers papering parlours and entombing pianos and pets under layers of William Morris. But as most Victorians lived in rented accommodation – Wilkie Collins, for instance, never owned a house in his life – the scope for making alterations was limited. Mr Wemmick in *Great Expectations* (1861), with his moated villa and his cheery assertion, 'I am my own engineer, and my own carpenter, and my own plumber, and my own gardener, and my own Jack of all Trades', is an early incarnation of the Home Improvement hobbyist.[11] However, George and Weedon Grossmith's suburban satire, *The Diary of a Nobody* (1892), offered the most influential literary treatment of this new social type – people who lived beyond the main drags of the city and did their own interior design.

Charles and Carrie Pooter are key figures in the history of the British suburb, and continue to embody our ambivalent attitudes to these liminal regions. Such attitudes, however, were fixed almost half a century before they moved into their unexceptional end-of-terrace home in Holloway, north London. Indeed, commentators (most of whom lived in well-appointed townhouses) began to express their dislike of these developments as soon as speculative builders threw up the first swathe of out-of-town Doric-style terraces. Wilkie Collins's suspicion of the suburbs has already been noted. As Basil walks through the north London fields newly churned and smothered by the Sherwins' Hollyoake Square, he confesses, 'Its newness and desolateness of appearance revolted me.' Nine years later, Alan Ruthven, the Cumbrian hero of F. G. Trafford's novel *City and Suburb* (1861), wondered at the palaver of the daily commute enforced by life in semi-rural dormitory districts, exclaiming, 'I could not live as the Londoners do; the mass of the business people I see take a journey for the sole purpose of going to sleep; they eat and drink, and walk, and read in the city, and then they get into a close ill-ventilated omnibus, and drive five or six miles to bed ...'[12] Suburban alienation, it seems, is another Victorian invention. 'It is', reflected Mabel Keningdale Cook in a *Woman* magazine article of 1872, 'a very evident fact that the suburbs of London are filled with wives of well-to-do city men, &c., middle-aged matrons, as well as youthful brides, whose existence is little more than a mere round of inanity.'[13] In these marginal areas, the terms of what it still means to be a member of middle-class consumer society were being defined: shaped by the temptation to landowners to sell their acreage to make some fast money, by the desires of moderately prosperous families to breathe clean air and by the sometimes arbitrary progress of the transport system. Amazingly, the distribution of rich and poor households across modern London is still being determined by the ticket-pricing policies of the Victorian railway companies. Enfield, for instance, is still a largely working-class area; Ongar is much more affluent. The reason? The Great Eastern Railway provided cheap rail fares to the former suburb, but not the latter, and effected a haphazard exercise in social engineering. Victorian householders were sensible to these processes. From the 1870s onwards, the inhabitants of Edgbaston, Hampstead and Kelvinside all attempted to prevent the horse-tram network making progress through their streets, fearing that it would alter the demographics of their areas, which suited them very nicely. In doing so, they became the progenitors of modern Nimbyism.

The Pooters, as residents of Holloway – a territory sandwiched between the inner city and the more genuinely suburban areas of Hampstead and Crouch End – would have been too close to the centre of London to prevent the incursion of undesirables. Instead, they concentrated upon the embellishment and beautification of their home. When Charles Pooter gets hold of a pot of enamel paint, he daubs a coat on the coal scuttle 'and the backs of our *Shakespeare*, the binding of which had almost worn out'. The next day, he goes to work on the bathroom. 'Painted the bath red, and was delighted with the result. Sorry to say Carrie was not, in fact we had a few words about it. She said I ought to have consulted her, and she had never heard of such a thing as a bath being painted red. I replied: "It's merely a matter of taste." ' He soon has reason to regret this outburst of creativity. Nursing a Sunday morning hangover, which his wife believes is the result of inhaling paint fumes, he climbs into the bathtub and soaks in the hot water for some time:

> On moving my hand above the surface of the water, I experienced the greatest fright I ever received in the whole course of my life; for imagine my horror on discovering my hand, as I thought, full of blood. My first thought was that I had ruptured an artery, and was bleeding to death, and should be discovered, later on, looking like a second Marat, as I remember seeing him in Madame Tussaud's. My second thought was to ring the bell, but remembered there was no bell to ring.[14]

The Grossmiths' book proved sufficiently Zeitgeistish to inspire a whole streetful of imitators. The narrator of Alfred Walter Barrett's *Martha and I* (1898), for instance, leases a six-year-old house on very reasonable terms (a murder, it seems, has taken place in one of the bedrooms and knocked down the rental value) and is soon attacking the new property from every angle: 'I promised to stain that floor or perish in the attempt,' he vows.[15] Although such fictions were comic exaggerations, they reflected much genuine truth about suburbia, and the lengths to which its inhabitants went to transform their mass-produced dwellings into expressions of their own taste and sensibilities. Magazines aided and abetted them in the realisation of their desires. 'Elsa' of *Practical Housekeeping and Furnishing* told her readers how to create a comfortable drawing-room seat by replacing the canvas on a three-shilling folding deckchair with crimson serge and enamelling the woodwork a glossy ebony.[16] 'M. E.' of the *Ladies Home Journal* urged her readers to turn 'ordinary drain-pipes' into 'an elegant stand for a plant or fern'.[17]

And the diaries of Jeannette Marshall, an inhabitant of Savile Row for most of the second half of the nineteenth century, offer an insight into the ways in which these projects and ideas were disseminated from the arty set to the inhabitants of the new suburban estates. In 1874, Marshall visited the home of Ford Madox Brown, the Pre-Raphaelite painter, and was none too impressed with the neo-medievalism of his interior décor. Three weeks later she found herself visiting a friend of her mother's and having uncharitable thoughts about her aesthetic ideas. 'I don't altogether admire her drawing room,' she wrote. 'The walls are too cold a colour, & I don't like either the stained floor, the mixed furniture or the peacock feathers.' Only a few years later, however, she had overcome her misgivings and embarked upon a programme of enthusiastic modernisation along these fashionable lines. Though the Marshalls were reasonably well off, they achieved the transformation from mid-Victorian brashness to moody high-Victorian exoticism with a modest budget. They bought one new item of furniture – a bentwood rocker – and used black Japanese varnish to orientalise their old chairs and tables. They stripped and polished the floorboards. They put up William Morris paper. They used filoselle silk and bright wool yarns to tart up reams of towel fabric with intricate, faux-Asiatic designs. Lengths of this were hung either side of the fireplace and used as table-mats and antimacassars. A Japanese screen was ordered from Whiteley's department store to complete the effect. 'Leightonesque' was how Jeannette's father described the new look.[18] If you want to get an idea of what he meant, take a trip to Holland Park and visit the house of the painter Frederic Leighton. Walk through the gift shop and into the hallway, and turn left. In front of you, you'll see the most gorgeous, extravagant chamber, clad with Turkish tiles and adorned with an indoor lily-pond. You can imagine Aubrey Beardsley, Lillie Langtry and a phalanx of odalisques here, lolling on satin cushions embroidered with parrots, puffing languidly away at their hookahs. It remains one of London's most impressive rooms.

For advice on design matters, the Victorians turned to authorities such as R. K. Philip, Lucy Orrinsmith, Charles Eastlake and Oscar Wilde, who all produced guides or delivered lectures on how to decorate and maintain the home. Read through these works, and you soon begin to notice a surprisingly consistent line of rhetoric, maintained between disparate authors throughout the last five decades of the nineteenth century, which advocates a war on the darkness, fuss and clutter proverbially associated with the Victorian home. The gurus of nineteenth-century interior design argue for simplicity. They don't go quite so far as urging their readers to a proto-IKEA scorched-earth policy regarding chintz, but they are as sceptical as Mitchell Bates about trying to fit a country house into a suburban terrace. When Hubert von Herkomer constructed his peculiar Bavarian-style lodge in Bushey, he considered that the 'Shibboleth of the English [was] plenty of light in a room, ignoring the fact that repose is positively extracted from a room that is overlighted'.[19] His English visitors, however, considered his home a 'glorified dungeon'.

In *The Practical Housewife* (1855), R. K. Philip advised, 'Never crowd a bedroom with furniture; have that which is really useful and requisite, and no more ... A dining-room requires little furniture; but that little should be good and handsome, and of mahogany. A little furniture tastefully arranged, is far better than a crowd of articles.' There were practical reasons for this: 'Never place a carpet under a bed, or you provide a resting-place for all the dust and flock which daily falls from the mattresses, and establish a nice hot bed for fleas.'[20] George Armitage considered the over-filling of rooms a positive health hazard: 'Do not overcrowd, do not have large bulky things that are hard to move, that are too high to reach to the top of and dust, and take up too many cubic feet and inches of precious air which in small rooms is a matter of great consideration.'[21] In *Hints on Household Taste* (1868), Eastlake condemned the standard Louis Quatorze-style settee of many Victorian homes as 'a piece of ugliness which we ought not to tolerate in our houses', and argued that 'a room intended for repose ought to contain nothing which can fatigue the eye by complexity.' Designs encumbered by 'extravagant curves' and 'strips of paltry and meaningless scrollwork' were a particular hate.[22] Oscar Wilde's lecture 'The House Beautiful', delivered on his tour of America in 1882, gave precise instructions to those who wanted to improve the aesthetic coherence of their domestic environment. These were his rules: the entrance hall of a house should not be wallpapered, it should not be carpeted, but tiled (the Leighton House gets two big ticks here); artificial flowers should be banished from the home; large gas chandeliers should be ripped out and replaced with less imposing side brackets; blown glass should be used in favour of elaborate cut glass (Charles Pooter, very proud of his hall windows – 'ground glass ... with stars'– would have lost points here).

It is debatable how much influence Wilde's ideas had upon nine-teenth-century decorative practice. Many people came along to his lectures simply to gawp at his clothes and mannerisms, and even he found that living up to these dictums could be an expensive and time-consuming business. The real heavyweights of the period were Ruskin and William Morris, who established themselves as champions in the campaign to rid British homes of Frenchified frills and clutter. Try to imagine Jacques Derrida or Camille Paglia writing weighty books about festoon blinds and picture rails, and you begin to appreciate how important the discourse of interior design was in Victorian culture.

In *The Stones of Venice* (1853), Ruskin explained to his readers that the choices they made in home furnishing had a direct part to play in the construction of a good and healthy society. There were, he argued, 'three broad and simple rules' for home aesthetics: 'Never encourage the manufacture of any article not absolutely necessary, in the production of which *Invention* has no share. 2. Never demand an exact finish for its own sake, but only for some practical or noble end. 3. Never encourage imitation or copying of any kind, except for the sake of preserving record of great works.'[23] In other words, don't buy useless gadgets, don't go mad with stencils and varnish and stippling when something simple will do, and don't fill your living room with naff reproductions of *The Hay Wain*. William Morris – whose printing firm, the Kelmscott Press, published this work – transformed Ruskin's advice into a catchy slogan in *Hopes and Fears for Art* (1882): 'Have nothing in your houses that you do not know to be useful, or believe to be beautiful.'[24] The edict was enormously influential, but not necessarily in the way that Morris had anticipated. Not only did it encourage Victorians to recognise their homes as a medium for artistic expression, but it also gave them *carte blanche* to fill them with as much vulgar junk as they pleased, as long as they could justify their belief in its beauty. The domestic aesthete Dorothy Peel, however, was certainly grateful for his campaign against cheap and nasty baubles. 'William Morris having saturated himself with the achievements of past centuries,' she reflected in *The New Home* (1898), 'set to work upon the gigantic task of reforming the Victorian era, and removing from it that reproach, which, had he not laboured, would certainly have been meeted [*sic*] out to it by posterity.'[25]

Posterity, unfortunately, has done more than reproach: it has derided, demolished, destroyed. 'Victorian arts and their foreign equivalents', reflects Peter Thornton in *Authentic Decor* (2001), 'have until fairly recently been viewed with ... abhorrence.'[26] When, in the 1980s, many middle-class Britons relinquished this abhorrence, seeing a revival of

Victorian aesthetics as an escape from the Formica and linoleum emphasis of post-war housing, all these fixtures and fittings were resurrected in peculiar, updated forms. What, I wonder, would Morris or Peel or Eastlake think if they could see the results of this process? If they could swish down the aisles of the DIY superstores that now fill the suburban retail parks of England, and gaze upon their contents: movement-sensitive security lights in the form of Victorian coach lamps; PVC windows threaded with the leaded lattice popularised by Morris; self-adhesive dado rails? They are exemplars of bad taste, but they are everywhere: contemporary imitations of domestic features which the Pooters would have bought the first time around, material that is policed from the smart interiors pages of the twenty-first-century Sunday newspapers, but which – as IKEA and St Luke's have discovered – still clutters the suburbs of England.

CHAPTER NINE

A Defence of the Freak Show

There's a quality of legend about freaks. Like a person in a fairy
tale who stops you and demands that you answer a riddle. Most
people go through life dreading they'll have a traumatic
experience. Freaks were born with their trauma. They've
already passed their test in life. They're aristocrats.

Diane Arbus, *An Aperture Monograph* (1972)

Coney Island ain't what it used to be. The faux-Arabian towers of Luna
Park have been demolished to make way for an undistinguished housing
development. The wooden skeleton of the Loop-the-Loop rots slowly
inside a barbed-wire enclosure. The Dragon's Gorge indoor scenic
railway, which rattled its passengers from Hell to the North Pole and
back, burned down half a century ago and was never rebuilt. Surf
Avenue, once a parade of food parlours and amusement booths, has now
been colonised by bric-à-brac stalls run by Russian immigrants. Great
place to buy an electric samovar or a set of second-hand spark plugs. Not
so great if you want the thrill of your life.

In its heyday, Coney Island was where America went for just such
stimulation. In particular, it went to gaze upon the extraordinary bodies
of freak-show performers. Punters could gratify themselves by stepping
inside the booth to come face to face with The Toad Man with Two
Noses, The Penguin Boy, The Barracuda Ape, The Lobster Boy or The
Alligator Skin Girl. They might visit Samuel W. Gumpertz's Lilliputia, a
half-scale metropolis with a population of three hundred dwarfs, or his
'Congress of Freaks', a big top extravaganza with a cast of 3,800
physically bizarre performers.

In the summer of 1999, I took the B Train to Coney in order to see
America's last freak show. It is housed in a featureless concrete building,
tucked between Astroland, a tatty amusement park, and Nathan's
Famous Hot Dogs, a great, greasy Brooklyn institution. The façade is
hung with garish banners, painted in a naïve style that has remained the
preferred sideshow aesthetic since the end of the nineteenth century. In

one picture, a monocled Nimrod figure peers at a two-headed creature, captioned 'Nature's Mistakes'. Another poster trumpets the presence of a 'Real Human Shrunken Head', with a crude image of a decapitated body, prone and bloodied by the side of a bubbling cannibal cooking pot. Most eye-catching of all, perhaps, is the banner for 'The Freak Bar', which depicts a pair of Siamese twins toasting each other with foaming glasses of cartoon beer, and an armless woman perched on a bar-stool clutching a pint of lager with her painted toes.

Misleading the customers is, of course, a time-honoured tradition of the freak show. After I'd parted with three dollars and entered the tiny auditorium, I wasn't too surprised to find that none of these attractions materialised. Instead, Frank Hartman, Blockhead and Sword Swallower, hammered a six-inch nail up his nose, Serpentina the Snake Woman sucked the head of a fifteen-foot albino python, Electra the High Voltage Lady illuminated light bulbs with her tongue and Madame Twisto sidled around the long, flat blades slotted into her Cabinet of Death. Koko the Killer Clown, of whom I had great hopes – his publicity claimed that he 'spent five years in prison for murdering his wife and her lover' – turned out to be a surly dwarf with an unremarkable line in balloon sculpture. To give Koko his credit, however, he did saunter onstage to the blare of Chic's 1970s disco hit 'Le Freak'.

The sparse crowd – mainly giggly college kids and a handful of poor-looking families – didn't seem much interested in the only 'real' freak in the place. Hidden away in a corner, half-concealed by the rickety seating stand, sat a glass case containing a dark-skinned creature about the size of a small dog. Coil-shaped eyes goggling out from a desiccated, simian face; fur giving way to scales and a blackened piscine tail. To the cynical eye, this was just a few pieces of monkey and salmon skin sewn together for monstrous effect. To those in the know, however, it was something more unique: Phineas T. Barnum's Fejee Mermaid.

There are at least seven Fejee Mermaids known to exist, and nobody can be entirely sure which is the one that Barnum unveiled to a curious American public on 8 August 1843. Several alternative candidates are held by the Ripley's Believe it or Not company, which runs a chain of thirty-odd dime museums across the States. Harvard University's Peabody Museum of Archaeology and Ethnology also claims to possess the original, where it shares a locked storage cabinet with a similar creature and is rarely put on public display. The first specimens of this kind to

12 The marriage of Tom Thumb and Lavinia Warren, photographed by Matthew
Brady, 1863. The wedding reception was attended by Abraham Lincoln

reach the west were the object of intense interest, but by the last quarter
of the nineteenth century the novelty had worn off, as large quantities of
the beasts had been imported into Europe, mostly from Japan. The
Belgian painter James Ensor, whose parents owned a seaside souvenir

shop in Ostend, spent his childhood surrounded by these grotesque little creatures. (In the shop window on Ostend's Vlaanderenstraat, now a museum, sits a glass case containing several examples: three mummified monsters with glaring glass eyes and cobweb-coloured beards, fixed in a fake underwater scene.)

The original Fejee Mermaid was first exhibited in London in October 1822, at the Turf coffee house on the corner of Jermyn Street and St James's Street. A Captain Eades of Boston acquired the specimen while visiting either China or Calcutta – and embezzled $6,000 of his ship's money to make the purchase. The Japanese fisherman who netted the mermaid, Eades claimed, had been warned by the dying creature that if its image was not distributed around the world, terrible plagues and years of infertility would descend upon the local population. Eades hoped that the monster would make his fortune. Instead, it became the locus of a legal dispute which left him penniless. All he had to bequeath to his son when he died was the shrivelled body of the Mermaid – which Eades junior sold to Barnum's collaborator Moses Kimball for a few pounds.

Kimball and Barnum succeeded where Eades had failed. They used one of the most extravagant publicity campaigns in American history to make the Mermaid the hot topic of conversation in the summer of 1843. They planted stories in the press, they went on a PR offensive to gain the favour of influential newspaper editors, they circulated engravings of the beast and they hired a stooge to impersonate an English academic – 'Dr Griffin' of the 'Lyceum of Natural History' – who was said to be bringing this remarkable creature to New York. They also used sex to sell the dried-up little creature, placing a huge placard of a semi-naked aquatic voluptuary outside their venue, the Concert Hall at 404 Broadway. Disappointed lechers were usually too meek to complain. By the end of the affair, Barnum was a million dollars richer. Even when the public began to suspect something fishy, he was able to exploit this scepticism to his own advantage. One advert read:

> Engaged for a short time, the animal (regarding which there has been so much dispute in the scientific world) called the FEJEE MERMAID! Positively asserted by its owner to have been taken alive in the Fejee Islands, and implicitly believed by many scientific persons, while it is pronounced by other scientific persons to be an *artificial* production ... At all events, whether this production is the work of *nature* or *art*, it is *decidedly* the most stupendous

curiosity ever submitted to the public for inspection. If it is artificial, the senses of sight and touch are useless, for *art* has rendered them totally ineffectual. If it is natural, then all *concur* in declaring it THE GREATEST CURIOSITY IN THE WORLD.[1]

The ploy had worked before. In 1835, Barnum had exhibited Joice Heth, a grotesquely wizened old lady whom he billed as the 161-year-old nursemaid of George Washington. When common opinion began to turn against the veracity of these claims, Barnum wrote anonymous letters to the newspapers, claiming that Heth was a clockwork automaton operated by the showman himself. The crowds came flooding back, hoping to hear the mechanism whirr or click and catch the humbug out. Naturally, they heard nothing.

In Britain, the exhibition of bizarre curiosities – some living, some dead, some animal, some human – was a thriving industry throughout the eighteenth and nineteenth centuries. London events such as the Hyde Park Fair (which celebrated Queen Victoria's accession) played host to appearances by 'numerous fat men and women, spotted boys, natural and unnatural, fair Circassians, the Hottentot Venus, dwarfs, Miss Scott, the two-headed lady, Yorkshire Jack, the Living Skeleton, and learned pigs and fortune-telling ponies galore'.[2] During the following decade, under Barnum's influence, the traffic in human oddities developed into one of the most lucrative branches of the entertainment industry. Today, its personalities – dwarfs, giants, baboon women, dog-faced boys and hirsute missing links – are all but forgotten, and we regard their careers as a barbaric embarrassment. Their textual remains – posters, contractual documents, visiting cards – are preserved in the collections of libraries and private individuals. Some of their physical remains – skeletons, pickled body parts, clothes, plaster *moulages* – reside in the archives of hospitals, museums and forensic laboratories. In their day, however, they were granted royal audiences, invited to smart parties and sold their photographs to eager admirers from all over the world.

The professional world of the freak has come to exemplify the worst excesses and ignorances of our Victorian ancestors. It offers a thumbnail sketch of their brutality, their credulity, their willingness to exploit the unfortunate. It's difficult for us to concede that nineteenth-century audiences may have pursued an ironic relationship with a phoney exhibit such as the Fejee Mermaid, perhaps in the same way that we enjoy impossible tabloid headlines involving sightings of Elvis or alien abduction. And the suggestion that human freak-show performers might have embraced a career in carnivals and sideshows is even more difficult to stomach: especially as post-Victorian medicine has effected the possibility of terminating the kind of foetuses that produced the freak show's personnel, and the post-Victorian media has so successfully suppressed images of human physical deformity.

The remaining chapters of this book will attempt to recover a number of aspects of Victorian sensibility which have been lost in time, or obfuscated by history: their attitudes to sex and gender roles, to their bodies, to their physical desires. Reclaiming Joseph Merrick as an eminent Victorian is a good place to begin. It is time for the freakish history of the nineteenth century to be reclaimed; for the reputations of its personalities to be recuperated and allowed to repopulate accounts of the period. Everyone knows about Lillie Langtry and Henry Irving, but Hassan Ali the Egyptian Giant and Julia Pastrana the Nondescript need talking up with a bit of showman's ballyhoo. The lives of the lost tribe of Victorian dwarfs, for example, should be returned to the position of prominence they once enjoyed. Its most lauded members included Charles Stratton, known as General Tom Thumb, the nineteenth century's most celebrated dwarf performer, who earned enough to retire to a specially scaled-down country house with his equally diminutive wife, Lavinia Warren; Count Boruwlaski, an aristocratic Polish dwarf who became a close confidant of King Stanislaus, went on a guitar-playing tour of Lapland and died in Durham at the age of ninety-eight, during the year of Queen Victoria's accession; the Dutch dwarf Jan Hanemma, exhibited as Admiral Van Tromp, who attracted widespread press interest on a visit to London in October 1848, and inspired approving paragraphs in publications ranging from *The Times* to the *Lady's News*.

The Giants, too, have now sunk from view. In 1853, Edward Smith, the landlord of the Lion and Ball public house in Red Lion Street, Holborn, engaged an American giant named Freeman to serve behind the bar. The erstwhile star of the Olympic Theatre extravaganza *The Son of the Desert and the Demon Changeling* – in which he had played opposite Hervio Nono, a celebrated legless acrobat – now resides in a glass case in the Museum of the Royal College of Surgeons.[3] In 1866, the Chinese giant Chang Woo Gow made the first of several visits to Britain, before he, his Liverpool-born wife and their two sons Edward and Ernest retired to Southcote Road, Bournemouth, from where they ran a teashop and Oriental bazaar. The couple died within a year of each other, and were buried together in Wimborne Road Cemetery. They were not cringing victims: they were stars.

Other performers offered more a more outré kind of wonder: Krao Farini, the Missing Link, exhibited between 1880 and 1920 as living proof of Darwin's Theory of Natural Selection; Madame Babault, the Lobster Claw Lady ('instead of Hands and Feet she has the Perfect Claws of a Lobster'), who delighted audiences by knitting and crocheting with her crustaceoid hands;[4] and Miss Atkinson, the Pig Woman, an Irish heiress with a fetching pink snout, to whom at least one respectable gentleman made an offer of marriage via the personal columns of the *Morning Herald:*

> Secrecy. A single gentleman, aged thirty-one, of a respectable family, and in whom the utmost confidence may be reposed, is desirous of explaining his mind to the friends of a person who has misfortune in her face, but is prevented for want of an introduction. Being perfectly aware of the principal particulars and understanding that a final settlement would be preferable to a temporary one, presumes he would be found to answer the full extent of their wishes. His intentions are sincere, honourable, and firmly resolved. References of great respectability can be given. Address to M.D. at Mr Spencer's, Great Ormond Street, Queen Square.[5]

Another Pig Woman, Miss Stevens, was in fact a strategically shaved bear, dressed up in crinolines and strapped into a chair (nobody proposed to her).

Study this material for a little while, and you start to develop favourites. Top of my dinner-party wish list is Miss Julia Pastrana the Nondescript, variously known as The Bear Woman and the Baboon Lady. She was covered from head to toe in thick brown hair, and her gums and jaw were as massive as an ape's. It was claimed that she was discovered inside a cave in a monkey-infested area of Mexico – the implication being that she was the hybrid product of some simian-human coupling. She sang, she acted, she danced the Highland Fling, and by special arrangement, she would visit members of the public in their own homes to entertain them with operatic arias. Although she was dead by 1860, her career was far from over. After her appearances in Britain during the late 1850s, her manager – a man named Lent – married her and took her to Moscow, where she died in childbirth. In 1862 Lent returned to London, exhibiting the mummified remains of his family as a miracle of the embalmer's art, the triumph of a Muscovite scientist named Professor Suckaloff. The biologist Francis Buckland, who examined her for a book on natural history, had his suspicions: 'As regards the history of the embalmment,' he noted, ominously, 'there were some queer stories told.'[6] Queerest of all, perhaps, was the true story that the embalmed Pastrana was soon touring Europe in the company of a second Mrs Lent – a German woman who enjoyed the same unusual physiognomy as her predecessor.

The story seems ghoulish and horrid, but it is worth noting that the longest part of Julia Pastrana's career took place in the twentieth century. For a hundred years after their deaths, mother and child were toured around the carnivals of Europe. The pair were exhibited as late as 1973, when the baby was eaten by mice and the body of its mother stolen by vandals while being exhibited at a fairground in Norway. Pastrana's mummy was thought lost for ever, but in 1991, the Norwegian authorities admitted that the body was being stored in the vaults of the Institute of Forensic Medicine in Oslo. She is still there, coffined underground in a refrigerated chamber.

The strategies that Victorian showpeople used to drum up custom were a long way from the whip-cracking Grand Guignolism of legend. An air of gentility and scientific enquiry pervades its advertising material. Exhibitors were keen to emphasise the popularity of their spectacles with the female public – specifically the middle-class female public. Tom Thumb's posters, for instance, frequently depicted a respectable-looking young woman admiring him on his pedestal. Handbills published prices for 'ladies and gentlemen', 'working classes' and even 'schools'. One 1836 advertisement for an audience with the Spanish dwarf Don Santiago de los Santos announces that 'Persons not wishing to take a Cigar are entitled to a Muffin or Crumpet.'[7]

The case of the 'Wonderful and Highly-Trained Sea Leopard or TALKING FISH!!!', illustrates that, in the advertising at least, the Gothic was not an element of the freak show's appeal. The Talking Fish was an African seal schooled to bark up to three and pronounce the name of its keeper (fortunately called John) – the forerunner of modern performing seals and dolphins who turn tricks in zoos for a fishy bribe from the keeper. Eager for business, the publicity attempts every strategy of enticement available to the exhibitor, offering the potential patron nine different ways to justify a voyeuristic interest in the prodigious animal. The spectacle will appeal: to the initiated freak show visitor ('All who take an interest in Natural Curiosities'); to the pious ('All who admire the Wonders of the Creation'); to the connoisseur of animal intelligence ('All who appreciate a wonderful development of Instinct'); to the student of science ('All who wish to know and understand Nature'); to those in search of Useful Knowledge ('All who desire Amusement with Instruction'); to those looking for genteel pleasure ('All who wish for Extraordinary Novelties'); to the sceptical ('All who disbelieve its Speaking powers'); to the sporting ('All who want Recreative Excitement') and – noted in one of the smallest typefaces on the sheet – the thrill-seeker ('All who crave for Sensations should see the TALKING FISH').[8] When the 'Fish' was exhibited in the capital at 191 Piccadilly, its owners decided to emphasise its scientific appeal, offering 'complimentary cards to Naturalists and Gentlemen of the Press'.[9]

An appeal to scientific interest was not necessarily spurious. Francis Buckland and Frederick Treves (the doctor who became the patron of the Elephant Man) both visited exhibitions of human oddities out of professional interest. A handbill in the John Johnson collection at the Bodleian Library, Oxford, advertising the appearance of a 'Seven Year Old Child with Huge Head', contains a sad little note made by a visitor with some medical knowledge: 'probably hydrocephalous – she was generally lying down, and seemed heavy and sleepy.'[10] Some showmen went aggressively for the scientific market. In June 1840, 'An Antediluvian child, Found in supercritary [sic] soil' was exhibited in rooms at 18 Leicester Square, with the exorbitant admission fee of £1:

> Until now there never was found but the bones of animals to have turned into a fossil state. Cuvier, the most celebrated of his age, has denied the existence of human fossil remains; and others pretend that previous to the Deluge the human race had no existence. Here, then, is at once a demonstrative evidence of the falsity of their opinion, and a clear indication of the truth of the Holy Bible.[11]

Once evolutionary theory had been broadly accepted, certain performers used the interest in this new science to draw in middle-class punters. In 1887, Krao Farini appeared at the Aquarium, Westminster, as 'A living proof of Darwin's Theory of the Descent of Man'. Farini was offered as the missing link between simian and human life: 'The usual argument against the Darwinian theory that man and monkey had a common ancestor, has always been that no animal has hitherto been discovered in the transmission state between monkey and man.'[12] Far from being a throwback to some barbaric past, the freak show was – in this case – marketed as an adjunct to the culture of scientific rationalism.

In the case of the Talking Fish, the strategy was signally successful. The gentleman of the press from the *Illustrated London News* was enraptured. 'It is no pretence, no delusion, no stuffed skin,' he enthused, alluding to a certain aquatic hoax from the South Seas. 'Between it and a man a mesmeric sympathy has been instituted . . . it can not only dance, but it can act, – go right through a scene.' Echoing the sentiments of the Oxford publicity, he proclaimed, 'Let every naturalist or lover of nature's marvels pay it a visit.'[13] A month later, the same newspaper claimed that the 'Fish' had 'excited much curiosity, and been visited by multitudes'.[14] Other commentators were less impressed. *Punch* remarked that 'Another Talking Fish is, *Mr Punch* understands, caught, and in course of education for next season. The proprietor's motto is, "*Sealum, non animum, muto*".'[15] Charles Allston Collins, writing as 'The Eye-Witness' in an article that first appeared in *All the Year Round*, condemned the performance as exploitative of both the animal and the public. 'Where was the talking?' he demanded. 'Was this the animal for whose feats of dialogue the public had been prepared by a placard, stuck on every wall in London, representing a British sailor in earnest conversation, not to say argument, with an enormous codfish standing upright on the tip of its tail?'[16]

At least Collins actually came face to face with a live exotic animal. When punters paid to see the 'Wonderful Performing Fish' re-enacting a famous naval battle and a 'Tame OYSTER that sits by the fire and smokes his yard of clay,' they were treated to the sight of a tank of terrified goldfish, noosed to paper boats containing live fireworks, and a daft piece of legerdemain by showman George Sanger – who attached a concealed set of bellows to an inert bivalve mollusc and declaimed, 'Now, sir, let the company see that you really are trained and intelligent by showing how you can smoke a pipe!'[17]

Histories like this, both mournful and comic, demonstrate the cultural importance of the freak show. Such entertainments seem to contravene every rule of decency and dignity to which we, as twenty-first-century people, wish our society to aspire. Able-bodied Victorians paid to poke their 'disabled' contemporaries with sticks; we have wheelchair ramps and induction loop systems. However, the fact that the category 'freak' makes no distinction between an animal act like the Talking Fish and a human performer such as Julia Pastrana does not necessarily mean that the Victorians were turning up to gloat over monstrosity they regarded as subhuman. Consider the alternative view: that Giants and Bearded Ladies commanded respect and hefty fees; that many Victorians did not regard the physical quirks and bodily abnormalities of their peers as disadvantages or misfortunes, but celebrated them – to the extent that they were willing to hire such people for parties like conjurors or after-dinner speakers.

The term 'freak', moreover, is very difficult to find in Victorian texts dealing with such figures. True, Joseph Merrick was touted as 'The Great Freak of Nature!', but this was in a pamphlet of his own authorship.[18] Most of his colleagues – even the Lobster Claw Lady and the Bear Woman – remained unassociated with the word. In 1899, when the Barnum and Bailey Circus brought a collection of extraordinary human specimens to London, the management was keen to distance itself from the term, and accepted Canon Basil Wilberforce's recommendation that these attractions be retitled 'prodigies'. Wilberforce, whose father, Bishop 'Soapy' Samuel of Oxford, had been one of the most venomous opponents of Darwin's theory of evolution, may well have preferred that such evidence of random human development had been hidden altogether. Perhaps he also wished to focus on the metaphysical dimension of prodigy status, which suggested that the unusual body offered a link with the divine. Clarence L. Dean explained this process in the souvenir brochure that accompanied the show:

> We turn first to the family of strange human beings, of whom it has been the habit of the public to speak of as 'freaks'. The name is a harsh one, and the people themselves object to it. At two meetings held by them in protest last January, they decided, on the suggestion of Canon Wilberforce of Westminster, that they should be called 'prodigies'.[19]

This done, the Barnum's paying customers could gawp with a clear conscience at Lalloo the Double-bodied Hindu Boy, Jo-Jo the Human Skye Terrier, Annie Jones the bearded lady and Hassan Ali, the Egyptian Giant. Ali was seven feet eleven inches high and a seventy-cigarettes-a-day man. His stage name seems to be a playful reference to the faithful manservant of General Gordon of Khartoum. 'I am no freak!' he declared, quoted in Dean's brochure. 'My father was a mere soldier of the Mahdi, and died the death of a brave man in the Soudan, and he was twenty-five millimetres (nearly an inch) taller than I. A pretty sort of freak I am!'[20]

All the Barnum and Bailey prodigies were veterans of the circuit. Lalloo, born in either Lucknow or Oudh, India, in about 1874, had a small twin attached to the lower part of his breastbone. Hoping to add a hermaphrodite angle to his show, the museums that employed him advertised that the twin was a sister and dressed the tiny body in female clothes. The twin grew directly out of Lalloo's body and had two arms and legs. Although it lacked a pulse, the parasite's bloodstream was connected to its host's. The twin's limbs were also sensitive: Lalloo could tell where his little brother was being touched.

Annie Jones, born in 1865 in Virginia, is said to have emerged from the womb with a beard and two feet of hair. When Barnum heard about this unusual birth, he wired her mother and offered her a contract to exhibit her daughter as 'The Infant Esau'. Mother and daughter moved to New York, but when a family crisis called Mrs Jones back to Virginia, she left Annie in the care of a phrenologist named Wicks. On her return to Manhattan, Mrs Jones learned that her daughter and her temporary guardian had disappeared. Six months later, Annie was reported to have been found in upstate New York. When Mrs Jones arrived to claim her child, Wicks insisted that the girl was his, forcing Mrs Jones to take the matter to court. At the age of sixteen, Annie secretly married a circus barker named Richard Elliott. She divorced him fifteen years later and married William Donovan, a wardrobe man with Barnum's circus. Eventually, the couple left the circus to tour Europe on their own. Dean's book describes her as 'the very impersonation of daintiness ... Miss Jones would never be taken for a "freak", as she dresses in fine taste.'[21] The man from *The Times* was certainly impressed, and perhaps even a little intoxicated by Jones's physical ambiguity: 'but for Mr. Barnum's well-known professional rectitude [she] might be taken for a young man of somewhat effeminate cast.'[22]

Were these performers exploited by their managers? Their rates of pay compared favourably with those of others in the entertainment industry. In the United States in the late nineteenth century, stage actors received about thirty-five to eighty dollars a week. The top performers on the Dime Museum circuit might take home five hundred dollars per week. In

Britain, freak show managers and their clients struck similarly mutually advantageous bargains. This aspect of sideshow life, however, is usually ignored. The case of Joseph Merrick, for instance, is often used as an exemplum of the freak show's sawdusty cruelty. Through the play by Bernard Pomerance and the movie by David Lynch, we know Merrick's biography as the story of a monstrously deformed man who was rescued from his snarling, gin-soaked keeper by a forward-looking medical philanthropist, Frederick Treves. They are perfect examples of the paradigm that structures most twentieth-century dramas on nineteenth-century subjects. Treves expresses the viewer's attitude to Merrick: compassionate, scientific, rational. The figure of the showman embodies all those qualities we imagine to be more typical of the Victorians than of ourselves: cruel, exploitative, hypocritical. If Merrick could have fitted up chimneys, this character would no doubt have been sending him up them in his lunch-hour. As Raphael Samuel has argued, Lynch's biopic of Merrick:

> invites us to consider the penny exhibition as a symbol of old-time barbarism, and the gawping crowd as a world we are lucky to have lost. The film thus flatters our sense of moral superiority towards the past, moving us sentimentally to tears at the thought of our own benevolence, and allowing us, at very little cost, to celebrate our own humanity.[23]

Both Pomerance and Lynch use Treves's own account of the case, *The Elephant Man and Other Reminiscences* (1923), as their main source. Treves provides the only evidence that the Elephant Man was cruelly used by his agents: 'Locked up in an empty shop and lit by the faint blue light of the gas jet, this hunched-up figure was the embodiment of loneliness,' he wrote. 'The showman – speaking as if to a dog – called out harshly: "Stand up!"' As Merrick's biographers, Michael Howell and Peter Ford, have shown, this version of the story is flawed, and was controversial when it was first published. The showman in question, Tom Norman, wrote letters to the press complaining that Treves had described him unfairly. 'Had I attempted to be harsh with him,' he protested, 'I would very soon have had the show wrecked, and me with it.'[24] (To avoid repeating the slander, Lynch's movie creates a fictional showman, Bytes, who, liberated from the responsibilities of historical accuracy, is the very archetype of drunken villainy.) In his autobiography, Norman asserted:

I can honestly state that as far as his comfort was concerned whilst with us, no parent could have studied their child more than any or all the four of us studied Joseph Merrick ... The big majority of showmen are in the habit of treating their novelties as human beings, and in a large number of cases, as one of their own, and not like beasts.[25]

As Treves's account actually gets Merrick's name wrong – he calls him John rather than Joseph – there is no reason to suppose that the surgeon is a more reliable witness than Norman. Moreover, Treves neglects to mention – or never knew about – Merrick's comfortable financial arrangements with Norman's management syndicate. At the end of his first twenty-two-week tour of Britain in 1885, the Elephant Man had saved £50 from his earnings. Howell and Ford argue that 'Joseph was certainly quietly affluent, far better off than ever in his life, and better off than many who crowded the freak shows to view him.'[26] True enough, he was later robbed of this money and abandoned in Brussels by an unscrupulous Austrian showman, but his British management seem to have treated him with respect.

Was this unusual? Charles Stratton ended his days in Bridgeport, Connecticut, the owner of a yacht and several racehorses: his towering tomb in the Mountain Grove Cemetery is evidence of a financially profitable life. Chang and Eng, the Siamese Twins, retired to a farm in North Carolina, as did Millie-Christine, another pair of conjoined celebrities (strikingly, both sets of twins owned slaves). At the height of his career, Chimah the Chinese Dwarf earned a weekly fee of five hundred pounds and, according to an article in the *Strand* magazine, bought himself a twenty-thousand-acre property in Ohio.[27] (The same writer assigned a weekly two hundred dollars to Miss Grantly, the Albino Princess.)[28] Commodore Nutt, a popular dwarf performer, was hailed as 'the thirty-thousand dollar Nutt', thanks to his three-year contract bearing that figure.[29] Another dwarf, Lucia Zarate, who with her co-star General Mite visited Britain in November 1880, commanded a fee of twenty dollars an hour. Born in Mexico in January 1863, and billed as the smallest woman in the world, she was twenty inches tall, weighed five pounds and had a fourteen-inch waist. In 1890, the managers of a dime museum to which she was contracted offered a diamond ring to any parent whose baby had a smaller ring-finger than the star exhibit, which indicates either that they were confident that no baby would fulfil these requirements, or that Zarate's box office was big enough to absorb the loss. (That same year she was caught on a train in the middle of a blizzard, and died of exposure in an unheated compartment.) Early in her career, she was exhibited as part of an act named the 'Fairy Sisters', under the management of an impresario named Fred A. Pickering, who operated from offices inside Boston's Old State House. Pickering's surviving contract sheets and his press releases, which avowed that the sisters had 'attracted large audiences of the most refined and cultivated people', suggest that, at its most sophisticated, the exhibition of human curiosities was a highly professionalised industry, which paid taxes, issued invoices and made marketing plans.[30]

As Raphael Samuel demonstrates, we tend to assume that such figures were the helpless victims of their employers because it suits us to regard the Victorians as cruel and unusual characters. Take the case of Maximo and Bartola, the 'Original Aztec Children', a pair of central American microcephalics who were exhibited in London in 1853 and continued to visit until the end of the century. 'In appearance they were certainly extraordinary,' wrote one commentator. 'They had small but long heads with little or no chins, and their deformity was exaggerated by an enormous bunch of black hair, which they wore at the back of their heads.'[31] At first, they were advertised as brother and sister, and their publicity material explained that they were indentured to a Spanish trader named Ramon Selva, who had sold them to an American impresario, who then brought them to England. In 1867, however, they were married at a London registry office, and treated to a lavish breakfast at Willis's on Old Compton Street, the fashionable Soho supper club beloved of Oscar Wilde. By 1889, *The Times* was referring to them as 'old friends of admitted respectability'.[32]

Were they really brother and sister? If so, this sounds like a textbook case of Victorian brutality: you can imagine Mr Bytes slapping one of these unfortunates on the back, making lewd remarks about the wedding night through a mouthful of game pie. These relationships between performers and their agents, however, have modern analogues. Compare the fate of the Aztec Children with this remark from an interview with the film actor Dirk Bogarde in 1972, when he reflected upon how he nearly became indentured to a Hollywood movie studio:

Twentieth Century Fox were buying up everyone willy-nilly. And when I say bought, I mean bought. They were going to call me Ricardo something or other Spanish and I was going to do a crash course in Spanish so that I could be discovered in Mexico for some extraordinary reason – I think they'd got enough Englishmen at the time. And the contract stipulated that after a certain period of time in Hollywood, I think it was 18 months, I would have to marry one of the girls who were also under contract to them.[33]

The exhibition room in which Joseph Carey Merrick was once displayed may now be part of a respectable sari shop on the Whitechapel Road, but the exhibition of human oddities still goes on. It has simply been evacuated into other, younger media. At the end of the nineteenth century, movies and monstrosities shared the same pitch: kinematograph booths and sideshows exhibiting deformed performers could be found side by side on the American carnival circuit. 'Ten years ago,' reflected the film writer Valentia Steer in 1913, 'the "cinema" was mostly nothing but a "penny gaff" – an adjunct to the "Fat Lady" or the "Two-Headed Calf".'[34] As picture houses became more luxurious and began to attract a more mainstream, respectable audience, the carnival went into terminal decline. Why queue with the mugs to gloat over a monster in a draughty tent when you could sit in the upholstered dark and watch Boris Karloff rise from the operating table in a shower of sparks? Why schlep out to Coney to visit Lilliputia when you could coo over the Munchkins in *The Wizard of Oz* (1939)? The American freak show survived just long enough for Diane Arbus to photograph its old retainers in the 1960s, but cinema eventually replaced these attractions.[35] It provided the same thrills much more efficiently, in a neatly sanitised package.

Although cinema embodies many of the same attractions as the freak show, when the medium presents such entertainments in its narratives, it always takes the moral high ground. In *Freaks* (1932), Tod Browning (a former sideshow contortionist) uses a cast of physically bizarre sideshow performers to demonstrate that beauty is no guarantor of virtue. In Alfred Hitchcock's *Saboteur* (1943), Robert Cummings and Priscilla Lane hide out in a caravan of bearded ladies, giants and human skeletons, who seem to be the one source of decency in an America made paranoid by the Cold War. In *X – The Man with the X-Ray Eyes* (1963), Ray Milland secures a comforting anonymity in the sideshow world. In *She-Freak* (1967), a drive-in remake of Browning's film, a young waitress is punished for her aversion to carny folk when deformity is visited violently upon her.

Television has other examples to offer. Middle-class viewers, myself included, will happily watch the freakery offered by *The Jerry Springer Show*, in which women with rhinoceros bodies engage in foul-mouthed slanging matches with their slatternly daughters, fist-fights break out between overpumped male strippers, and deeply weird human specimens try to outrage their loved ones with bolt-from-the-blue revelations about their true identities. They scream, weep and shout for the delectation of millions of viewers, and all they get for their trouble is a weekend of shopping in Chicago. The Springer show's relationship with the freak exhibition is a close one. A journalist visiting the production office once spotted this list of rejected publicity slogans pasted up on the wall: 'The Shallow End of the Gene Pool'; 'Talkin' to Freaks, So You Don't Have To!'; 'You Don't Have to Live in a Trailer, but It Helps'; 'Jerry's Been Shaking the Freak Tree ... and Look Who Fell Out!'.[36]

In Brazil, the TV compere Carlos Massa, known as 'Ratinho', oversees a show with a line-up more grotesque than those paraded by any Victorian carnival. The nightstick-waving host has introduced a woman whose eyes had been poked out by her jealous husband, an abnormal toddler with pubic hair and a mature penis, a child with hundreds of tumours in his body, and an 'Elephant Boy' whose deformities were so grotesque, it was claimed, that he had to be shown in profile behind a screen. There is a game-show element to proceedings: viewers pledge money that is supposedly used in therapeutic medical treatment for Ratinho's guests. 'I don't want to hide these people,' Massa has said, in an interview with the Reuters news agency, 'I want to show that the Brazilian health system is a failure, that these people suffer from a lack of money, not from a lack of available technology. I want to show a part of Brazil that the government tries to hide.'[37] For Ratinho, the voyeurism of his programme is justified because it reveals his guests as victims of medical incompetence. How sad and disempowered these people seem in comparison with the nineteenth-century prodigies, many of whom pursued a career in freak shows precisely because they wanted to resist being cast as pathological specimens.

The Hilton Sisters, a Brighton-born pair of Siamese twins who enjoyed success as a vaudeville act in the 1920s, carried this tradition into the twentieth century, but suffered when the carnival tradition declined and died, leaving them to do the same, in obscurity. They danced with Bob Hope, and starred in their own biopic *Chained for Life* (1951), the tagline for which was 'Siamese Twins – Playthings of Desire!' Towards the end of their careers, they suffered numerous indignities at the hands of their exhibitors and agents – including being stranded in the middle of nowhere after a drive-in screening of Tod Browning's *Freaks* – and ended their days working as checkout operators in Charlotte, North Carolina. Theatrical exploitation, however, was still preferable to being the subject of medical interest. 'We loathed the very tone of the medical man's voice,' they wrote in 1947, and feared that their family would 'stop showing us on stage and let the doctors have us – to punch and pinch and take our pictures always.'[38]

The Hilton sisters left a written autobiographical record, and they are unusual in this respect. The voices of their predecessors were often enthusiastically silenced by their managers, who liked to drum up custom by generating exotic – and bogus – narratives around their stars. To some extent, what will survive of them is lies. We'll never know whether Tom Thumb and Lavinia Warren, sitting in their miniature mansion in Bridgeport, were truly happy with their lives. We will never be able to judge the veracity of the claim that Julia Pastrana was rescued by cowboys in the Mexican jungle, or whether Miss Emma Atkinson, the Pig-Faced Lady, was really an heiress who had all that money stashed away in Ireland, and ate her bran mash from a silver trough.

That there was pathos and exploitation in their sector of the entertainment business is undeniable. There is little worth celebrating in the sad tale of 'The Human Tripod, or the Three-Legged Child and First Bipenis ever seen or heard of' – a dead little boy preserved in a jar of formaldehyde, whose mother would discourse upon his short life for a shilling. 'The Nobility and Gentry, and lovers of natural Science are respectfully invited to view,' declared the Tripod's publicists.[39] However, condemning the freak-fancier's attitude as patronising or barbaric will simply not suffice; nor will assuming the freak performer to be the pathetic victim of exploitation. The culture of the nineteenth-century exhibition circuit was too complex and ambiguous to allow for such a reductive reading of the relationship between freaks and their fans. To dismiss it all as the shame of our callous great-grandparents would be an undeserved insult to the Victorians. And, as we have the excesses of TV and Hollywood to match any cruelty of their sideshows and fairground booths, it would make us guilty of the hypocrisy that we are so fond of identifying in them. The Fejee Mermaid was, briefly, one of the most reified objects in the western world. It was a byword for weirdness, wonder and creepy titillation. Now it sits, unregarded, in a rundown seaside resort surrounded by tower blocks. And in those blocks, dazed citizens are slumped in front of daytime television, as twenty-first-century showmen lead a fresh parade of freaks into their living rooms.

CHAPTER TEN

Presumed Innocent

It is a dangerous thing to make your children afraid of you.
Anything is almost better than reserve and constraint between
your child and yourself; and this will come in with fear. Fear
puts an end to openness of manner; fear leads to concealment;
fear sows the seed of much hypocrisy, and leads to many a lie.
  John Ryle, *Thoughts for Parents* (1886)

There is nothing natural about childhood innocence: it is as artificial as
Arctic Roll. This, presumably, is the reason why early twenty-first
century popular culture is encouraging us all to buy into it; to surround
ourselves with its paraphernalia; to snuggle up to its uncomplicated
comforts. So twentysomething women wander about with their hair in
pigtails, and balding fortysomethings zip themselves into the combat
pants that their teenage sons ought to be wearing. Children, conversely,
are moving to meet them half-way: they have acquired tough, marketable
new competences that their parents do not possess. They calculate in
metric weights and measures; they can follow fast-cut, hare-eyed TV
narratives which only baffle their elders; they know how to deal with the
Internet (and prevent anyone finding out what they have been viewing);
they know how to handle a gun (albeit an arcade one). Being a child is no
longer an incapable state. The Chicago-born sculptor Charles Ray has
offered the most striking articulation of this process, in a work that
depicts an average American nuclear family, all of whom are levelled to a
standard size based on the height of a young adolescent. The four figures
join hands, standing upright, stripped of their clothes. Baby is the same
height as her older brother. Mom and Dad have come down to the level
of their eldest child. The expressions also tell a story. The parents appear
worried about what the future will bring; their offspring seem preterna-
turally confident and alert. The title is Family Romance – a term coined
by that hopelessly unfashionable old guy Sigmund Freud to describe the
sexual plot he detected unfolding between mothers, fathers, sons,
daughters.

13 According to the writer Edgar Jepson, 'a cult of little girls' sprang up
in Oxford in the 1880s

Childhood innocence is a comparatively recent entrant into western
culture. Crudely, the story of its progress goes something like this. Before
the eighteenth century, there was very little interest in the idea of
childhood as a separate category of experience. Children were simply
regarded as small people who couldn't hold a scythe properly, and were
put to work as soon as they were able – usually at about the age of seven,
which, traditionally, was also the age of criminal responsibility. There
seems to have been less of the coochy-coo stuff, too. The doctrines of
John Calvin (1509–64) successfully promulgated the idea that children
were creatures of innate evil, whose damnation (or otherwise) was

[156]

predestined from birth. Only by schooling children in the habits of virtue and thrift could parents prepare them for inevitable immolation in the Hereafter. It was not until John Locke argued, in *Some Thoughts Concerning Education* (1693), that 'children should be treated as rational creatures ... All their innocent Folly, Playing and *childish Actions are to be* left perfectly free and *unrestrained*', that the concept of childhood began to be discussed in terms which we would recognise.[1] Similar arguments in Jean-Jacques Rousseau's *Emile* (1762) encouraged families to think of their tiniest members as individuals whose sensibilities needed to be formed, nurtured and insulated from the horrors and complexities of the adult world. In Britain, Romanticism did an immense amount of public relations work for this point of view, particularly in Wordsworth's gargantuan meditation upon himself, *The Prelude* (1805), which established that the experiences of childhood formed the adult mind in subtle and dramatic ways. An earlier poem, 'My Heart Leaps Up', expresses this idea in terms which have become very familiar:

> The Child is father of the Man:
> And I could wish my days to be
> Bound each to each by natural piety.

The Romantic movement renegotiated the terms of childhood, transforming it from a condition besmirched by Original Sin to one that embodied prelapsarian innocence; possibly the greatest switcheroo in the history of western culture. It was the Victorians, however, who developed and expanded childhood's new status, gave it a privileged position under the law and generated an iconographic system through which we still articulate images of the youngest members of our society. The notion of the preciousness, vulnerability and moral sanctity of children was circulated so enthusiastically – in books, photographs, prints and journalism – that the concept has become axiomatic. To take issue with it today is to invite mistrust: childhood innocence has been so effectively naturalised that its history has disappeared from public consciousness.

Mary Martha Sherwood's didactic *History of the Fairchild Family, or The Child's Manual* (published in three volumes between 1818 and 1847) supplies a good account of how the Calvinist iceberg melted. Volume One is an utterly uncompromising document, and reflects the regime of chilly discipline under which Sherwood, a clergyman's daughter, lived out her childhood in 1770s Worcestershire. 'When she was in the presence of her parents,' says the biographical introduction of a Victorian

[157]

reprint, taking a rather Stracheyite line with Georgian culture, 'she was neither allowed to sit, nor approach the fire, nor take any part in conversation. Besides this, following the preposterous practice of those days, she had an iron collar round her neck, to which a back-board was attached, and thus accoutred, straight and stiff, the child had to stand the greater part of the day, and learn and repeat her lessons.'[2] In the 1818 volume, God punishes young Emily Fairchild with a near-fatal fever for the unauthorised consumption of two preserved damsons; the Fairchilds' playmate Augusta Noble is incinerated after looking at herself in the mirror by candlelight ('The unhappy young lady was so dreadfully burnt, that she never spoke afterwards, but died in agonies last night – a warning to all children how they presume to disobey their parents!'); and Mr Fairchild takes his children deep into the woods to see the morally instructive (and hideously decayed) cadaver of a hanged man:

> It had on a blue coat, a silk handkerchief round the neck, with shoes and stockings, and every other part of the dress still entire; but the face of the corpse was [so] shocking, that the children could not look upon it.
>
> 'Oh, papa, papa! What is that?' cried the children.
>
> 'That is a gibbet,' said Mr. Fairchild: 'and the man who hangs upon it is a murderer; one who first hated and afterwards killed his brother! When people are found guilty of stealing, or murder, they are hanged upon a gallows, and taken down as soon as they are dead; but in some particular cases, when a man has committed a murder, he is hanged in iron chains upon a gibbet, till his body falls to pieces, that all who pass by may take warning by the example.'[3]

By the time Sherwood had completed two further volumes of Fairchild family history, her attitudes seem to have softened. Volumes Two and Three, published in 1847, are markedly less severe. The most shocking event in the concluding volume is a tumble taken by young Henry Fairchild into a tub of pig swill ('The odour', notes Sherwood, 'caused by the stirring up of this foul mass was overpowering'[4]). The book remained a popular Sunday school prize throughout the nineteenth century, and was reissued in 1902 in a version bowdlerised by Mary Palgrave. By this time, the scene of the gibbet and the corpse had been extracted, and the death of Augusta Noble toned down. In 1908, another, more aggressive rewrite by Jeanie Lang, published under the retro imprint Grandmother's

Favourites, had policed both stories from the text. A final reprint, with excisions by Lytton Strachey's mother, appeared in 1913

Many of the late- and mid-Victorian manuals that considered a child's religious education would have made Sherwood split her backboard in disgust. 'Kindness, gentleness, long-suffering, forbearance, patience, sympathy, a willingness to enter into childish troubles, a readiness to take part in childish joys, these are the cords by which a child may be led most easily, these are the clues you must follow if you would find the way to his heart,' advised the touchy-feely evangelical bishop of Liverpool, John Charles Ryle, in *Train Up a Child the Way that He Should Go* (first published in 1846, but reprinted into the 1880s).[5] 'Children are weak and tender creatures, and, as such, they need patient and considerate treatment. We must handle them delicately, like frail machines, lest by rough fingering we do more harm than good. They are like young plants, and need gentle watering, often, but little at a time.'[6] Ryle's attitudes reflect a middle-class Victorian consensus about child development and welfare; his musings were so popular that they inspired a hymn and an advertisement slogan for a hair-cream named Carter's Thrixaline: 'Train Your Moustache in the Way it Should Go.' The ubiquity of his views is one reason why so many of nineteenth-century fiction's favourite villains – beadles, schoolmasters, stepfathers, landlords – express their villainy in cruelty towards children. Ryle's advice is as conscious a rejection of Calvinist rigidity as, say, Dickens's portrait of the glacial Mrs Clennam in *Little Dorrit*. Dickens's novels contain a gallery of child-crushers, the neurotic residue of his experience of being put to work in a blacking factory when he was twelve – an age which the previous generation, and most of his own, would not have considered unreasonable.

Real abuses also helped purify and angelicise the popular image of the child. Middle-class opinion was galvanised by a scandal that emerged from the dozens of adverts which, in the 1860s, were published each day in the *Daily Telegraph*, offering child care on terms that, realistically, were too low to provide for the service. As interested parties knew, the payment was made for the nursemaid to starve an unwanted child to death. For many working-class women, it was a less hazardous alternative to abortion. Special rates were charged for sickly infants or those under two months, whose expiry would arouse little suspicion. Baby farmers would keep their charges docile with laudanum, which, if given in large enough doses, would eventually cause the fatal accumulation of fluid on the brain. The first attempts to curb these practices were made in the early 1860s by pressure groups such as the Association for the Preservation of Infant Life and the National Society and Asylum for Prevention of Infanticide. In 1865, their campaigns were brought to wider attention by the trial of Charlotte Winsor, a Torquay baby farmer who was found guilty of smothering a four-month-old boy, wrapping his body in a copy of the *Western Times* and dumping it by the roadside – a service she was happy to perform for between three and five pounds per child. Two doctors, John Brendon Curgenven and Ernest Hart, editor of the *British Medical Journal*, initiated a programme of research into the problem, and the resulting paper, *The Waste of Infant Life* (1867), was instrumental in fostering the opinion that the state should intervene in matters of child care. The Brixton baby-farming scandal of the summer of 1870 – in which two sisters, Sarah Ellis and Margaret Waters, were convicted of drugging, starving and disposing of over a dozen babies in a few weeks – and a similar scandal in Greenwich led Curgenven and Hart to form the Infant Life Protection Society, whose lobbying was instrumental in the drafting of the Infant Life Protection Bill (1871), which proposed a state registration system for nurses involved in child care. Opposition from the Commons and – more surprisingly, perhaps – Lydia Becker, editor of the *Women's Suffrage Journal*, reduced the bill to an ineffectual compromise. It took another criminal trial that of a Mrs Dyer, who, in 1896, was caught dumping bodies in the Thames at Reading – to yield legislation that gave local authorities the power to remove children from households in which they were being mistreated.

Throughout the entire Victorian period, similar bursts of activity, equivocation and argument produced an accretion of measures which aimed at regulating the hours worked by children and later – once the idea of state intervention in family life had been broadly accepted – formed the basis for the establishment of a system of universal education. The Mines Act of 1842 ended the employment of children under ten in the subterranean parts of coalmining operations. The Factory Act of 1844 cut the hours of work for children aged between eight and thirteen to six and a half a day, and initiated an inspection system to check that these restrictions were being observed. In 1867, the Children's Employment Commission unanimously recommended the extension of the system of factory inspection to children in any workplace where fifty or more persons were employed – it became law the same year. Slowly and fitfully, legislation began to remove children from their roles in the manufacturing and agricultural economy, which they had occupied since prehistory, and place them under the jurisdiction of official bodies: ragged schools, board schools, reformatories and barrack schools.

Mass media reports of crimes against children helped speed their sanctification. One particular murder was so horrific and notorious that a fragment of the story is still lodged in the language. In the Hampshire market town of Alton, at half past one on the blazing hot afternoon of 24 August 1867, eight-year-old Fanny Adams, her younger sister Lizzie and their friend Minnie Warner went to play in the meadow adjoining Amery Farm, a few yards from their parents' cottages. After half an hour, they noticed a man sitting on the gate, observing them. He struck up a conversation with the girls, and offered Fanny a halfpenny if she would take a walk with him to the hop-garden planted at the top of the meadow. She concurred, but her companions insisted on following, hoping for some reward. So the stranger agreed to take all three girls to pick strawberries from the field of a farmer named Chalcraft, distributed more halfpennies among them, then told Lizzie and Minnie to run away and buy some sweets. Later, they remembered that as they dashed from the field, they heard the man say to Fanny, 'Don't cry, my dear; keep quiet, and if you will come up into the hop-garden I will give you some more money.'[7]

When Fanny failed to return home, Harriet Adams assumed that her daughter had gone to watch her father play cricket at the Butts, a grassy area south of the town. At around five o'clock, however, Lizzie told her mother the story of the generous stranger in the hop-field. Harriet and a neighbour, Jane Gardner, rushed up towards the meadow, where they saw a young man sauntering down the footpath on the side of the River Wey. They called to him, and he crossed the meadow to meet them. Mrs Gardner demanded to know what he had done with the missing child. 'I have not seen her,' he replied. At that moment, Minnie Warner also appeared. 'Did this gentleman give you any money today?' asked Mrs Gardner. 'Yes,' she replied, 'Threepence.' 'No, three-halfpence,' interjected the stranger. Mrs Gardner took hold of the man, and demanded to know his name. 'No matter what's my name,' he retorted. 'You will find me at Mr Clements' office if you want me.' The women returned home, and the stranger continued his journey in the direction of the Basingstoke Road.

Between seven and eight o'clock that evening, a farm labourer named Thomas Gates was crossing the hop-field when he noticed some bloodied scraps of clothing scattered on the ground, and a strange object lying by the hedge, resting upon two hop-poles. It was the severed

[161]

MURDER AND MUTILATION OF THE BODY!

14 Frederick Baker decapitates sweet Fanny Adams, from *The Alton Murder!*, 1867

head of a child, the eyes gouged from their sockets, the right ear sliced away. He picked it up, and ran to the row of cottages at the foot of the meadow, where a gaggle of neighbours immediately identified it as that of Fanny Adams. 'With a coolness which would seem almost incredible,' noted one contemporary account, 'the man Gates took the head to the father's cottage. All doubts were then set at rest, the poor mother identifying the head as that of her daughter, and immediately falling into hysterics.' A police search of the hop-field yielded a grotesque harvest. A leg and a thigh, the stocking and boot still in place; the right arm and hand, severed from the elbow; the left hand, severed from the wrist; the remains of the trunk, savagely mutilated. In the next field, the girl's left foot was discovered, the left arm, and the heart, torn from Fanny Adams's body and hurled over two hedges and the intervening lane.

By the time Superintendent William Cheyney went to the office of Mr Clements, Alton's solicitor, the townspeople had already identified the suspect as Frederick Baker, a clerk employed in the practice for the past twelve months. Cheyney found the clerk working quietly at his desk, and asked him if he had heard anything about the murder. 'Yes,' replied Baker. 'And they say it is me, don't they?' His trousers, cuffs and waistcoat were marked with blood; his socks and boots were wet, as if they had been recently washed. A search of his desk revealed a private diary. The entry for Saturday 24 August was brief, and written in a bold hand: 'Killed a young girl; it was fine and hot.'

The Fanny Adams case was a milestone in the history of British childhood. The story offered such an affecting mixture of pathos, atrocity, sadism and moral outrage that it established a vocabulary of popular sentiment in whose terms responses to violent crimes upon children have been articulated ever since. 'Three happy English girls at their small sports among the ripening blackberries and hop-gardens of Alton,' exclaimed one commentator, 'their mothers' cottages within hail, the public footpath close by! – what harm, in pity's name, could happen to such an innocent triplet – everybody's friends – except perhaps if a bumble bee should sting them, or a great frog frighten them on his way to the water? One might think that all the world would love and protect the little simple playmates, and that even devilish passions would go, reproved and calmed, past their sweet ignorance and glad young eyes, not wise enough to be afraid or ashamed.'[8] As has already been noted, naval ratings produced their own, less deferential tribute, in the form of a nickname for their rations of chopped mutton.

The first summer of the twenty-first century gave British culture the opportunity to rehearse these responses once again. Nobody who followed the dreadful case of eight-year-old Sarah Payne – kidnapped in July 2000 from the Sussex cornfield where she was playing with her brothers and a sister, and found dead two weeks later by the side of the A29 – can read about Sweet Fanny Adams without a sense of déjà vu. 'It was the summer's great tragedy,' observed one broadsheet columnist. 'And it isn't hard to see why Sarah Payne held our attention and our sympathy last July. There was something about her fresh, smiling face, about her disappearance from a sunlit, pastoral scene, about the love and anguish of her parents, and about the horror of the eventual discovery of her body, that held a real, tragic pull.'[9] The homes of suspected paedophiles were attacked in her name, the *News of the World* boosted its circulation by printing the names and addresses of men on the national register of sex offenders, button badges were distributed bearing the face of the murdered girl. Press coverage of her funeral inspired an outpouring of unselfconsciously sentimental religiosity which seemed to reproduce and amplify the language of nineteenth-century responses to innocence destroyed. 'Yesterday,' declared a typical example, 'her little body came home at last, in a white coffin carried in an ornate black Victorian carriage. The funeral was a chance for people who had been touched by Sarah's death to meditate over her short life... A touching tribute read: "Sometimes God sends a little girl from Heaven to earth to show us how to laugh and smile and care for each other, but most of all how to love. He calls them his angels. Sometimes he sends very special angels and when it is time, calls his special angels home."' Attempts to interpolate some kind of religious narrative into the biography of the dead child were common: 'Sarah had visited St Peter's Church in Hersham, Surrey, many times before. There she had sung hymns and said prayers. There, in the months leading up to her death, she discovered her own faith in God.'[10] In comparison, reports of Fanny Adams's funeral – which, like Sarah Payne's, inspired public riots, sermons and acres of newspaper coverage – seem appreciably restrained. 'The burial service was impressively read by the Rev. W. Wilkins, curate of Thedden,' noted one report, 'and a large number of persons assembled to witness the funeral. Wreaths of flowers were placed upon the coffin, and subsequently upon the grave. The parents of the unhappy victim followed, and their grief appeared to be almost unbearable.'[11]

The grave of Fanny Adams lies on the western side of Alton's cemetery, facing the Old Odiham Road. It is an ornate cross, carved with an inscription that makes no attempt to conceal the violent nature of her death. An epigraph warns, 'Fear not them which kill the body but are not able to kill the soul but rather fear him which is able to destroy both soul and body in hell'. Here, in the months after her murder, a local photographer set up his tripod, and shot some plates of a pretty eight-year-old girl standing solemnly by the headstone. Sold as a cabinet photograph, it became a popular object of meditation, an icon of the sanctity of childhood, celebrating the eventless life of an ordinary little girl, immortalised by adult savagery and adult horror at that savagery. Today, the grave, splotched with yellow lichen, remains well tended. Schoolchildren study the case in their history lessons, and leave the occasional card and bouquet. Since the murder of Sarah Payne, such offerings have been deposited more frequently, modest echoes of the mountains of flowers and white teddy bears left by the side of the A29.

Dreadful events in our own time have an impact upon the way we view the past. After summer 2000, after the anti-paedophile riots on the Paulsgrove estate in Portsmouth, after the news footage of protesting parents teaching their children to chant 'Murder the pervert!', after a mob attacked the home of a Welsh doctor because they were unable to understand the difference between the words 'paediatrician' and 'paedophile' – what are we to make of the Victorians' images of, and relationships with, children? How do we look at a painting like Millais' *Cherry Ripe* (1879), in which the doe-eyed pre-teen sitter is wearing lacy fingerless gloves of the sort now only seen in the window of Ann Summers? How do we interpret those strange, quasi-erotic relationships between Victorian adults and children? How do we continue to read the works of Lewis Carroll when he is routinely described as – to take a few random examples – a 'repressed paedophile in love with his petulant heroine'; 'a repressed, stuttering, platonic paedophile who befriended little girls and dropped them when they made the mistake of growing up'; 'a paedophile who turned his erotic love of a child into *Alice in Wonderland*'?[12]

From an early twenty-first century perspective, there seems to be a substantial amount of evidence against the Rev. Charles Lutwidge Dodgson. The odd series of letters he sent to the family of his Oxford colleague Andrew Mayhew, for instance, asking permission to make nude photographic studies of his three daughters, aged between six and

[165]

thirteen, specifying that they should be unchaperoned. His persuasion of the parents of Beatrice Latham, Frances Henderson and Evelyn Hatch to let their daughters whip off their drawers to be snapped in swimsuits, in 'primitive dress' and sprawled naked on blankets. His dreamy obsession with Alice Liddell, the model for the heroine of *Alice's Adventures in Wonderland* (1865). His sudden decision in 1880 to give up his photographic hobby, return pictures to their subjects' families and destroy most of the remaining plates. Any modern jury would suspect him of encouraging the sullen Lolitas of suburban Oxfordshire to do six improper things before breakfast. Indeed, when the home of the artist Graham Ovenden was raided by the Obscene Publications Squad in March 1993, the officers who falsely suspected him of being part of a child pornography ring drove back to Scotland Yard with a haul consisting mainly of Ovenden's collection of Dodgson photographs.[13]

The romanticised images of children which enjoyed such a vogue in the mid- and late- nineteenth century might now appear creepy and saccharine: Dodgson's four surviving child nudes; the Pears Soap child – half-boy, half-Bambi; frilly-frocked, apple-cheeked girls in kitschy domestic narrative paintings by George Bernard O'Neill; Kate Greenaway's illustrations of cherubic children playing ring-a-roses. Put these side by side with those other familiar images of young Victorians – Thomas Barnardo's photographs of cadaverous street arabs, William Daniels's pictures of starving match girls – and they seem to articulate one of the key injustices with which the Victorians have been charged: generating a sentimental eroticism around childhood at the same time as enjoying the fruits of child labour – idealising the young but still expecting them to deliver their coal.

The sentimental adoration of girl-children was particularly popular in Victorian Oxford, where, by the time Dodgson had thrown away his camera, it had become a student fad, like self-mutilation or reciting scenes from *Withnail and I*. 'There was at Oxford in the eighties', recalled the crime writer and Balliol alumnus Edgar Jepson, 'a cult of little girls, the little daughters of dons and residents: men used to have them to tea and take them on the river and write verses to them.'[14] Jepson's contemporary, the poet Ernest Dowson, was an enthusiastic votary, as were – beyond the confines of the university – Frederick Leighton, Dante Gabriel Rossetti and John Everett Millais (whose children were photographed by Dodgson). The cult was a logical consequence of the newly privileged status of children and childhood: a self-consciously intense, impeccably educated equivalent of the cooing with which the broader mass of Victorians had greeted Millais's cutesy painting *Bubbles* (1886) when Pears began pasting it up at railway stations. At around the same time, Christmas cards bearing pictures of naked ten-year-old girls were commercially produced for circulation between middle-class families. Other images became ubiquitous in print-shops and illustrated magazines: the soot-smeared chimney sweep; the barefoot match girl; the small boy crawling through the narrow galleries of the coal mine; the five-year-old girl nipping into a whirling mass of industrial machinery to retrieve a dropped spanner or a stray shuttle. Icons of a sentimental revolution that gradually took children out of the factories; propaganda for a reformulation of childhood which eventually abolished child labour in Britain.

Recent analyses of some of the most popular paintings of Victorian childhood have argued that we should regard such images with suspicion. When, in 1991, Laurel Bradley produced a reading of *Cherry Ripe* which argued that, despite modern distaste for the picture, the Victorians saw this work as an embodiment of innocence, she was reproached by two other academics, Pamela Tamarkin Reis and Robert M. Polhemus, for ignoring its erotic content.[15] As Anne Higonnet recounts in her book *Pictures of Innocence* (1998):

> Arguing that the Victorians thrived on a (barely) repressed pedophilia, both latter-day interpreters read a sexual metaphor (hymen) into the title of the image, and saw curvacious [*sic*] adult female forms in the child's billowing dress. Most importantly, they saw female genitalia beneath pubic hair in the child's hands below black wristlets, pressed palm to palm between her thighs.[16]

Such overzealous identification of sexual codes is common in the discipline of Victorian studies: little wonder that so few academics working in the field have ever taken issue with the myth of the covered piano leg.

The pervasion of the cult of little girls generated, for a few brief years, a new kind of relationship between adults and children: one which would have been inconceivable at the beginning of Victoria's reign, and one which was quietly forgotten by the beginning of the twentieth century and regarded with intense suspicion by the beginning of the twenty-first. Wilkie Collins's mock marriage with the eleven-year-old Anne le Poer Wynne was one such alliance. Their gently flirtatious correspondence began in 1885, when Nannie and her widowed mother were living in the

London suburb of Little Venice, on the banks of the Regent's Park Canal. Francis Carr Beard, who was doctor to all three, provided the introductions. Over the next four years, Collins wrote to Nannie twice a month, maintaining the conceit that they were a married couple. 'Dear and admirable Mrs Collins,' he enthused. *'Mia sposa adorata.'*

> Dearest Mrs Wilkie,
> Don't bully me. Mother-in-law will tell you that I am already prostrate. Besides, I don't approve of your conduct since I have been away. I hear you have got tall. Have you forgotten that I am short? News has also reached me that you have got a waist. Have I got a waist? And, greatest disappointment to me of all, I am positively assured that your back hair is on the top of your head. My back hair hangs on my shoulders. I have not had my hair cut for the last four months to please you. A good wife follows her husband's example. What right have you to hide the top of your head from Me. I have a right to see (and, if I like, admire) the top of your head. There may be one excuse for you. Are you getting bald on the top of your head? If that is the case, I pity and forgive you. When I come to see you, I will bring with me 'Mrs Allen's Hair Restorer' and rub it in myself. But don't allude to 'Galantine and Truffles' – your mother, your excellent mother, will tell you why. With all your faults, I love and adore you.
>
> W.C[17]

They exchanged photographs. Nannie sent her admirer flowers and Christmas cards. Collins peppered his correspondence with slightly smutty humour. He is 'delighted to receive [her] conjugal embrace'; she is a 'sly little hussy'; the 'Amyl' he has been forced to 'sniff at' is, he assures her, 'not the Christian name of another wife. It is only a glass capsule.'A twenty-first-century social worker casting an eye over these letters would probably argue for an exclusion order to be slapped on their author sharpish. Especially, perhaps, in the light of Collins's advice to Nannie that she combat the effects of hot weather by adopting 'the costume of a late Queen of the Sandwich Islands – a hat and feathers and nothing else'.[18] William Clarke, who edited these letters for publication, was assured by Wynne family descendants that Nannie's mother was well aware of the correspondence, that she accompanied her daughter on visits to Gloucester Place, where Collins lived with his common-law wife Caroline Graves, and that the family never considered the letters to be inappropriate in any way – much to the disappointment of Clarke's publishers, who were keen to generate a bit of Dodgsonian scandal.

Unfortunately for them, the suggestion that Collins had a carnal interest in children is not corroborated by any source – and quite a lot is known about his sexual peccadilloes. His letters to Napoleon Sarony – a Manhattan photographer famous for his pornographic postcards – are full of such frank confessions as 'I too think the back view of a finely-formed woman the loveliest view.'[19] Sarony sent Collins parcels of photographs under plain brown wrappers; Collins dedicated his novel *Heart and Science* (1883) to him in gratitude. Although it predates the Nannie correspondence by two years, *Heart and Science* contains a portrait of a relationship between an older man and a young girl that reads like a Gothicised account of Collins's Little Venice mock romance. Its principal villain is Dr Benjulia, a sadistic vivisectionist who keeps a monkey in his coat and enjoys a strange intimacy with a precocious ten-year-old named Zo. 'One of his favourite recreations was tickling her ... He put two of his big soft finger-tips on her spine, just below the back of her neck, and pressed on the place. Zo started and wriggled under his touch. He observed her with as serious an interest as if he had been conducting a medical experiment.'[20] Of course, the reader is led to believe that if Zo is ever foolish enough to enter Dr Benjulia's windowless laboratory, she will be dissected in a jiffy.

Better documented is John Ruskin's interest in very young girls. Ruskin knew Alice Liddell, and took a keen interest in the female pupils of a girls' school in Cheshire, but this side of his personality found its principal outlet in the disastrous affair with Rose La Touche, a family friend to whom he developed a passionate attachment in his forties, when she was nine. She called him 'Dear St Crumpet' and 'Archigosaurus'. He called her his little 'Mouse-pet'. Unsurprisingly, it all ended in tears. She developed a religious mania and died in her twenties from the physical effects of some quasi-anorexic mental illness; his sexual obsession with her caused a falling-out with her parents and contributed to the collapse of his sanity. By the end of his life, Ruskin had returned to a second childhood of helplessness and unreason: exploding into foul-mouthed tantrums, referring to his loyal nurse Joan Severn as 'mama' and himself as 'a little donkey boy', composing incoherent diary entries about Rose La Touche, the Devil and Gothic architecture, sitting out in the garden wondering vaguely who he was.

Ernest Dowson's attraction to young girls was rather more self-conscious and self-torturing. The fascination remained with him all his life. When employed as a theatre critic in the 1880s and 1890s, he enjoyed a long correspondence with a child star called 'Little Flossie'. Minnie Terry, the little star of *Bootle's Baby*, also charmed him, to the extent that he collected an album of her souvenir photographs. (Terry later married Edmund Gwenn, best known for his Oscar-winning performance as Santa Claus in the 1947 version of *Miracle on 34th Street*.) Dowson had regular sex with prostitutes his own age, usually after an alcoholic binge ('absinthe makes the tart grow fonder,' he once said), but he does not seem ever to have formed a significant emotional attachment to anyone over the age of fifteen. Indeed, the most important relationship of his adult life was with a Soho restaurateur's daughter named Adelaide Foltinowicz, who caught his eye when she was eleven. With her parents' tacit co-operation, Dowson courted the girl throughout her teenage years. As the age of consent had only recently been raised from thirteen to sixteen, the propriety of this action does not seem to have concerned anyone unduly – except Dowson himself, who, after reading in the *Star* about the case of Lucy Pearman, a little girl kidnapped and raped by a man named Newton, wrote an anxious letter to his friend Arthur Moore: 'The worst of it was that it read like a sort of foul and abominable travesty of pah, what is the good of hunting for phrases. You must know what I mean, and how I am writhing.'[21] News stories about such atrocities offered variations on a theme sounded in W. T. Stead's tale of Lily, and their eager consumption by the public made the adoration of girl-children an increasingly contentious impulse. (Carroll, interestingly, wrote a letter of protest to the *St James's Gazette*, condemning the 'Maiden Tribute' articles running in its rival's pages.) Perhaps Dowson's anxiety about the Pearman case doomed his relationship with Adelaide Foltinowicz: she rejected her suitor in 1896, and married the family lodger one year later. With hindsight, she might have done better to have thrown in her lot with Dowson, as her married life was tragically unhappy: in 1903, she had an affair with a second lodger, became pregnant, and died from the after-effects of a botched abortion.

Even with the knowledge of all this humiliating and compromising detail, can we really decide – as many recent commentators have done, despite the term being an anachronism – that these men were paedophiles? The history of the British consent laws has already been given some attention, but a brief sketch of the law in America gives a stronger sense of how recently such boundaries have shifted. Until the last years of the nineteenth century, the age of consent in most of the American states was set at ten years old. In some areas it was even lower. California was one of the first to raise the age of consent – upping it from ten to fourteen in 1889, then from fourteen to sixteen in 1897. (In 1913, it rose to eighteen.) Other states – including Arizona, Colorado, Florida, New York, South Dakota and Wyoming – followed their example, and Tennessee raised it to twenty-one. An economic plot underlies these developments. In the first years of the nineteenth century, the average age of the American population was sixteen; it did not rise above twenty-one until the beginning of the twentieth century. The emergence of the USA as an economic superpower was a product not just of child labour, but of sexual relationships that today would be considered illegal.

In Britain, Charles Booth calculated that between 1851 and 1881, children under fifteen outnumbered the adult population. Victoria's kingdom was a nation of children. It was also a nation in which the concept of childhood was being actively developed and redrafted. The paradoxes and inconsistencies in that concept are still being negotiated today. They are present in the angelicisation of the child – heard most explicitly in the expressions of public grief after the murder of Sarah Payne – and in the equally discomfiting sexualisation of childhood, telegraphed by the ubiquitous media images of teenage pop starlets in school uniforms and catwalk models who would look just as much at home in an NSPCC ad. They are present in the decision of the *News of the World* to launch its anti-paedophile campaign just a few pages away from a photograph of a sixteen-year-old 'glamour model'. They are present in the decision that ensured that, in the Royal Academy's Sensation exhibition, works depicting naked children were forced into an anteroom – the door of which was hung with a warning about the possible offence its contents might cause – while in the main chamber sat a Damien Hirst installation: a glass box containing a putrefying cow's head from which thousands of maggots and blowflies buzzed and bubbled. How will we justify *that* to the future?

CHAPTER ELEVEN

Whatever Happened to Patriarchy?

Strive to be vulnerable with your husband by baring your most
tender feelings. When you feel the fear of being rejected welling
up, find your courage by reminding yourself that you are safe
with your husband ... Make yourself available for sex at least
once a week, whether you feel like it or not.

Laura Doyle, *The Surrendered Wife* (2001)

When I turn up at the Dog and Partridge, the afternoon girlie acts are
grinding to a conclusion. A bottle-blonde woman is rubbing herself
against a bentwood chair on a stage set that demonstrates the limits of
what can be achieved with scrunched-up aluminium foil. A cohort of
male pensioners are goggling at her, pints in hand, silently shifting their
dentures around their mouths. A number of younger men are scattered
through the audience, and, tellingly, they're on halves. They don't stay
for long. There's a women-only event on in the evening, and the
afternoon crowd know they're not encouraged to linger. They return
their well-nursed glasses to the bar, and file out through the door, back to
their families. On his way home, a balding punter comes over to the bar
to congratulate the landlady and a man who turns out to be the stripper's
husband. 'Got a couple of good shots there,' he says. 'Your missus
doesn't half turn me on.' As he's wearing a pair of blue terylene slacks,
there's no real need for him to point this out.

The Dog and Partridge sits on the Attewell road, midway between
Sheffield and Rotherham. What was once a bustling Victorian street is
now a drag of empty warehouses, closed factories, fast-food outfits and
windowless massage parlours offering special discounts for the unemployed. Walk down here in the dusk, and it's like watching a magic
lantern show of Sheffield's economic decline: a rather more realistic
spectacle than *The Full Monty*, the most popular account of the same
process. But the worldwide success of this film – the story of a gang of
former Sheffield steelworkers who bolster their self-esteem by turning to
stripping – has had an appreciable impact on the city's nightlife. Male

Order, tonight's headlining act, are just one of a number of troupes of male strippers whose routines are based explicitly on scenes from the film. 'They're going round all over,' their choreographer Chera Kincaid tells me. 'Gay as well as straight venues. To start with it, it was like "We're all married, there's no way we're doing gay." And now they enjoy gay – because they don't get touched by the men, as they get fondled by the women.' And the women are now here: a louder, dressier and visibly more affluent crowd than the afternoon punters. The pub is a riot of sequins, blonde highlights and wet-look cocktail dresses. 'Does changing room needing cleaning?' a punter in a feather boa enquires of the landlady.

Male Order are preceded by two warm-up acts. Jeff Deja Vu, a seven-foot drag queen in a glittery Afro wig ('You're looking at a lady with two weeks to live. Me husband's gone away for a fortnight!') and Decker ('the biggest schlong in Yorkshire,' according to one admirer), a stripper in naval uniform who squirts cream on to his semi-hard penis like a milk-bar waitress preparing a banana split, and spatters the whooping crowd with dairy products. By the time Male Order make their appearance, the audience are banging pint-pots on the tables like sailors slamming their mah-jong cups in a Shanghai bare-knuckle fight club. Finally, the troupe strut on to the tiny stage – dressed in the uniforms that the men of this area used to wear to dig coal and work steel.

It's the crisis in masculinity, mister. You must have read about it in the papers. At the beginning of the twenty-first century, heterosexual maleness looks decidedly shabby, besieged, discredited. Men find it more difficult to secure work than women. Boys are outstripped by girls in examination results. Gay men have undermined the confidence of straight men by colonising images of heterosexual masculinity, queering the macho attributes their fathers and grandfathers could identify as the distinguishing marks of real maleness: muscles, uniforms, crew-cuts. Zeitgeist-watchers have lined up to chisel the inscription on the tombs of traditional masculinity and of patriarchy, too – for how could men remain in control when the tokens of their power were so devalued? When Susan Faludi was researching the demise of 'traditional codes of manhood' for her book *Stiffed: The Betrayal of Modern Man* (1999), she found an andropausal Sylvester Stallone crying on her shoulder, still traumatised by the tyrannies of his father, revealing that powerful, pumped-up maleness – the patriarchy of

15 'The Libertine's Death', from *Rose Mortimer; or, The Ballet Girl's Revenge*, 1865

Rambo, Reagan and Frank Stallone – as empty posturing, an outmoded drag act.

Twenty-first-century man's collective sense of cluelessness has yet to right very many inequalities – as any female production line worker who has bumped into her firm's all-male board of directors on the way to lunch will tell you. Male power is everywhere. Its claim to be an expression of the natural order of things, however, now appears deeply phoney. Feminism, as the theorist Harry Brod puts it, has effected 'the emasculation of patriarchal ideology's masquerade as knowledge' has been swift and successful.[1] Male dominance has been exposed as a kind of cultural artefact, a scripted performance – not the monolithic, ahistorical, utterly plausible entity that was once invoked by supporters and enemies of male power alike. 'Culture', argues Faludi, 'is the whole environment we live in; to acknowledge its sway is to admit men never had the power they imagined.'[2] The conclusion has not simply been reached in the gender studies departments of Anglo-Saxon universities. You can see it on television every day. What can a term like patriarchy mean if Homer Simpson is the most widely broadcast image of fatherhood in the modern world?

When, from some angles at least, twenty-first-century masculinity seems to be in fragments, it seems a sensible time to re-examine what it meant to be a man in the nineteenth century – a time when patriarchy, it is often insisted, was at its zenith. The previous chapter examined the influence of Victorian images of children, and the suspicion with which we now regard them, even as we subscribe to their advocacy of childhood innocence. Images of Victorian men, however, perform a much more satisfying role in our culture: they are there to be booed and hissed. Characterised as the police force of obsolete, chauvinistic ideologies, Victorian men have been forced to embody many of our negative views of nineteenth-century culture. Among the most negative was that expressed in Virginia Woolf's *Three Guineas* (1938), which asserted that Fascism was some mutation of Victorian patriarchy. Nineteenth-century campaigners such as Josephine Butler, Woolf contended, and 'those queer dead women in their poke bonnets and shawls' were opposing the same forces against which the anti-Nazi campaigners of the 1930s were ranged. 'They were fighting the same enemy that you are fighting and for the same reasons. They were fighting the tyranny of the patriarchal state as you are fighting the tyranny of the Fascist state. Thus we are merely carrying on the same fight that our mothers and grandmothers fought; their words prove it; your words prove it.'[3] (The reflection is ironic, considering that she and Oswald Mosley had so many friends in common – Vita Sackville-West, for example, was the gardening correspondent of *Action*, the newspaper of Mosley's New Party.) There is a flavour of Woolf's comparison in many recent histories of Victorian gender relations. Reay Tannahill's *Sex in History* (1989), for instance, identifies Gretchen, the idealised matron of Nazi culture, as a development of 'Victorianism'.[4]

There they stand, these domestic totalitarians, stern-browed at the mantelpiece or at the head of the dinner-table, in some of our favourite images of the period – both those culled from Victorian culture itself, and those fashioned in its image during the following century. Mr Murdstone dealing out tough love in *David Copperfield* (1850); Mr Gradgrind squeezing the life out of his wife and children in *Hard Times* (1854); the solemn patriarch in Augustus Egg's series *Past and Present* (1858) staring impassively from the fireplace, as his adulterous wife crawls for mercy across the hearthrug; the forbidding father in Richard Redgrave's *The Outcast* (1851), banishing his errant daughter into a snowdrift. In pastiche form, the crimes of Mr Murdstone's peers became even more extravagant. Most twentieth-century narratives set in the Victorian period prefer their male authority figures to be tyrannical hypocrites – from Judge Turpin in Stephen Sondheim's *Sweeney Todd* (1979) to the whole synod of drunks, sadists and deviants who ran the families, churches, schools and asylums of Hammer horror films. In Roland Pertwee's play *Pink String and Sealing Wax* (1943), the autocratic Brighton pharmacist Edward Sutton punishes his daughter with extra catechism classes when she takes pity on the guinea pigs he is starving to death for some chemical experiment. Watch the 1945 film version, and you'll see that, for most of his performance as Sutton, Mervyn Johns refuses to remove his hands from their tight-threaded position at the tails of his frock coat. His behaviour is only slightly more subtle than that of Victorian Dad, the comic-strip character from *Viz* magazine, who protests against smut while indulging in clandestine sexual perversions. Victorian Dad is an extreme example of the type, but the deep suspicion with which nineteenth-century men have been regarded in the post-Victorian era continues to emerge from all sorts of unlikely contexts. The *Daily Express* declared that, in the view of his former girlfriend Justine Frischmann, the musician Damon Albarn 'has more in common with a Victorian patriarch than a caring New Man'.[5] According to his most recent biographer, Jack Kerouac 'became a Victorian patriarch' once he was married, 'treating his second and third wives with a callous brutality which would these days probably have landed him in court'.[6]

Is it possible to make any generalisations about the behaviour of Victorian men? Did the majority of them possess such arrogant certitude that they felt that they could, like Jack Kerouac, casually treat their wives with 'callous brutality'? Strikingly, the editors of the correspondence of Charles Darwin offer their subject as a textbook example of nineteenth-century man. 'Darwin', they write, 'emerges as a typical Victorian patriarch, retiring to his study for the day's work on his book, emerging only to visit the greenhouse and walk in the garden, the children accompanying him on the daily round of experimental plots, the pigeon houses, and the "Sandwalk".[7] This, however, is a reading of the domestic routine of the Darwins that lets its preconceptions about Victorian family life occlude the facts of the case. Darwin rarely worked much past lunchtime, giving over the rest of his day to activities with his family. Visit the Darwins' Kent home, Down House, which has now been carefully restored to its mid-Victorian condition and restocked with many of their belongings, and you will see some compelling physical evidence for Darwin's lack of authoritarian uptightness. In his study, the room in which he struggled to read the scrawl of his notes from the *Beagle*, and in which he spent many years studying the physiology of simple marine life (prompting his son to ask of a school friend, 'Where does your father do *his* barnacles?'), there is a leather stool mounted on castors. Darwin had the wheels added so that he could scoot between his writing desk and his work table, where his microscope and his specimens were placed. The side of this stool is scuffed and scraped – there are great scores in the wood, as if it had been dragged along the wall at speed. This is exactly what happened. Once Darwin had concluded his morning's work with his jars of molluscs, he gave the stool over to his children, who punted it up and down the hallway, pretending that it was a boat. The *Beagle*, perhaps.

The power of Victorian men has been consolidated retrospectively by a parallel insistence upon the relative powerlessness of Victorian women. The nineteenth century is remembered as a time when women's lives were more severely policed and circumscribed than in other historical epochs. Post-Victorian culture has been inexpressibly keen to dwell upon images of women housebound by stern husbands, restricted by forbidding social codes, trussed up in underwear that was a physical embodiment of their cultural position. If this was so, it begs the question why the nineteenth century was the era in which women first found their political voices, penetrated male-dominated professions, won property rights and carved out their own spheres of professional competence in high-tech jobs that were wholly unrelated to their traditional domestic and sexual roles. Might the widespread presence within Victorian culture of a scepticism towards and mistrust of male power not explain the preponderance of heavy stepfathers, vicious schoolmasters and weak, deceitful men in its fiction, theatre and art? Who, do we imagine, of the original readership of *Hard Times*, cheered for Mr Gradgrind?

Emblematic of the Victorians' bad attitudes to male and female roles is their doctrine of 'separate spheres', a notion which used contemporary research into the biological differences between the sexes to demarcate their different social functions. The idea was fostered in dozens of conduct and advice manuals, but it received its most popular expression in Ruskin's essay 'Of Queen's Gardens', a lecture first delivered at Rusholme Town Hall, Manchester, in December 1864. The argument ran thus – in language that has since become notorious. Man, according to Ruskin, 'is eminently the doer, the creator, the discoverer, the defender. His intellect is for speculation and invention; his energy for adventure, for war, and for conquest, wherever war is just, wherever conquest necessary.' Conversely, 'woman's power is for rule, not for battle, – and her intellect is not for invention or creation, but for sweet ordering, arrangement and decision.' It is a split between aggressive field work and measured domestic legislature: man pursues 'rough work in open world,' encounters 'peril and trial'; as for woman, 'by her office, and place, she is protected from all danger and temptation.' Womanhood and domesticity, Ruskin claims, are inseparable concepts. 'And wherever a true wife comes,' he continues, 'this home is always round her. The stars only may be over her head; the glowworm in the night-cold grass may be the only fire at her foot: but home is yet wherever she is; and for a noble woman it stretches far round her, better than ceiled with cedar, or painted with vermilion, shedding its quiet light far, for those who else were homeless.'[8] This, at least, is the part of the lecture most often quoted today. Kate Millett's *Sexual Politics* (1977), for instance, singles out this passage, commenting upon 'the wonderful license such a system grants to the male to exploit other human beings ... It is the perfect ethic for a harsh business society.'[9] In common with most commentators, she has less to say about the rest of the lecture, which advocates the teaching of science, history, mathematics and sport to young women, and contends that 'the idea that a woman is only the shadow and attendant image of her lord, owing him a thoughtless and servile obedience, and supported altogether in her weakness by the pre-eminence of his fortitude [is] the most foolish of errors.'[10]

'Of Queen's Gardens' was published as part of the collection *Sesame and Lilies* (1865), a book whose over-representation in the second-hand bookshops of the United Kingdom and the States bears testament to its status as the greatest bestseller of Ruskin's career. By 1882, the book had gone through eight editions in Britain. In America, the number of editions reached thirty-five by 1900, and inspired a sorority organisation called the Queens of Avalon, which flourished between 1902 and the 1930s and regarded Ruskin's essay as 'the textbook of the society, to be studied as thoroughly attractively and devotedly as possible, its mottoes to be illuminated by the members and its choicest lines memorized'. Unfortunately, the Queens' founder (or 'Mage Merlin'), a martyrologist named William Byron Forbush, used Ruskin as a bulwark against the progressive approach to girls' education for which the Rusholme lecture had argued. 'Organized before the word "flapper" was invented,' proclaimed Forbush, 'the Queens is distinctly an antidote to flapperism, an antidote so sensible, joyous, and good-humored that it is acceptable to even the most thoughtless lass who, usually innocently, affects boyish mannerisms or adopts a misunderstood and dangerous license of behavior.'[11]

The publishing success of *Sesame and Lilies*, however, may not be entirely attributable to the reading public's receptiveness to the book's ideas. Millett suggests that ' "Of Queen's Gardens" is an expression of the more normative beliefs of the Victorian middle class at the moment of their most optimistic and public profession,' but in fact the book was widely perceived as an attack on middle-class complacency and the limitations of the syllabus customarily taught to girls by governesses at home.[12] Moreover, as Ruskin was also the disgraced party in the most notorious marital failure of the nineteenth century, his production of an essay exploring the ideal relationship between man and woman would have piqued the interest of some readers for all the wrong reasons. Ruskin's brief married life with Euphemia Gray was at farcical variance with the ideals adumbrated by 'Of Queen's Gardens'. Ruskin seems to have lost interest in his wife during their Venetian honeymoon, possibly as a result of discovering she wasn't going to listen to any of his patronising attempts to reshape her personality – 'a schoolgirl's life ... of early hours ... and mental labour of a dull and unexciting character' was what he prescribed for her.[13] (Instead, she went partying with soldiers while he clamped his ruler to the Gothic spandrels of the Gran Via.) After several unhappy years, Gray had the marriage annulled on 15 July 1854 – citing grounds of 'incurable impotency' – and left her husband for the painter John Everett Millais. The couple produced eight children, and – just to add to the air of malicious fecundity – one of their sons became a prodigious breeder of basset hounds. Many of the original readership of 'Of Queen's Gardens' must have been amused by the thought of a man with such a disastrous track record preaching to the middle classes about marriage.

Kate Millett describes the ideology of separate spheres as 'the period's most ingenious mechanism for restraining insurgent women'.[14] If this is so, its success was limited. The doctrine is hardly adequate to express the complexity of the relationship between the Victorian domestic and professional worlds as they actually existed, the rich diversity of the lives that men and women led. It fails to register the paid and unpaid work performed by women in the home; the large numbers of professional men whose workplace was the domestic environment; the armies of women who found employment in new sectors of the Victorian economy such as retail and information technology. Telegraphic offices on both sides of the Atlantic preferred to engage women, and their speed and skill in these jobs facilitated the development of global capitalism. These insurgent women created their own on-line communities, sharing information and jokes, conducting friendships and affairs through the cables. (One Boston woman even initiated the world's first on-line marriage by wiring instructions to her lover, who was working in England, to go to the nearest telegraph office with a magistrate.) From the 1870s, typewriting became another distinctly female high-tech profession, particularly identified with self-sufficient middle-class women; the divorced Laura Lyons, tapping out letters on her Remington in *The Hound of the Baskervilles* (1902), and the jilted Mary Sutherland in 'A Case of Identity' (1891) are two examples from the Conan Doyle canon.

Other details suggest that the 'restraint' of the separate spheres ideology was limited. Census records, for instance, reveal that one-third of the regular paid labour force were women, employed as – among dozens of other professions – actors, blacksmiths, bookbinders, leech dealers, pawnbrokers, pen grinders, ropemakers, schoolmistresses and whipmakers. This figure excludes those housewives who contributed to the family's income by taking in lodgers or laundry, or fulfilling an administrative role in the family business. Strikingly, the majority of economic migrants in the nineteenth century were women. ('As to *sex*,' wrote Adna Ferrin Weber in 1899, 'it may be confidently declared that woman is a greater migrant than man, – only she travels shorter distances. In considering the sex of city population, we shall see that the excess of women among the immigrants is one of the causes of the general surplus of women in cities, which exceeds that of the rural districts.')[15] It was true that, as Mabel Keningdale Cook and others had noted, the suburbanisation of the middle classes had marooned many women in half-built ghettos on the city limits. Statistically, however, women outnumbered men on the city streets. Even the most finicky etiquette writers saw nothing irregular in a woman walking the streets unchaperoned. 'We can only say', pronounced Mme Marie Bayard, 'that as long as the lady has reached a steady age – say two or three and twenty – and is quietly dressed, and walks with a self-possessed demeanour, neither looking about her, nor behind her, not staring into the shop windows, there can be no impropriety in her walking alone ... a lady who knows how to conduct herself may walk alone in London with perfect safety, and without transgressing any social rules.'[16]

It is easy to pick out extracts from the didactic works of the period and construct the nineteenth century as a historical moment at which women were discouraged from economic activity, deterred even from venturing beyond the confines of the home. Such texts are a problematic source: if these rules needed to be urged or restated, it suggests that they were not universally obeyed. For instance, the popularity of today's neo-conservative self-help books such as *The Surrendered Wife* (2001), *A Return to Modesty* (1999), *The Rules* (1995) and *The Smart Woman's Guide to Staying at Home* (2001) could be used to imply the same about the twenty-first century, but it seems clear to us that such books go against the grain of our times. To some extent, the same was true for comparable Victorian works: although the ideology of separate spheres was in circulation, its impact upon women's lives was far from total. Despite propaganda like 'Of Queen's Gardens', despite the now-notorious popularity of Coventry Patmore's domestic epic *The Angel in the House* ('Man must be pleased; but him to please/ Is woman's pleasure ...'), despite the misogynist medicine being formulated by William Acton and his colleagues, Victorian women were making unparalleled advances, socially and politically.[17] They may have had to wait until 1928 to secure the right to vote in British elections, but the statute books – the Contagious Diseases Acts excepted – describe a steady broadening of women's rights and opportunities. The Infants and Child Custody Act (1839) allowed divorced or separated women who had not been proved adulterous to sue for custody of children under seven; previously, fathers had been granted custody automatically. The Matrimonial Causes Act (1857) allowed wives who could prove extreme cruelty, or desertion, to obtain a divorce, and enabled courts to force estranged husbands to pay maintenance to their former wives. The Married Women's Property Act (1870) allowed women to inherit property without ownership passing immediately to their husbands; a further Act in 1882 extended these reforms. The Custody Acts (1873) allowed women to be awarded custody of children up to age sixteen, even if they had been divorced by their husbands for adultery. The Matrimonial Causes Act (1884) allowed a deserted wife to petition for divorce immediately, without waiting for two years, as previously required.

If nineteenth-century women were leading more complex and productive lives than the widely circulated stereotype suggests, so too were Victorian men, who were involved in the domestic sphere to a much greater extent than is customarily acknowledged. John Tosh, in his landmark study of gender in nineteenth-century domesticity, *A Man's Place* (1999), argues that 'Victorian middle-class family life was far more varied than the popular stereotype allows ... Fatherhood encompassed every variant from the almost invisible breadwinner to the accessible and attentive playmate.' Many Victorian men, he argues, following the example of Prince Albert, were happily and successfully domesticated; others were unable to resolve the competing demands of home and furiously homosocial professional, sporting and educational environments. 'The recent attempt by Robert Bly to recover a "deep" masculinity on behalf of men who have grown up in feminized homes would have been instantly recognizable to all those Victorian fathers who patronized the new public schools in order to remove their sons to a more manly environment.'[18] Other organisations also answered this need. Friendly Societies, the progenitors of the trade union movement, were joined by more Victorian men than any other kind of organisation. By 1905, nearly half of all men in England had signed up to their mixture of social insurance and fraternal initiation, which combined sickness benefit and pension schemes with peculiar blindfold rituals involving red-hot pokers. Less weirdly, the Mechanics' Institutes, which flourished in Britain and the USA between the 1820s and 1860s, aimed to provide education for male manual workers. A model Institute would offer courses of lectures and contain a laboratory, a library, a museum and lectures by A-list names such as Edward Bulwer-Lytton, who addressed the Royston Mechanic's Institute in June 1852.

Nineteenth-century texts support John Tosh's view of the male role as complex and multiplicitous, but they also reveal something surprising about Victorian images of masculinity – that they didn't make a great deal of sense. Even at their toughest and most conservative, Victorian theorists and polemicists failed to offer a uniform, coherent blueprint for proper masculine behaviour. That Victorian men were somehow more confident in their roles as husbands, fathers, lovers, than their twenty-first-century counterparts is not borne out by the literature. They were, I think, as puzzled about the nature of their social role as twenty-first-century men. The crisis in masculinity had already begun.

A huge amount of prescriptive literature from the period survives, which gives some indication of how certain sections of Victorian society wanted their men to behave. Even the most minor of these publications is available to the researcher, as their authors (who were generally pushy evangelical clergymen and schoolmasters attempting to sharpen their media profiles) were extremely diligent about depositing them in libraries – where they remained, unread, until twentieth-century academics identified them as a legitimate medium through which to read Victorian culture.

Conduct books and tracts prescribing the regulation of the behaviour of young women have often been used to make claims about the repressive energy that went into the construction of Victorian female identity, but many young men were invited to consume an analogous literature of control, often compiled by the same authors. William Henry Davenport Adams, for example, offered homilies for schoolboys in *The Boy Makes the Man* (1867) and gave girls the benefit of his advice in *The Sunshine of Domestic Life* (1867). (He also wrote a history of lighthouses, a concordance to Shakespeare, a study of Pompeii and a handbook on party games – nearly 150 titles in all.) Adams was a prolific producer of a significant sub-genre of boys' conduct literature, the compendium of hagiographic tales: stories relating acts of heroism selected from the boyhoods of famous men. In these peculiar texts, small boys save lives, tackle monsters and discover various scientific principles – and the reader is asked to emulate them in his daily life. The seven-year-old Nelson's attempt to take on a polar bear with a musket-butt is a particular favourite, and is retold in William Martin's *Heroism of Boyhood, or What Boys Have Done* (1865) and Adams's *The Boy Makes the Man*. This is Adams's version of the anecdote:

'Sir,' said he, pouting his lip, as he was wont to do when agitated, 'I wished to kill the beast that I might carry home his skin to my father.' Nelson's own words afford the best commentary on his career: 'Thus,' he says, 'may be exemplified by my life that perseverance in any profession will most probably meet its reward. Without having any inheritance, or been fortunate in prize-money, I have received all the honours of my profession, been created a peer of Great Britain; and I may say to the reader, Go thou and do likewise.'[19]

Quite how the reader was intended to emulate this Arctic adventure is not made clear. And there is evidence that these exhortations were regarded as ridiculously naïve by some of their contemporary readers. Thomas Morell Blackie, master of Chipping Hill school, Essex, and author of *What is a Boy? And What To Do With Him* (1858), was abused in the pages of *Punch* for his naïve belief that virtue could be inculcated in schoolboys.[20] The Rev A. K. H. Boyd acknowledged in his lecture 'A Young Man: His Home and Friends' (1884) that his audience was likely to be indifferent to his opinions. 'There is a greater difficulty which I am aware of, young men, in speaking to you,' he admitted. 'You do not care much about this that I have been saying.'[21] Any didactic text must be read with scepticism, but many of the recommendations in these conduct books would have been impossible to implement, even for the most unblinking zealot. Their incoherence, however, may be more eloquent than their matter, as the literature which young men and boys read for pleasure offered a similarly garbled message about proper masculinity.

Take, for example, *The Boy Detective; or, The Crimes of London* (1865–6). It is a typical example of the cheap serial fiction that boomed after the abolition of the Newspaper Stamp Tax in 1856. Its plot is intermittently comprehensible, and constitutes a series of violent and bizarre incidents linked by the involvement of the hero Ernest Keen, a young aristocrat expelled from the family home through the machinations of his wicked stepmother, Barbara. Week by week, Ernest and his faithful troupe of followers find themselves in a variety of scrapes: the heroine, Fanny, is half-stripped, then bound and gagged in the attic of a burning house as a chained lunatic thrashes below; Ernest's acolyte Inky Bob is tied to a grinning skeleton in Bluebeard's death-chamber. Ernest Keen is a malleable entity in a work of fiction whose cogency is local at the best of times. Depending on the demands of the plot, he flickers uncertainly

THE BOY DETECTIVE;
OR, THE CRIMES OF LONDON.

16 Ernest Keen drags up to smash a counterfeiting gang, from *The Boy Detective; or, The Crimes of London* (1865–6)

between the states of androgynous youth, small child and aggressive young man. He is also capable of flooring villains twice his size, and participates in the romantic strand of the plot with Fanny.

The events of the serial begin on London Bridge, where Ernest is saved from a suicide attempt by his old friend Joe Whiffins, 'a serio-comic wocalist at the Harmonic Cripples, hup the Walworth Road', after which they go on to form a gang of juvenile crime-fighters called the Band of Light.[22] They unite specifically to combat a counterfeiting organisation led by Barbara Keen and her evil French lover, Gaspard Massillon, who has murdered Ernest's father. Ernest's big plan involves dragging up as 'Miss Sharp', a governess, in order to infiltrate the hideout of the Band of Darkness. Once inside the house, he confronts a member of the criminal gang, William, and makes an unusual request:

'Now, take off your clothes.'

What a command from a young lady!

Poor William almost fainted.

Yet, more shocking to relate, Miss Sharp began to undress herself.

Presently, from the coop of rustling silk, expansive crinoline, and delicately-broidered petticoats, leapt a graceful form in shirt and trousers tucked up to the knees.

'You – you are Ernest Keen, the Boy Detective!' gasped the page.

'Yes, William,' answered our hero, stepping up to the glass, and disturbing the arrangement of a most exquisite coif of ringlets.

He took out a pocket comb, and parted his hair neatly.

'Now, make haste, give me your jacket,' he said, while on one knee he was rolling his trousers down from his knees.

They were black, with a red stripe down each side.

'And let me try on your half tops.'

The boy did not offer the least resistance; he threw off his jacket and kicked off his boots.

Our hero put them on.

Both boys being dark and of equal stature, there was no small resemblance between them.

'Now, Miss Sharp, let me assist you to dress yourself.'

Our hero then dressed the page in the clothes he himself had discarded.

This done, our hero said with a smile,

'I'm sorry to be obliged, miss, to act so rudely, but I shall be forced to tie your hands.'

Ernest then walked to the window.

He cut down the cord of the blind.

He tied the page's hands behind him.

Then he drew from his pocket an elastic band with a square piece of bone sewed upon it.

He placed this over the head of his victim, and by fixing the bone in the boy's mouth, effectively gagged him.

He then led him to the cupboard, locked him into it, and taking up the letters, left the room.[23]

Ernest Keen is a typical hero of the mid-century boom in young men's fiction. These odd man-boy amalgams were a staple of such literature in the 1860s. Sift through the blackened pages of the periodicals in the British Library's Barry Ono collection, and figures such as Galloping Dick, the Boy Highwayman, and Kit Foundling, the Boy Pirate, come careering, blood-slaked, out of their pages. The more of these stories you read, the more peculiar their heroes seem to become. They are boys playing at hyper-masculine roles with which they cannot become comfortable. They face 'peril and trial', pursue 'adventure, war, and conquest', like good little Ruskinians. But they all seem to suffer from depression, too.

As he engages with the enemy, Kit Foundling, hero of Irving Lyons's *The Boy Pirate; or, Life on the Ocean* (1864–5), is energised by the violence of the slaughter. 'His cheek was blanched', the text boasts, 'not by fear, but only with intense excitement.' Later, however, he exclaims, 'Why – why was I forced to do this?' The role of piratical hero is one whose contradictions seem to madden him: 'Fight as he would; display whatever qualities he might that belong to the conventional conception of a hero, his desperate valour, his cool prudence and foresight, his masterly discipline, would bring him no triumph.'[24] He is, it seems, no more a pirate than Decker, owner of modern Yorkshire's biggest schlong, is a naval officer. Both are just playing dress-up with stereotypical modes of masculinity.

The hero of 'Galloping Dick, the Boy Highwayman' (c.1865) seems no more happy. The narrative opens in mid-flight. Dick is being pursued across the rooftops by a squad of policemen. He is grabbed by one of his pursuers: '. . . with a desperate effort, Dick freed the hand containing the loaded pistol – as quick as lightning the barrel touched the man's temple – there was a startling explosion, and the upper part of the unfortunate man's head was shattered.' Dick takes the fight on to the roof of the house, where, in another attack, he sends a Bow Street runner tumbling from the rafters to his death. The text insists that he is a 'daring boy' and a 'fearless youth', but it seems that Dick himself has other ideas. 'Great God,' he cries, 'the second life sacrificed through me; and in so short a time.' A few paragraphs later, he seems to have changed his tune again. Having all but evaded his enemies, he allows himself a declaration of triumph. 'Hurrah!' he shouted, 'I'll trick them yet – they will yet find more than a match for them in Galloping Dick the Highwayman!' No sooner has he made this declaration, than the text rounds on him. 'His past career moved before his mind's eye like a panorama . . . each sin and wicked deed assumed the shape of a hideous, taunting demon . . . Alas! The boy was RAVING MAD!'[25]

These boys' stories did not need to worry too much about internal consistency. They were liberated by their loose form from the need to maintain psychological continuity, and no figure in them can ever really act out of character: the consequences of the plot do not, strictly speaking, need to take their toll on the hero. However, both Kit Foundling and Galloping Dick both exhibit some form of mental malaise. The 'conventional conception of a hero' was so evidently dysfunctional that even the hack writers of violent boys' stories could not insulate their protagonists from its contradictions.

If Kit or Dick had checked into a hospital for the insane, they would have found themselves in good company. The wards of Britain's mental health institutions were packed with men whose madness revolved around the very notions of heroism, of strength, of hypermasculinity with which these fictional heroes struggled. In an 1862 article by C. L. Robertson on cases of paresis, one W. B. thinks 'he is King of the Earth', and J. J. 'says he is a hundred ton man, and proposed to show his strength by lifting the fireguards, &c. Says he weighs six millions of tons, that he has not eaten since 1834, &c.'[26] John Millar's handbook *Hints on Insanity* (1861), which collected and criticised doctors' certificating comments on suspected cases of madness, quotes other examples of the superhuman bravado of the psychotic male subject: one patient 'states that he is a Prince of France'; another, whose 'countenance is expressive of great anxiety and restlessness . . . says all the public-houses in London belong to him; also that he is going to marry the Queen.'[27] In their madness, these men become exemplars of patriarchy: unlike most of Davenport Adams's readers, they would certainly have dared to tackle a polar bear with a musket butt.

Victorian masculinity, far from being an unassailable source of power, was riven with internal contradictions, beset by the knowledge of its own weakness and incoherence. Standing at the bar of the Dog and Partridge, watching Chera Kincaid's boys pick their way across the floor between the tables, women's hands clawing at their groins with every step, it would be easy to be seduced by the idea that this scene represents some narrative of the decline of masculine power. True, Sheffield's industrial collapse, and the disappearance of thousands of labouring, bureaucratic and administrative jobs, may have removed one source of male pride from which their great-great-grandfathers might have taken comfort – but were they any more certain that they wielded the natural authority of their sex, that they were in charge of their women? Or did they return to the conduct books they had been made to read as children, puzzle over the illustrations of the boy Nelson's impossible feats and shake their heads in resentful disbelief?

CHAPTER TWELVE

Monomaniacs of Love

Of course I have seen people recover from homosexualism. A boy at Eton assaulted my elder brother in the bath there and was later expelled for repeating the offence on another boy. Later he became a pillar of county society and captained the county cricket team. So one can undoubtedly recover from homosexualism. But if I were the parent of a boy who had been seduced by some middle-aged gentleman, I should feel that his life had been taken a long way towards ultimate ruin.

Lord Longford, *Hansard Parliamentary Debates* (13 April 1999)

Aubrey Beardsley had an intense preoccupation with sex. In his brief, brilliant career – which saw him celebrated, disgraced, passé and dead before his twenty-sixth birthday – he created a unique illustrative style, which was contemporary, monochrome and lubricious. He collected explicit Japanese prints and framed them for his bedroom wall; he delighted in books that detailed carnal curiosities; his intimates were sodomites and smut-peddlers to a man. In 1894, he began *Under the Hill*, a pornographic novel in which – to take one example – Venus works up an appetite for lunch by masturbating a unicorn called Adolphe. ('Adolphe had been quite profuse that morning. Venus knelt where it had fallen, and lapped her little aperitif.')[1] His biographers, however, have searched in vain for hard evidence that he didn't die a virgin. There are vague suggestions that he might have enjoyed some libidinous fumbling during a drunken coach accident on the streets of Paris, and there was certainly an unsuccessful attempt to 'ravish' Muriel Broadbent, the mistress of art historian Herbert Horne, in a room at the Thalia supper club. There is probably no truth, however, in W. B. Yeats's claim that Beardsley shared the favours of a 'painted woman' with the poet Ernest Dowson, or that he had been intimate with a well-known London prostitute with the frank *nom de guerre* of 'Penny Plain'. There is even less evidence that Beardsley's remark to the publisher John Lane that he was planning to go to the St James's restaurant 'dressed up as tart' amounted to a taste for transvestism. The same can be said for Frank Harris's claim that the artist had an incestuous relationship with his sister Mabel. A modern reader would conclude that Beardsley was basically heterosexual. 'Don't sit on the same chair as Aubrey,' his mentor Oscar Wilde declared. 'It's not compromising.'[12]

So, you might ask, why did Beardsley spend all his spare time with the decade's most notorious sexual deviants? Why did he turn against Edward Burne-Jones, the elderly Pre-Raphaelite painter who gave him his first major commission, and move firmly into the orbit of figures like Oscar Wilde, Robert Ross, John Gray, Bosie Douglas, Max Beerbohm and Will Rothenstein? Why was he, in his final years, financially supported by Marc-André Raffalovich, author of *Uranisme et Unisexualité*? Why, at the age of nineteen, did he accept a commission for an 'atmospheric' picture of Hermaphroditus from the louche Julian Sampson, or hang out with Count Eric Stenbock, a thirtysomething half-Estonian aristocrat who once fell madly in love with a male music student whom he had met on the top deck of an omnibus?

When Oscar Wilde was escorted by two detectives from the Cadogan Hotel on 5 April 1895, the newspaper headlines used the association between playwright and artist to compromise them both: 'OSCAR WILDE ARRESTED: YELLOW BOOK UNDER HIS ARM'. It might have been a French novel in yellow wrappers. It might even have been a Yellowback, one of the cheap reprints of popular novels sold on railway bookstands. The assumption, however, was that this volume was *The Yellow Book*, the journal of Aesthetic art and literature with which Beardsley was strongly identified. Sufficient numbers of people made that assumption for a sizeable crowd to assemble outside the Vigo Street offices of its publisher, the Bodley Head, and pelt the windows with stones. Some are still happy to hurl them. In September 1998, the *Daily Mail* columnist Paul Johnson denounced the Royal Academy's controversial art show *Sensation* as the product of a 'perverted, brutal, horribly modish and clever cunning, degenerate, exhibitionist, high-voiced and limp-wristed' culture, and identified this tendency as Beardsley's legacy. 'The Naughty Nineties,' he raged, 'saw an upsurge of intellectual degeneracy whose taste was for opium, cocaine and obscenity, whose symbol was the Yellow Book, the leading avant-garde publication of the day, and whose talismans were the drawings – some published, most privately circulated – of Aubrey Beardsley. These precious creatures were riding high until, in 1885 [*sic*], the conviction

17 Two Sicilian boys pose for German photographer Baron Wilhelm von Gloeden,
c.1890 (courtesy Mark Lee Rotenberg, www.vintagenudephotos.com)

and imprisonment of Oscar Wilde, the paedophile, brought the edifice of
fashionable degeneracy down in shameful ruin.'3

For the remaining chapters of this book, Oscar Wilde is our lead
character. Since the 1960s, the story of his fall and martyrdom has been
one of our favourite parables of Victorian intolerance, circulated in
countless books, films and plays, and on tea towels and greetings cards.

[192]

Whether he deserves this iconic status is debatable: not because he could still be arrested today for the things he got up to with teenage boys, but because the sexual sensibility he represented – curious, adaptable, versatile – was much more typical of his times than our own. We tend to see him as a proto-modern figure who was unlucky enough to have been born in the nineteenth century, forgetting that the freedoms he enjoyed were not available to post-Victorian men.

In the aftermath of the Wilde scandal, Beardsley, fired from the Bodley Head at the insistence of William Watson (the most successful poet on its lists, now quite forgotten), took up with a pasty-faced pornographer by the name of Leonard Smithers. The most memorable – but perhaps not the most accurate – description of Smithers is by Oscar Wilde: 'he is usually in a large straw hat, has a blue tie delicately fastened with a diamond brooch of the impurest water, or perhaps wine, as he never touches water – it goes to his head at once. His face, clean shaven, is wasted and pale. He loves first editions, especially of women: little girls are his passion. He is the most learned erotomaniac in Europe. He is also a delightful companion and a dear fellow, and very kind to me.'[4]

Shortly after accepting a series of commissions from Smithers, Beardsley moved away from his mother and sister and into rooms at Geneux's Private Hotel at 10 11 St James's Place. He set up home in a suite that Wilde had taken in 1893, ostensibly in order to write *An Ideal Husband* away from the noise and distraction of family life in Tite Street, but more probably as a place to explore his growing interest in rent boys. As a result of the Old Bailey trials, the address had been made notorious. 'Quite what perverse desire', wonders his most recent biographer, Stephen Calloway, 'thus to invite further association – of the worst kind, and with the most infamous part of Wilde's life in London – can have possessed Beardsley at this moment remains unfathomable.'[5] There is an answer to this question to be found in the very pornographic material upon which Smithers and Beardsley collaborated.

Pornography was one of the major textual industries of Victorian Britain. It first became a mass-market product in the 1830s and 1840s, when Chartist activists used profits from the production of erotic prints and fiction to subsidise their political pamphleteering. Some of these publications were hybrids of both genres: *Town* (1837–42), the *Crim. Con. Gazette* (1838–40) and *Exquisite* (1842–4) used graphic descriptions of upper-class sex scandals to agitate against the political *status quo* – like a sort of *Socialist Wanker*. When, in 1848, the Chartist movement collapsed, and it became clear that the British Revolution was not going to happen, this lucrative sideline became the central business: a business which grew and grew. The irrepressibly mouthy Stockport-born printer William Dugdale, for instance, was a political radical who had been involved in the Cato Street Conspiracy, an unsuccessful attempt to assassinate Lord Liverpool's Tory cabinet as they dined in Chelsea in 1821. Thirty years later, he had the best stock of dirty books on Holywell Street, Victorian London's street of a thousand pornographers. When he was raided in 1851, police seized 822 books, 3,870 prints and sixteen hundredweight of unsewn letterpress. The ninth raid on his shop, in 1856, garnered three thousand books. Order up some of these texts in the few British libraries that hold them, and there is still the sense that you have transgressed some unwritten moral code. In the Bodleian Library, you are issued with a warning ticket in Beardsleyan yellow that exhorts you not to leave the book on your desk for fear of it corrupting the morals of a passing academic. In the old reading room at the British Museum, anyone wanting to consult a book from the 'private case' was made to sit at a special frontless desk, so that the librarians could watch out for any unauthorised self-abuse.

Stephen Marcus's *The Other Victorians* (1966) is perhaps the most widely read account of Victorian pornography. There is a central eccentricity in the book, however: 'there is almost no literature of a homosexual kind surviving from the period,' he declares, disregarding the obvious examples of *Sins of the Cities of the Plain* (1881) and *Teleny* (1883). A good Freudian, Marcus suggests that the taboo against sex between men was so strong that Victorian pornographers sublimated it into a sub-genre focused on scenes of flagellation. Pornographic stories such as *The Romance of Chastisement* (1866) were, he argues, 'a kind of last-ditch compromise with and defence against homosexuality.'[6] However, sexual encounters between men do take place in the nineteenth century's most reprinted pornographic text – *The Pearl*, 'a monthly journal of facetiæ and voluptuous reading'. Originally published by William Lazenby, one of London's most prolific pornographers, it went through many reprints and reincarnations, and is still in print today. The protagonists of its lurid stories are frequently aristocratic, always educated and articulate. For all its fleshly obsession, *The Pearl* is not an entirely unintellectual publication. Its unsigned contributors included Algernon Charles Swinburne, who supplied its pages with several flagellant poems and an obscene parody of the National Anthem, and George Augustus Sala, a prominent Fleet Street journalist and close friend of Mary Elizabeth Braddon. A late Victorian reprint actually claims to have been produced by the Oxford University Press. This attribution is only the sniggering joke of printer Edward Avery, who reproduced this edition from Lazenby's stereotype plates; but in making it, he evokes the idea of this pornography being consumed in the single-sex enclave of the university – and this is not without significance. In 1875, William Money Hardinge was sent down by Benjamin Jowett, Master of Balliol, for 'keeping and reciting immoral poetry', a series of sonnets addressed to a male lover. In 1880, *Boy-Worship*, a pamphlet published anonymously by Charles Edward Hutchinson, revealed that it was possible to pick up boys in 'Oxford's fashionable book shops' and argued that 'few men, indeed, are proof against the fresh young voice and pretty petulance of a boy of fourteen or fifteen.'[7] Between November 1892 and December 1893, Bosie Douglas turned the student magazine *The Spirit Lamp* into a journal dedicated to the exploration of sexual relationships between men. 'If Bosie has really made Oxford homosexual,' wrote George Ives, founder of the all-male coterie the Order of Chaeronaea, in his diary on 15 November 1894, 'he has done something good and glorious.'[8]

What is startling about *The Pearl* to a modern readership is its willingness to stage erotic encounters between men, without the imputation that the participants are compromising themselves by doing so. None of these men are what we would call homosexual; they simply have sex with men, usually as a sort of kinky side salad or anticipatory hors d'oeuvre to more central acts of carnality with women. In 'Sub-Umbra; or, Sport among the She-Noodles', for instance, Walter offers to loan his friend Frank a deluxe copy of *Fanny Hill*. Walter's graphically illustrated edition is stowed in a secret compartment of his dressing case. 'Here it is, my boy, only I hope it won't excite you too much; you can look it over by yourself, as I read the *Times*.' Of course, it does excite him too much, and soon the pair are, as Walter puts it, 'having a mutual fuck between the thighs on the bed' – which, incidentally, was Oscar Wilde's favourite position. In a later chapter, a similar scene is initiated when Frank's lustful intentions towards the improbably named Rosa Redquim become all too apparent to Walter. 'The sight was too exciting for me to restrain myself,' he confesses, and in *The Pearl*'s only intimation of the feminisation process that might be expected to accompany the expression of such a desire, reveals that 'the cigarette dropped from my lips.' In another long-running serial, 'Lady Pokingham; or, They All Do It', Beatrice, the heroine-narrator, is forced into marriage with one Lord Crim-Con, a virtuoso of perversion who has regular anal sex with his butler and other male servants ('Crim-Con' being a punning reference to the charge of 'Criminal Conversation' that was used to indict seducers). On their wedding night, Lord Crim-Con penetrates the butler, as the butler does the same to Beatrice. In the middle of this colourful scene, she reflects that 'he seemed to have rather an easy task in getting into the man's bottom, no doubt having often been there before.'[9]

You have to be careful about drawing too many conclusions from texts like these. Extrapolate twenty-first-century male sexuality from the letters pages of *Men Only*, and you would conclude that Britain was a nation of tumescent plumbers and pizza delivery boys. However, *The Pearl's* willingness to countenance such acts suggests that sexual desire between Victorian men was not considered sufficiently marginal to exclude it from representation within non-specialist pornographic texts. It might also suggest new ways of reading those passionate same-sex friendships that exist in the Victorian novel: the intimacy between Mortimer Lightwood and Eugene Wrayburn in *Our Mutual Friend* (1865), for instance, or the passion that exists between the two heroes of Wilkie Collins's *Armadale* (1866):

> . . . I do love him! It *will* come out of me – I can't keep it back. I love the very ground he treads on! I would give my life – yes, the life that is precious to me now, because his kindness has made it a happy one – I tell you I would give my life –'
>
> The next words died away on his lips; the hysterical passion rose, and conquered him. He stretched out one of his hands with a wild gesture of entreaty . . . his head sank on the window-sill, and he burst into tears.[10]

For nineteenth-century readerships, the opposition between homosexuality and heterosexuality which we regard as pivotal did not exist. The term 'homosexual' was coined in 1868 by a German-Hungarian named Hans Benkert, a campaigner against punitive German anti-pederasty laws who wrote under the name of Karoly Maria Kertbeny. It did not get into print in English until 1892, in a translation of Richard von Krafft-Ebing's *Psychopathia Sexualis*, a study that rejected Benkert's liberationism in favour of generating a taxonomy of morbid psychosexual disorders. (According to Lord Alfred Douglas, this was among Wilde's favourite reading.) In Britain during the 1880s and 1890s, before the H-word caught on, same-sex lovers were known as Uranians, Satodists, Inverts, Urnings and persons of 'contrary sexual instinct'. To speak of 'homosexuals' in contexts before this date is like using the word Nintendo to describe everything from 1930s fruit machines to 1980s Pac Man games.

This is more than a semantic quibble. The absence of medico-legal definitions for what the Victorians did in bed was reflected in the relationships they conducted and in the peccadilloes they indulged. Victorian sexuality was much less systematised and tribalist than our own. Attempting to apply modern jargon to what went on between nineteenth-century lovers can only yield a limited understanding of how their relationships were constituted. In Victorian medico-legal texts dealing with same-sex sexual relationships, the notion of sexual orientation was a function of the assignment of male/female identity. Men who had a sexual interest in other men were held to be phenotypically male and psychologically female, and their growing representation within psychiatric and legal discourse supported this assumption by emphasising their adoption of feminine characteristics and social codes. In 1895, one American commentator wrote of 'peculiar societies of inverts' who ran 'coffee-clatches, where the members dress themselves with aprons, etc., and knit, gossip and crochet'.[11] It was not until 1899 that the sexologist Magnus Hirschfield made a radical distinction between homosexuality and transvestism, in his specialised journal *Jahrbuch für Sexuelle Zwischenstufen*, but this clinical opinion was slow to diffuse into mainstream thought. A sympathetic study from 1908 asserts that transvestism is the 'perennial trait of effeminate Uranians'.[12] The pioneering social theorist Edward Carpenter admitted that an 'extreme specimen' of Uranism could be 'mincing in gait and manners ... skilful at the needle and in woman's work, sometimes taking pleasure in dressing in woman's clothes'.[13] The elision is repeated by 'Walter', the pseudonymous author of the immense pornographic memoir *My Secret Life*. When spying on prostitutes through a cellar-grille, he observes to his 'astonishment a prick and balls hanging down between the legs' of a petticoated figure.[14] Similarly, Henry Spencer Ashbee – who was probably the man behind the pseudonym – in his lavish porno-bibliography *Index Librorum Prohibitorum* (1877) informed his readers of 'balls of sodomites and catamites where women were not admitted, but where the men came in male or female attire indiscriminately', even going so far as to quote names and addresses.[15]

Ashbee's reference is a topical one. In April 1870, Ernest Boulton and Frederick William Park, two middle-class men in their early twenties, became the most famous transvestite goodtime boys of their age. Indeed, a later publisher of *The Pearl* included an obscene limerick about the pair until 1900:

> There was an old person of Sark
> Who buggered a pig in the dark.
> The Swine in surprise
> Murmured: 'God blast your eyes,
> Do you take me for Boulton or Park?'[16]

The story of Boulton and Park illustrates the fluid nature of Victorian sexuality. They were charged with frequenting the Strand Theatre with the intention to commit a felony, and their first court appearance – clad in the silk and satin dresses in which they were arrested – caused a public sensation. Crowds clamoured at the doors of the court, and were enraged to discover that, on the second day's hearing, the accused pair had left their hairpins and costume jewellery at home. As the trial progressed, examination of the accused pair's letters and papers revealed their intimate connections with several members of the aristocracy, including Lord Arthur Clinton MP, who committed suicide during the trial, probably in order to avoid making a humiliating court appearance. The jury heard how Boulton and Park put on their glad rags and tripped around the Burlington Arcade, visited the Casino at Holborn and cheered the teams of the Oxford and Cambridge boat race from the banks of the Thames. The verdict was Not Guilty, delivered after an hour of deliberation and received in the court with a round of applause. They went to the theatre in frocks, they were known to friends and correspondents as 'Stella' and 'Fanny' respectively, but nothing strictly criminal was ever proved of Boulton or Park. What Park referred to in a letter to Lord Arthur Clinton as his 'campish undertakings' did not amount to proof of the criminal conspiracy with which the pair were charged. The amorous terms of endearment used in the letters did not prove they had committed the prohibited act of buggery – no matter how hard the court doctors gazed up their anuses. There was simply nothing on the statute books with which they could be charged.

Buggery, which had a variety of meanings, not exclusively related to sex between men, had been an offence since 1533 and remains so today. It was not until the passing of the Labouchere Amendment to the Criminal

Law Amendment Act (1885) that the courts were enabled to pursue the more ambiguous offence of 'gross indecency' between men. The Amendment facilitated the prosecution of the telegraph boys implicated in the Cleveland Street affair, Oscar Wilde and every collared cottager between the 1890s and – thanks to the survival of Labouchere's expression in current legislation – the present day. The fuzzily-worded clause, debated lamely in a sparse House of Commons late one August night in 1885, states:

> Any male person who, in public or private, commits, or is a party to the commission of, or procures or attempts to procure the commission by any male person of, any act of gross indecency with another male person, shall be guilty of a misdemeanour, and being convicted thereof shall be liable at the discretion of the court to be imprisoned for any term not exceeding two years, with or without hard labour.[17]

It must be the most mythologised legal paragraph in British history. Bonnie Zimmerman's *Lesbian Histories and Cultures* (2000) keeps the oldest chestnut warming: 'In 1885,' she writes, 'when the Criminal Law Amendment regarding homosexual behaviour was passed in England, Queen Victoria (1819–1901) refused to sign it until all references to women were removed. She did not believe female homosexuality existed and did not wish to blemish women by referring to them in this law about public or private homosexual acts.'[18] Several British publications regurgitated it again on the centenary of the monarch's death, a *Times* editorial explaining that lesbians escaped prosecution 'since no one liked to explain to the Queen what exactly might be involved', and a *Radio Times* article asserting that 'Queen Victoria's famous denial that such a thing as lesbianism could exist in her empire may well have provided an effective smokescreen' for sexual relationships between women.[19] This story, which relies on a constitutional impossibility, seems to have made its way into the popular imagination after a statue of Victoria in Wellington, New Zealand, was made the focus of a demonstration on International Women's Day 1977. (Members of the Lesbians Ignite Fire Brigade draped the effigy with a banner proclaiming 'Lesbians are Everywhere'.)

The Labouchere Amendment was not the queer-baiting instrument of received history; in fact, the clause had the effect of reducing the sentence for buggery from life to two years. The rest of the Bill was concerned with the suppression of brothels and the protection of children from pimps and their punters. It was hurried into law in response to Stead's 'Maiden Tribute' articles, which, as has been noted, made wildly exaggerated claims about the extent of child prostitution in London. Labouchere's motives in drafting the Amendment remain obscure. The MP and his wife Henrietta Hodson, a retired actress, were good friends of Oscar Wilde (the playwright introduced Lillie Langtry to their regular am-dram evenings in 1881) and no friends of the social purity movement. Labouchere expressed his hope that 'the law should be used equally against high and low', suggesting that he was most concerned to limit aristocratic sexual exploitation of working-class men, and Wilde's friend Frank Harris even claimed that the MP had intended the Amendment to be a wrecking clause. Whatever the case, it was used by others after Labouchere to enforce the sexual norms by which we now define ourselves. Between them, apologists for same-sex desire and those who wanted to see it pathologised and policed ensured that a series of disconnected acts, traits and practices became organised into a new type of human being. This is not to argue that same-sex sexual relationships did not occur before the 1890s, or that there were not names for those who enjoyed them. British history teems with examples of such liaisons. In the early years of the eighteenth century, members of the Society for the Reformation of Manners launched a series of raids on male brothels, and acted as *agents provocateurs* in order to entrap men whom they had observed cruising each other on London Bridge and in the Royal Exchange. In July 1772, Robert Jones, a lieutenant in the artillery corps of the British army, was convicted at the Old Bailey for committing sodomy upon the person of thirteen-year-old Francis Henry Hay. Jones, the author of a popular treatise on skating, was sentenced to death, but given an eleventh-hour reprieve on condition that he transport himself abroad for the term of his natural life. Henry Spencer Ashbee claimed he could name 'a long list of celebrities' who indulged in such practices.[20] In the 1890s, however, medical and legal terminology describing and cataloguing different models of sexual behaviour emerged from obscure German textbooks and into avidly consumed court reports. By 1908, concerned men and women could complete a psychometric test, 'Am I At All a Uranian?', answer questions such as 'Do you whistle well, and naturally like to do so? Do you feel at ease in the dress of the opposite sex? Are you peculiarly fond of Wagner?' and calculate the nature of their sexual identity in terms of percentage points.[21]

For the previous thirty years, however, other writers had been attempting a similar project through more subtle means. During Oscar Wilde's first trial, there was a protracted discussion of whether his novel *The Picture of Dorian Gray* (1890) contained an address to a coterie of Uranian initiates. Edward Carson, speaking for the Marquess of Queensberry, suggested that the book was 'understood by the readers thereof to describe the relations and intimacies of certain persons of sodomitical and unnatural tastes and practices.'[22] This line of inquiry perplexed many of the book's admirers. Sir Arthur Conan Doyle, for instance, thought it 'a book which is surely on a high moral plane'. Other groups of readers, however, were used to scouring literature for Uranian content. In June 1891, John Addington Symonds, author of *A Problem in Greek Ethics* (1883), wrote to Edmund Gosse: 'What a number of Urnings are being portrayed in novels now! . . . I stumble on them casually & find the same note.'[23] Symonds seems to have devoted much energy to this kind of reading. 'I mean to get more of this man's books – and perhaps to write to him,' he enthused of Rudyard Kipling's *Soldiers Three* (1889). 'When I first read it I felt the lover in it . . .'[24] Kipling, for his part, was unimpressed by Symonds's 'sugary gushing' attentions. Magazines such as *The Artist* (edited by Wilde's friend Charles Kains-Jackson), *The Spirit Lamp* (edited by Bosie Douglas) and *Woman's World* (edited by Wilde), contained articles with more definite signs of Uranism, as did an extraordinary anonymous novel, now utterly forgotten, which offers a strange snapshot of male sexuality in flux.

Arthur Howard, the hero of *The Monomaniac of Love* (1878), is a man struggling to define himself, within a text that seeks to address a coterie of readers undergoing a similar process. The book contains a large number of allusions to people, events, books and ideas which, although they amount to little individually, would have got Symonds's antennae twitching like mad. At the opening of the novel, Arthur is walking in Hyde Park, dressed in the Aesthetic uniform of a checked Ulster overcoat and a magenta necktie, discussing Darwin arm in arm with his friend Andrews, who tells him, 'You don't know a pretty girl from an ugly one.' He keeps his hair in 'the style displayed in the photographs of Mr Tennyson', whose poem *In Memoriam A. H. H.* was an exploration of passionate male friendship. (In 1908, Xavier Mayne argued that *In Memoriam A. H. H.* was a poem 'exhaling elegiacly so much psychological uranism' that it amounted to 'a homosexual threnody', and considered its addressee 'perceptibly of homosexual type'.) Andrews, amused when a pen becomes entangled accidentally in his friend's Tennysonian locks, jokes, 'Hang it, Howard, what are you about? Though you are a regular Mary-Ann, I never dreamt that you wore hairpins.' The insult is a colloquial term for a rent boy, and one of its earliest printed uses.[25]

The evidence continues to accumulate: Arthur expresses the desire to read Justin McCarthy's *Miss Misanthrope* (1878), a novel about a love affair in literary and artistic circles, and one of the earliest texts of British Aestheticism. (McCarthy was a friend of Robert Ross, and on the fringes of a group of Uranian writers and artists who referred to themselves as the Cénacle.) He allies himself with the Catholic Church, which attracted converts such as John Gray and Aubrey Beardsley, and (according to Mayne) was proverbially associated with effeminacy and 'similsexual scandal'. He chats about religion with Dubois, his Aesthete brother-in-law, on a bench in the notorious cruising-ground of Leicester Square. Dubois believes that the Christian church will make way for a new social order based on a conception of 'culture' developed from the ideas of Matthew Arnold. A reader like Symonds would have taken note here: Arnold's Hellenistic assertion that 'the εύφυής is the man who tends towards sweetness and light' accrued importance within the writings of High Victorian apologists for male love – so much so that its detractors, such as Swinburne, cast aspersions about 'Platonic love, whether imbued with "sweetness and light" by philosophic sentiment, or besmeared with blood and dung by criminal lunacy'.[26] Arthur is suspicious of this prediction, and denounces Arnold as an impostor, comparing him with a notorious figure in one of the nineteenth century's most celebrated trials: the Tichborne Claimant, the subject of the longest legal proceeding in British judicial history.

This is another point to tick off the list: the jury in the Tichborne case eventually decided that the man who claimed to be Sir Roger Tichborne, the long-lost heir to an enormous fortune and a large estate in Hampshire, was in fact Arthur Orton, an uneducated butcher from Wagga Wagga. They did not reach this conclusion, however, until the trail had forced an embarrassing exposure of what the aristocracy kept in its trousers. An important detail of the case was the fact that Sir Roger Tichborne had an 'extraordinary physical defect'.[27] This, it transpired, was a freakishly shrunken penis – retracted inside his body – which the presiding judge delicately classified as 'a peculiarity of formation' throughout the trial.[28]

Although not all the physical details were released to the press, enough was made available to make speculation about Sir Roger Tichborne's genital shortcomings the subject of public gossip, particularly when the court reports revealed that the real Sir Roger had, in 1851, written a letter to his relation Lady Doughty, referring to the 'impossibility' of his marrying and enclosing a withered leaf to symbolise his condition. The fact that his mother had not put him in boys' clothes until he was approaching his teenage years was also the source of much interest. A privately printed pamphlet circulated to MPs details the 'defect' and then makes an explicit link with his childhood couture: 'We can therefore easily understand why the undoubted ROGER TICHBORNE was kept by his Mother in *Frocks* till he was between ELEVEN and TWELVE years of age, when other boys were taken out of Frocks at *Seven* years'.[29] It is not recorded whether Tichborne was enough of a Mary-Ann to have worn hairpins.

By the 1870s, most of the great pornographers of the Chartist era were dead or out of business. Although its implementation was patchy and equivocal, the Obscene Publications Act of 1856 had not helped producers of pornography to flourish. Some transferred their operations to more liberal cities such as Amsterdam – or at least printed the name of a foreign city on the frontispieces of their books – to throw the police off the scent. Edward Sellon, author of *The Ups and Downs of Life* (1867), blew his brains out in a London hotel room shortly after selling his *magnum opus* to William Dugdale. A year later, after a lifetime in and out of prison, Dugdale, the man who ushered *Intrigues and Confessions of a Ballet Girl* into the world, expired in the Clerkenwell House of Correction. A mysterious and influential friend, probably a client in high office, had managed to have Dugdale's sentences rescinded in the past; his luck ran out in 1868. Dugdale's arch-rival John Camden Hotten – who, as a youth, was smacked over the head with a book by Thomas Babington Macaulay, and went on to become a prodigious producer of books on 'chastisement' – was buried in Highgate Cemetery in 1873. Henry Hayler, who photographed his wife and his two sons in explicit poses, fled to Berlin in 1874, after the police raided his two houses in Pimlico and went away loaded up with 130,248 obscene photographs and five thousand pornographic magic-lantern slides. A new generation of smut-peddlers, however, was ready to take their place.

Leonard Smithers was chief among these. An energetic Yorkshireman, he began life as a law student and, as has already been related, ended it on his forty-sixth birthday in an empty house in Palmer's Green. Smithers was connected with an aristocratic gang of porn-bibbers headed by Richard Monckton Milnes, Lord Houghton, a prominent Yorkshire MP. (Milnes also founded the Cannibal Club, which met at Bertolini's restaurant on Leicester Square, and whose membership included Swinburne and Sir Richard Francis Burton, translator of the *Kama Sutra*.) The Milnes family home, Fryston Hall near Ferrybridge – now converted into a swish country hotel – housed a gigantic collection of pornographic books and manuscripts, many of which were supplied by Smithers and by a Parisian agent named Frederick Hankey. Hankey, the son of a governor of the Ionian Islands and an enthusiastic student of de Sade, enjoyed a life of dissipation in Paris, staging lesbian *tableaux vivants* in his apartment at 2 Rue Laffite – known to his friends as 'the clitoris of Paris'. In order to get his acquisitions through customs, he persuaded the manager of the Covent Garden Opera, Augustus Harris, to make use of an unusual ability to manipulate his spine to create a large recess between his back and his overcoat, in which books and daguerreotypes could be stowed. Harris's greatest triumph was to conceal a statue, which Swinburne described as 'a Sapphic group by [James] Pradier of two girls in the very act and one has her tongue up *où vous savez*, her head and massive hair buried, plunging, diving between the other's thighs'.[30]

Smithers's relationship with the principal Cannibals was an important element in the early part of his career. During the time of their patronage he published extracts from Burton's translation of *The Thousand and One Nights* and smutty novels with titles such as *Aglae, An Erotic Fairy Story* (1889), *The Romance of My Alcove (*1889), Gallant Confessions of a Woman of the World (1889) and *Teleny*, a purple account of an Uranian affair which may have influenced *The Picture of Dorian Gray*. The zenith of his professional life, however, came in the last five years of the nineteenth century, when he emerged as the only publisher willing to give his support to the group of writers who found themselves ostracised after the fall of Oscar Wilde. He published *The Ballad of Reading Gaol*, brought out the first printed editions of *An Ideal Husband* and *The Importance of Being Earnest*, and bought the rights to an unwritten play by Wilde, *Mr and Mrs Daventry*, more as an act of charity to its author than as a financial speculation. He launched a new magazine, *The Savoy*, which provided work for refugees from *The Yellow Book* such as Ernest

Dowson and Arthur Symons. Most significantly, perhaps, he kept
Aubrey Beardsley in commissions until the end of the artist's brief life.
(The last book produced by Smithers's company was an edition of
Beardsley's pornographic retelling of the Venus and Tannhauser story.)

Beardsley and Smithers had much in common: chronic lung disease
and an interest in drugs, smutty limericks, erotic art and sexually explicit
literature. Ernest Dowson recalled an evening dining out in Paris with the
two men, during which Beardsley, whacked out on hashish, made them all
giggle so much that he feared they would be thrown out of the restaurant.
The Beardsley-Smithers correspondence is full of filthy remarks about –
among other subjects – the ejaculations of canaries, the supposedly phallic
shape of Beardsley's teeth, the arousing potential of the lacy edging on a
Christmas card of the Virgin Mary, and a peculiar fantasy about the
gendarmes of Dieppe carrying a photograph of Beardsley's penis in order
to bring him to justice for an unpaid hotel bill. In Smithers, Beardsley
found someone who shared his intense curiosity about anything carnal
and outré. (As Xavier Mayne concluded in 1908: 'All real friendships
between men have a sexual germ.')[31] For Smithers's deluxe editions of
works such as *Lysistrata* and Pope's *The Rape of the Lock*, Beardsley
inked pictures of satyrs lolling their heads against impossibly large
members, men masturbating behind curtains, plump nudes having their
bottoms patted with a powder-puff. When Beardsley knew he was dying,
he sent Smithers a scrawled note: 'Dear Friend, I implore you to destroy
all copies of *Lysistrata* and bad drawings . . . By all that is holy *all* obscene
drawings, Aubrey Beardsley, In my death agony.' Smithers did nothing of
the sort. He continued to sell prints of these drawings – and forged copies
of Beardsley's last letter – until his peculiar and depressing end in
suburban south London in December 1907. It was a more private death
than that of most of his friends and colleagues. The poet Lionel Johnson –
a cousin of Lord Alfred Douglas who suffered from paranoid delusions
and was in the habit of knocking back two pints of whisky a day – fell off a
bar stool in the Green Dragon on Fleet Street and died two days later. The
mystic John Davidson threw himself off a Cornish cliff and was washed up
at Mousehole in a state of advanced decomposition. The author Hubert
Crackanthorpe perished in Paris in 1896; he had been living in a *ménage à*
quatre on the Avenue Kléber with his mistress, his wife and her lover.
When the lover discovered he had venereal disease, he accused Crackanthorpe's wife, who in turn blamed Crackanthorpe. The mistress went
back to her husband; Crackanthorpe drowned himself in the Seine.

Smithers was buried in an unmarked grave in the Fulham Palace Road cemetery; the plot paid for by Lord Alfred Douglas.

In the century or so that has passed since this massacre of the decadents, Beardsley's work has gone in and out of fashion, his critical stock has fluctuated and the rumours about his erotic life have accumulated: a week after his final haemorrhage in a hotel room on the French Riviera in March 1898, *The Times* was condemning Beardsley's 'morbid imagination' and his former advocate Edward Burne-Jones was railing against his association with Wilde and his 'horrid set of semi-Sodomites', dismissing Beardsley's work – especially the drawings he completed under the aegis of Smithers – as 'detestable' and 'more lustful than any I've seen'.[32]

Stephen Calloway might consider Beardsley's decision to move into Oscar Wilde's 'bachelor apartments' in St James's Place to be 'unfathomable', but in the context of the matter of this chapter, his motives seem to be perfectly in tune with this unique era in sexual history. The 1890s were the high noon of erotic ambiguity, the last moment of freedom before the system of personae and pathologies through which we have come to view our own sexualities became fixed. With his own sexual tastes made a subject of public speculation by Wilde's arrest and imprisonment, it is little wonder that Beardsley needed to reflect on the impact of these events. You can imagine him sitting in the Geneux Hotel, pondering Wilde's downfall at the scene of his crimes; reflecting on his own sexual appetites; sniffing at the linen for traces of telegraph boy; and glancing over the columns of the *Daily Mail*, wondering if things would ever change.

CHAPTER THIRTEEN

Prince Albert's Prince Albert

The religion-ruled Englishmen then dominant in the governing, directing, professional and business classes spent, there can be little doubt, far less of their time and thought on sex interests than either their continental contemporaries or their twentieth century successors; and to this saving their extraordinary surplus of energy in other spheres must reasonably in part be ascribed.

Robert Ensor, *England 1870–1914* (1990)

According to Virginia Woolf, the modern world began on a spring evening in 1908, when she and her sister Vanessa received a visit from Lytton Strachey at their flat in Gordon Square. Strachey walked into the drawing room and pointed to a stain on Vanessa Stephen's dress. 'Semen?' he inquired. It is not recorded whether his guess was correct. Woolf's account, in *Moments of Being*, is more interested in the question than the answer:

With that one word all barriers of reticence and reserve went down. A flood of the sacred fluid seemed to overwhelm us. Sex permeated our conversation. The word bugger was never far from our lips. We discussed copulation with the same excitement and openness that we had discussed the nature of good ... It was, I think, a great advance in civilization.[1]

For this axis of the Bloomsbury Group, it was as if a bout of upper middle-class sex talk in WC1 had forced the Victorians to relinquish their grip on the present and recede back into history, genuinely afraid of Virginia Woolf.

There is an ironic coda to this story. As the career of William Stead demonstrates, the details of the sex lives of many prominent Victorian figures were subject to public exposure during their lifetime. The members of the Bloomsbury Group, however, were extraordinarily successful in their attempts to suppress reports of their own carnal

18 Erotic postcard, *c.*1890 (courtesy Mark Lee Rotenberg,
www.vintagenudephotos.com)

exploits. 'It is ironic', notes Gertrude Himmelfarb, 'that people who prided themselves on their honesty and candor, especially in regard to their much-vaunted "personal affections" – in contrast, as they thought, to Victorian hypocrisy and duplicity – should have succeeded for so long in concealing the truth about those personal affections.'[2] Himmelfarb has tracked the progress of these strategies of suppression, observing that the five volumes of autobiography published by Leonard Woolf in the 1960s remained silent on the extent of Bloomsbury partner-swapping; that Roy Harrod's 1951 biography of John Maynard Keynes chose not to mention its subject's homosexuality; that James Strachey refused to grant access to his brother's private papers until thirty years after he was dead, then raised loud objections to the ways in which they were used; that Quentin Bell, the son of Clive and Vanessa Bell, published an account of the Bloomsbury set – in 1968 – in which he declared that he 'suppressed a good deal that I know about and much more about what I can guess.'[3] Most incongruously of all, Woolf's story of how she and Strachey stormed the barricades of Victorian reticence remained unpublished until 1976.

Stephen Marcus's *The Other Victorians* used *My Secret Life* and other pornographic texts to take issue with the stereotype of Victorian prudishness, but absorbed its own argument into an equally limited paradigm, which suggested that aspects of the Victorians' sex lives which could not be accommodated within the institution of monogamous marriage were part of some clandestine nightscape; an underworld into which the Victorians policed every subversive element. Most subsequent treatments of Victorian sexuality have been written with reference to this duality, a model of sexual repression adapted from the pages of Freud. Ronald Pearsall's *The Worm in the Bud* (1969) argued that 'when sex ceased to be talked about openly it went underground. No society has been so eager to welcome pornography and indecent engravings as the Victorian.'[4] Fraser Harrison's *The Dark Angel* (1977) asserted that 'Victorian man could only contemplate sex through a fog of guilt and anxiety.'[5] Other studies which aimed to produce more sophisticated readings subtly reinforced these views. The first volume of Michel Foucault's *History of Sexuality* (1976) took an anti-Freudian tack, regarding the appearance of a massive body of sexually-orientated texts in nineteenth-century Britain as the product of 'the great process of transforming sex into discourse'. For Foucault, Walter was no 'fugitive from a "Victorianism" that would have compelled him into silence', but a 'representative of a plurisecular injunction to talk about sex.'[6] Rather than seeing this textual explosion as evidence of widespread rational inquiry into these subjects, other researchers interpreted it as another twist of pathology. Sex was put into discourse in order that it might be processed, regulated and controlled. A generation of cultural historians and literary critics based their work upon this pattern. There are some British academics who have made entire careers out of reading aloud misogynist passages from Victorian medical texts in a sarcastic voice. Their work has recruited a police force of Victorian personalities, identified as articulating that legislating power – William Acton, Isaac Baker Brown, Max Nordau, Sarah Stickney Ellis – and a concomitant set of dissidents – Oscar Wilde, Josephine Butler, Emily Brontë, Mary Elizabeth Braddon – who worked to undermine it. The latter receive Whiggish plaudits, the former genteel punishment beatings, and in the pages of academic works continue to pursue each other like chorus members from *The Pirates of Penzance*.

Gayle Rubin's influential essay 'Thinking Sex: Notes for a Radical Theory of the Politics of Sexuality' (1993) is a good example of the type. She begins with an old cliché, a description of hot irons being applied to the vagina of a young female patient, and follows it up with a quasi-pornographic litany of other abuses: 'to protect the young from premature arousal, parents tied children down at night so they would not touch themselves; doctors excised the clitorises of onanistic little girls.'[7] The rhetorical value is strong, but the historical accuracy is doubtful. The clitoridectomy has been enshrined as representative practice by many modern commentators, but it is a practice drawn from the cranky margins of Victorian medical culture. The most vocal British advocate of the therapy was Isaac Baker Brown, head of a private clinic called the London Surgical Home. He was widely condemned for his advocacy of the practice and eventually expelled from the London Obstetrical Society – hardly evidence for widespread subscription to his views. Moreover, it is rarely volunteered that the twentieth century can offer its own examples of this procedure. For instance, editions of Luther Emmett Holt's *Diseases of Infancy and Childhood* continued to discuss clitoridectomy as a therapeutic option in cases of 'vulvovaginitis' until 1936. To prevent masturbation in young infants, Holt argued, 'much may be accomplished by mechanical restraint. The kind of restraint which is necessary will depend upon the manner of masturbating. If by the hands, they should be tied during sleep, so that the child cannot reach the genitals. If by thigh-friction, the thigh should be separated by tying one to either side of the crib; in inveterate cases a double side-splint, such as is used in fractures of the femur, may be applied.'[8] Holt's work was not a quack pamphlet, but the standard American textbook on paediatrics until the 1950s.

Despite such evidence, the Victorians are required to play the villains in most histories of sexuality. Rubin characterises the nineteenth century as an era in which 'there were educational and political campaigns to encourage chastity, to eliminate prostitution, and to discourage masturbation, especially among the young. Morality crusaders attacked obscene literature, nude paintings, music halls, abortion, birth control information, and public dancing.' The aim was 'the consolidation of Victorian morality, and its apparatus of social, medical, and legal enforcement'.[9] Sex was a terrifying chaos, this argument suggests, to which the Victorians attempted to bring order – a spectre which they were determined to exorcise. Fraser Harrison contends that this was a function of the chilly cruelty of economic exploitation:

> In their eagerness to exploit to the full the advantages bequeathed by the industrial revolution, the bourgeoisie created a world of abject misery for the proletariat on whose labour they relied. By depriving working people of the means to clothe, feed, and house themselves, they also denied them their sexuality. By a just irony, the same eagerness caused them to institute a cripplingly harsh sexual code which prevented them, in their turn, from enjoying all but the most sterile and distorted forms of sexual relationship.[10]

The current edition of the *Encyclopaedia Britannica* is equally enamoured of the repressive hypothesis: 'Partly by taking thought and partly by instinct, they perceived that the drive to revolution and the sexual urge were somehow linked. Therefore they repressed sexuality; that is, repressed it in themselves and their literature, while containing it within specified limits in society.'[11] 'Sex', insists Christopher Wood's *Victorian Panorama* (1976) 'was the Victorian bogey.'[12]

It is hard to reconcile the image of a general climate of fear and reticence suggested by these accounts of nineteenth-century sexual attitudes with the bewildering multiplicity of opinions and ideas offered by the library of sex-related texts bequeathed to us by the Victorians. As has already been indicated, the body of 'top-shelf' publications (the phrase was already in use towards the end of the period) was extensive. Popular pornographic texts which could be procured from the booksellers of Holywell Street included *The Romance of Chastisement* (1866), *The Amatory Experiences of a Surgeon* (1881) and *Randiana* (1884). More practical information on sexual subjects could be found in standard household manuals, jostling with recipes for devilled kidneys and tips on how to repair cracked varnish. Henry Hartshorne's *Household Cyclopedia* (1881), for instance, assures readers suffering from erection problems due to fear, excess of passion, or want of confidence at the moment of coition that 'remedies ... must be sought for in calming excessive agitation and acquiring, by habits of intimacy, that confidence they are sure to produce.'[13] There is something utterly humanising about the recommendation: it conjures up the image of a nineteenth-century couple whose sexual problems are not caused by some crippling neurosis imposed upon them by their culture, but a pair of halting, nervous lovers getting to know each other in bed.

Less attractive advice was supplied in pamphlets produced by unlicensed quacks who attempted to sell unlikely cures for such conditions, incorporating them into bogus pathologies calculated to terrify the sufferer. 'It is a familiar physiological fact', boomed Alfred Field Henery in *Manly Vigour; the art of preserving, improving, and recovering it* (1861), 'that total impotence or incapacity ... is not only the constant accompaniment but constant cause of mania and insanity.'[14] It is easy to find eccentric medical texts giving detailed information on how to cure male masturbation by, say, slipping spiked rings on to the penis, or a sheath with an electric sensor that rang an alarm bell if the wearer experienced arousal during sleep. It is much less easy – virtually impossible, in fact – to find accounts of these therapies being put into action.

Beyond these quack pamphlets, more rational variations on the genre, such as the *Ladies' Manual of Practical Hydropathy* (c. 1880) issued by the proprietor of a clinic in Matlock, Derbyshire, warned their readers against exploitation by dishonest practitioners – the type who, according to Caroline Smedley, 'almost immediately informs them that a private examination is necessary, and then the unfortunate victim passes through all the "speculum" horrors'.[15] The Smedleys' hydropathic centre remained in operation as a spa until the 1950s, when the building was converted for office use by Derbyshire County Council. Here, in rooms where council employees now tap away at keyboards under the strip-lights, Victorian women recovered from miscarriages, received treatment for gynaecological conditions and munched on charcoal biscuits while waiting for a bath. The Smedleys were sufficiently popular for the London Stereoscope Company to depict them in a series of souvenir photographs, but they have received much less critical attention than Isaac Baker Brown.

The highly visible and much-debated world of nineteenth-century prostitution ensured that silence on sexual subjects was an impossibility. Paul Verlaine entertained happy memories of the women to be found in the bars at the Alhambra Theatre, from whom he claimed to have contracted syphilis during 1871, when he was in London as press spokesperson for the Paris Commune. William Gladstone toured the streets of nocturnal London, offering rehabilitation and cups of tea to women working the pavements of the Haymarket and Strand. Anatomical museums such as Dr Kahn's establishment just off the Haymarket (London's most thickly populated cruising ground) allowed the men who used prostitutes to gaze upon the possible consequences of their promiscuity in waxwork form. A female equivalent, Mme Caplin's on Berners Street, provided a similar service for women. In the 1860s, the debate raging around the Contagious Diseases Acts put extra-marital sex and the spread of venereal infection into the leader columns of every British newspaper. The Acts obliged women whom the authorities believed to be prostitutes to undergo compulsory health checks, in an attempt to reduce the number of cases of clap in naval and garrison towns, which had been increasing steadily since the 1820s. In many cases, the legislation was clearly used as a pretext for cruelty and abuse, but many prostitutes welcomed it as recognition of the legitimacy of their work. Had the Acts not been repealed in 1886, they might have become the basis for a licensed system of prostitution in Britain.

Accurate estimates of how many people sold their bodies during this period are notoriously impossible to formulate. As Michael Mason has shown, the total often revealed more about the prejudices of the enumerator than about any demographic reality. Several French commentators of the 1860s put the London total at 22,000; the figures offered by the Metropolitan Police in the same period hovered between 5,500 and 9,500. How such statistics compare with the extent of prostitution in twenty-first-century London is difficult to say – especially now that sex workers have, for the most part, moved off the pavements, conduct their business with mobile phones and e-mail, and even attract new clients by garnering good reviews on a number of prostitution-themed websites. In 1999, the Metropolitan Police investigated seventy-five brothels in Soho and calculated that they had a combined monthly turnover of £1 million, with each woman earning £350 a day on average. In 1994, an eight-week campaign to remove prostitutes' cards from pay phones in Westminster garnered more than one million cards.

There has been a tendency to see the history of Victorian extra-marital sex as a history of prostitution – an effect of the prominence of the profession in judicial and parliamentary records, and of the emphasis upon London's sexual economy in *My Secret Life*, the nineteenth century's most compendious erotic text. The eleven volumes of Walter's testimony cast a long shadow over most considerations of Victorian sexual mores. Cultural historians from Marcus through Foucault to Mason have certainly considered that this epic of (to use its author's favourite expressions) firkytoodling, lying in state, gamahuching and visits to the dumpling-shop represents a form of documentary truth. Jonathan Gathorne-Hardy, for example, states that '*My Secret Life* is not only almost certainly genuine, which is to say it is a work of autobiography and not of pornography, it is also extremely honest.'[16] Ian Gibson's biography of its probable author Henry Spencer Ashbee, however, detects the mediated remains of earlier journalistic and sociological accounts of prostitution, whose presence undermines the book's claim to bear 'the impress of truth on every page'.[17] The facts of Ashbee's life are rather less lurid than those of Walter's. He was the son of the manager of a gunpowder factory in Hounslow; he married into a Jewish family of textile exporters; he travelled in the Far East, Europe and America; he hated his artsy-craftsy son Charles, and cut him from his will; his wife walked out on him in 1891, possibly as a response to this antagonism. We must, I think, treat Walter's narrative of sex with over a thousand prostitutes as a combination of record and fantasy. Like modern pornography, it offers a repertoire of erotic situations that have a problematic relationship with genuine sexual practice. Certainly, it would be a great mistake to regard Walter's whoring activities as typical behaviour among middle-class Victorian men.

After all, there were many places to which Victorians could go to find casual partners. The Cremorne, for instance, a pleasure garden on the Chelsea embankment, was between 1846 and 1877 one of London's busiest cruising grounds. It occupied the squarish plot of land on the

Chelsea Embankment now taken up by housing between the King's Road and Lots Road. Walk west from Battersea Bridge down the length of Cheyne Walk, and you can see the sorry little plot of bedding plants and brickwork, marooned on the wrong side of the road, that now keeps its name alive. The original Cremorne, however, was one of the most popular public attractions of the Victorian mid-century, and operated in much the same way as a modern theme park or suburban leisure complex. Punters would pay the shilling admission fee for access to a variety of entertainments. Families might go to see puppet shows and a balloon ascent, steal a few strikes in the American Bowling Saloon and conclude with a drink at the lemonade stalls. Consenting adults would go to drink champagne under the gaslights and the arbours, polka around the dancing platform in the south-west corner (in the centre of which an orchestra played on an elaborate Chinoiserie bandstand) and pop back home with each other. From 1862, patrons were able to telegraph in advance to reserve advance seats in the booths around the dance floor. Music-hall entertainers such as Harry Wall belted out numbers which alluded to the sexual, social and narcotic pleasures of the Cremorne, and local residents complained about noisy drunks who filled the streets at kicking-out time, claiming that there were many prostitutes among their number. When, however, William Acton was despatched to report upon prostitution in the Cremorne, he could detect no evidence of soliciting, just a crowd of young people drinking and socialising.

The railway system, with its ranks of closed compartments, also offered exciting – and sometimes dangerous – possibilities for casual encounters. The railway companies ensured that the ticket-pricing regime reinscribed the structure of British society upon the train itself, but that did not prevent passengers from cruising each other within their own compartments. The existence of ladies-only carriages suggests that impropriety occurred in the unsegregated parts of the train – and railway porters, like telegraph boys, had a reputation for obliging gentleman travellers on the production of a silver shilling. Edward Carpenter met his long-term boyfriend, George Merrill, in a railway carriage in 1891. In fiction, Everard Barfoot, the anti-hero of George Gissing's *The Odd Women* (1893), is picked up by a woman on the train to London:

> I saw her at Upchurch Station, but we didn't speak, and I got into a smoking carriage. We had to change at Oxford, and there, as I walked about the platform, Amy put herself in my way, so that I was

obliged to begin talking with her ... At all events, Amy managed to get me into the same carriage with herself, and on the way to London we were alone. You foresee the end of it. At Paddington Station the girl and I went off together.[18]

Walter provides a good example of the kind of sexual encounter that must have taken place in these well-cushioned interstices between the public and private spheres. In a packed first-class carriage, he presses his legs surreptitiously against those of a female travelling companion, and when all the other passengers have disembarked, attempts to persuade her to have sex with him. ('I now tried to feel her notch, she resisted but laughing always.')[19] The woman declines to go farther than such fondling, but agrees to reconvene in a quiet lane near to her suburban home.

Such encounters sometimes led to violence. Colonel Valentine Baker of the 10th Hussars found himself accused of rape when, on 17 June 1875, he pressed his attentions on a young governess, Rebecca Dickinson, on the train from Portsmouth to London. Baker engaged Dickinson in some small talk in the early stages of the journey, and as the train progressed from Liphook towards Woking, started to make sexual advances. Whatever happened next produced screaming and an attempt to quit the carriage while it was still in motion. The Colonel was arrested at Waterloo, and hauled up before Croydon Assizes on 2 August – from where he was taken the Horsemonger Lane jail. The lurid pornographic story *Raped on the Railway: a True Story of a Lady who was first Ravished and then Flagellated on the Scotch Express*, reprinted throughout the 1890s, may owe a debt to this incident.

Within marriage, there was also plenty of scope for permutation. Trawl through the biographies of Victorian worthies, and the monogamous marital relationships which have been used to characterise the age begin to seem minority pursuits, like batik or well dressing. Wilkie Collins, for instance, divided his affections between two women, Caroline Graves and Martha Rudd, had children with the latter and acted as a surrogate father to the daughter of the former. Edward Carpenter lived in a *ménage à trois* with Albert Fearnehough and his wife, tending their Sheffield vegetable plot in open-toed sandals. Mary Ann Evans lived, unmarried, with her partner George Lewes; he was unable to divorce his wife, having given up his rights when he refused to condemn her affair with his best friend, Thornton Hunt. Charles Reade cohabited with a widowed actress, Laura Seymour, and seems to have refrained from marrying her simply in order to preserve his stipend from Magdalen College Oxford, which only paid out on condition of celibacy. John Stuart Mill and Harriet Taylor cohabited for a decade before the latter's husband died, leaving them free to legitimise their union. Mary Elizabeth Braddon cohabited with and had children by her partner, the publisher James Maxwell, while his first wife was living in Ireland. Ouida spent much of her spare time flirting with guardsmen in a series of grand hotel suites. Rhoda Broughton and Marie Corelli enjoyed intense relationships with female companions. And beyond the celebrity list, census records show that large numbers of working-class men and women took a very equivocal and pragmatic attitude to marriage and cohabitation, forming alliances that were much more influenced by economics than the demands of propriety. Clearly the prescriptive power of such ideas was weak enough to be resisted by vast numbers of Victorians.

However, the need to reassure ourselves that the Victorians were worse at sex than we are has generated a repertoire of popular myths about what they got up to in bed. That old story about John Ruskin's Venetian honeymoon, for example, is still repeated as fact in sources as diverse as Slovene critical theory and Canadian cinema.[20] Ruskin, it goes, having only seen marble representations of the naked female form, was unaware that women have pubic hair. On his wedding night, therefore, he was totally unprepared for the exuberant thatch lurking in his wife's cami-knickers. The story has been told and retold by generations of under-graduates. I first heard it from a PhD student working on Ruskin – who added details about how the author of *The Stones of Venice* had lifted Effie Gray's crinoline, shrieked in horror, pelted from the hotel and skittered across the Bridge of Sighs, white as a starched bed sheet. (Alex Chapple's film *The Passion of John Ruskin* has its hero lecturing his students in front of a classical statue, praising its 'delta . . . as bald as a hard-boiled egg.')[21]

This theory was first suggested in 1965, in a popular biography of the Ruskins by Mary Lutyens. It is extrapolated from a statement Ruskin wrote in 1854, two days after Effie walked out on him: 'Her person was not formed to excite passion,' he claimed. 'On the contrary, there were certain circumstances in her person which completely checked it.'[22] Lutyens speculated:

John must have been familiar with the female nude from his study of pictures. It is probable, though, that Effie was the only naked woman he ever saw. In what way could her body have been different from the one he imagined? In only one particular, it seems: the female nudes he saw in galleries – statues as well as pictures – were either discreetly veiled or depicted as children. For a man as sensitive as he it may well have been a lasting shock to discover the adult reality. Had he seen other women he would have realised that the unattractive circumstances in Effie's person were common to them all; in his ignorance he believed her to be uniquely disfigured.[23]

Lutyens did not know, it seems, that Ruskin had written to his parents, with a frankness which now seems creepy, that he had seen plenty of pictures of 'naked bawds' in his undergraduate days. But the sage's most recent biographers still seem stuck on vaginophobic possibilities – 'he was referring perhaps', muses John Batchelor, 'to menstrual flow or a smell he found unpleasant' – perhaps because the characterisation of the most Victorian of all Victorians as a sexual ignoramus satisfies a desire to see evidence of broader erotic dysfunction in Victorian culture.[24]

It is a narrative of sexual ignorance that seems at odds with the embarrassingly explicit public debate about the progress of the marriage that took place when, as has already been noted, Gray secured an annulment on the grounds of 'incurable impotency'. Given these circumstances, it seems plausible that Ruskin's remarks about her 'person' were simply the bitchy defamations of a man whose sexual inadequacy had become a subject of public gossip. 'All London has of course been in arms over the affair,' enthused John Everett Millais, who was soon to fulfil the role of which Ruskin was judged incapable.[25] As Effie's beauty was regularly remarked upon, the former husband's jibe would only have worked if it came in the form of an innuendo about a part of her body not on public show. There were many other reasons why he might have developed a distaste for his new wife. It can't have helped, for instance, that she had been born in the same room in which his grandfather, John Thomas Ruskin, had cut his throat. He was unimpressed with her talents as an amanuensis. And she may just have been a really irritating person. When Edward Lear dined with Gray, then Mrs Millais, years after the scandal, he recorded in his diary: 'The dinner was very good; but the 2 hours I passed there, a bore. Mrs R's – I mean Mrs M's – cold Scotch accent, her vulgar queries . . . her pity of bachelors – "it's just so melancholy!" – (as if one half of her 2 matrimonial ventures

in life turned out so happily!) – & her drawling stoniness disgusted me . . .
so that I don't care ever to see her again.'[26]

The stories which continue to circulate about the Ruskin marriage date
back to 1965, but other stories are of even more recent origin. The
assertion, for instance, that Prince Albert wore a ring through his penis –
a genital piercing to which his name is now irremediably conjoined. 'It
was called a "dressing ring",' insists Pauline Clarke's piercing manual
The Eye of the Needle (1994), 'originally used to secure the penis to either
side of the pant leg, thus minimising any show of natural endowment at a
time when the fashion was for extremely tight fitting, crutch binding
britches. Legend has it that Prince Albert wore such a ring to retract his
foreskin.'[27] It might appeal to our desire for the Victorians to be the
repositories of kinky secrets, but despite what your local backstreet
septum-splicer might tell you, there is no evidence of its truth. It seems to
have been made up in the 1970s by Douglas Malloy, an eccentric
Californian millionaire who, after having made his fortune as one of
the founders of the Muzak Corporation, went on to open a chain of
piercing parlours in the late 1960s. A pioneer in this field, he attempted to
dignify his then rather disreputable profession with historical precedent,
concocting a historiography of body jewellery in a series of articles for
Piercing World magazine. Roman centurions, he asserted, used nipple-
rings to secure their capes. (Anyone with the relevant adornment will tell
you that this would simply have left a trail of bloodied areolae all over
Hadrian's Wall.) The Cyprian Society, he claimed, was a Jewish men's
organisation whose members bore a genital piercing called a 'dydoe',
which was claimed to return the sensitivity to the penis lost after
circumcision. (No evidence for the existence of such a group has ever
been produced.) As for the Prince Albert, Malloy declared, 'Legend has it
that Prince Albert wore such a ring to retract his foreskin and thus keep
his member sweet-smelling so as not to offend the Queen,' but
'minimizing a man's natural endowment' when wearing 'crotch-binding
trousers' was the principal aim.[28]

If Albert's pants were so tight that he felt he was exposing himself in
public, it is doubtful whether slotting a gold ring through his penis would
really have helped to make his genitals *less* conspicuous. And what else, I
wonder, are tight pants for, if not to emphasise 'natural endowment'?
Victoria – who on her first romantic outing with Albert enthused about
'that beautiful figure of his' – may well have come to the same conclusion.
After getting lost with him in the countryside around Windsor one night

in October 1839, she retired to her room and wrote in her journal, 'It was with some emotion that I beheld Albert – who is *beautiful*.'[29]

It is highly likely that the piercing bears the Prince Consort's name because of its resemblance to a watch chain, a fashion accessory that he imported – like the Christmas tree hung with big shiny baubles – from his native Germany. The two meanings survive to this day. Ask for a Prince Albert in an antique jewellers on Hatton Garden, and you will be given a chain designed to secure a fob watch in place by fastening it through a vest or waistcoat button hole. Ask for a Prince Albert in a Soho fetish store, and – should you happen to have one – the proprietor will stick a needle through your urethra and through the skin of your glans.

In twenty-first-century Soho, where some of the most skilful practitioners of the Prince Albert have their workshops, a sex-focused culture much influenced by the Victorian past is still visible. The licensing laws and the drug dealing would have caused our nineteenth-century ancestors some puzzlement, but they would recognise the dayglo cards pinned to the architraves of doorways advertising the services of the first-floor tenants. This is Walter's territory. His creator, Henry Spencer Ashbee, knew these streets and alleyways; may even have sweated his way to orgasm in some of the flats still used today for such purposes. Although most of his two thousand-odd sexual encounters were probably no more than fantasy, some of these anecdotes that read more honestly than others.

At the beginning of *My Secret Life*, Walter is attempting to secure the services of two well-to-do French prostitutes who live in a square near Oxford Street. Camille and Louise are sisters; Walter cannot decide which of them he likes the best, and is attempting to resolve whether to put one of them on a retainer. He walks with Camille in the square, discussing the arrangements, then goes to the front door of their house to meet Louise. 'She kissed and hugged me in the passage, a minute afterwards she was on my knee and grasping my prick, my fingers were on her cunt, our lips together; in another with tongues lapping together I was up her; in two or three minutes we were quiet.'[30] After this encounter, Walter find himself musing, 'I should so like to experience the feeling a woman has as she sits and talks with her cunt full of sperm, does it feel so very pleasant sitting so?'[31] There is no record as to whether Lytton Strachey wondered the same thing of Vanessa Stephen, but there would be a nice irony in it if he had. Walter gives the location of Camille and Louise's lodgings as G**d*n Sq***. This is Golden Square, not

Gordon Square, but the asterisks make the point: the words of the address are the only ones about which Walter is willing to be coy. Everything else – the most savage desires, the most queasy biological details, the most searching descriptions of naked human bodies slapping together – is there in black and white on the page. If Ashbee is the author of these words, he probably wrote them in the 1880s in his study at 53 Bedford Square, only nine doors away from the address at which, in the following century, Lady Ottoline Morrell would hold extravagant parties for Woolf, Strachey, Duncan Grant and their Bloomsbury Group friends. If 'all barriers of reticence and reserve went down' with the utterance of the one word 'semen' in the spring of 1908, what exactly was happening in a similar flat on the other side of Oxford Street, several decades earlier?

Liberating the Victorians

> I know that there are many historians, or at least writers on
> historical subjects, who still think it necessary to apply moral
> judgements to history, and who distribute their praise or blame
> with the solemn complacency of a successful schoolmaster.
>
> Oscar Wilde, *Pen, Pencil and Poison* (1889)

There are places where the Victorian past will rush to meet you. The
ruins of the Crystal Palace at Sydenham, where the Vegetarian Society
held its annual meetings, where the first English game of baseball was
played and the first lick of asbestos paint was applied, where the Sacred
Harmonic Society performed Haydn's *Creation* with two hundred violas
and violins, ninety violoncellos and double basses and 2,500 voices, and
where Queen Emma of the Sandwich Islands, General Tom Thumb and
Tsar Alexander II strolled past rows of exhibits. The car park behind the
video shop in Rugeley, where you can gaze up at the window of William
Palmer's bedroom, in which he and his wife slept soundly before he
killed her. And Soho – Soho above all. At night, Old Compton Street and
Rupert Street, Wardour Street and Greek Street are luminous with a
sense of the 1890s. The pavements carry a mixture of media darlings,
fashion victims, rent boys, pimps and shiftless ne'er-do-wells. The
homeless wait hopefully outside the theatres. Knives and forks clatter
in Kettner's, where Wilde feasted with the 'panthers' who were used to
bring him down: Soho characters such as Alfred Taylor (a brothel-keeper
who was sentenced with Wilde at his trial), Sidney Mavor (a prostitute
who later became a Church of England priest) and Maurice Schwabe (a
nephew of the then Solicitor-General). Sitting in its shabby-genteel
dining room, it's hard not to speculate what Wilde would think if he
were suddenly to return to his usual table. He would miss the pink
lampshades and note the poor state of the paintwork. He would have to
content himself with feasting on pasta. But around the corner in Old
Compton Street, he would still find plenty of teenage escorts and lawyers'
sons waiting to be cruised. He would find noodle bars done out in his

favourite kind of Japonaiserie, absinthe on sale at the bars, and glammed-up wannabes trolling down the middle of the road, talking loudly about themselves. If he walked farther south, however, past the Palace Theatre (where *Salome* with Sarah Bernhardt didn't quite happen), past Lisle Street (where Jack Saul, the most celebrated male prostitute of the 1880s, had his lodgings) and over St Martin's Lane to Charing Cross, he would – were he not dead already – get the shock of his life.

Here, within sight of the martyrs' memorial, sits Maggi Hambling's sculpture *A Conversation with Oscar Wilde*, depicting the playwright emerging from his sarcophagus, fag in hand, ready to begin gossiping. I attended its unveiling in November 1998, jostling in the crowd of public servants, literary types, B-list celebrities and hacks who had assembled to do homage to a writer whose name could not easily be mentioned in public for the best part of the twentieth century. (E. M. Forster's *Maurice*, for instance, describes himself as one of the 'unspeakables of the Oscar Wilde sort.')[1] The actors Nigel Hawthorne and Judi Dench played a short scene from *A Woman of No Importance*, the culture secretary Chris Smith announced that it was fitting that there was at last a memorial to Wilde 'on the fringes of London's Theatreland' and members of the crowd – former Conservative ministers, a gaggle of critics and an actress from *Coronation Street* – applauded politely. Stephen Fry, who played the title role in Brian Gilbert's biopic *Wilde*, talked gently to gathered reporters about how he knew many gay Tory MPs who were afraid to come out, because it would break their mother's heart. The journalist Matthew Parris – who had his wrists slapped by the BBC for alluding to the homosexuality of the Labour minister Peter Mandelson during a news programme – hovered on the sidelines, as far away from Chris Smith as possible. The jazz singer George Melly, in a strange parody of Aesthetic gear (canary yellow fedora, black pinstripe suit and purple Tellytubby badge) signed autographs for ladies of a certain age. As Merlin Holland, Wilde's grandson, suggested to Channel Four News later that same day, some of the people most eager to sweet-talk him at this event were the very types who sent his grandfather to Reading Gaol. Only a few hours later, Nigel Hawthorne was silenced during a live BBC broadcast because he had made the mistake of suggesting that Wilde's situation was 'not a million miles away' from that of Peter Mandelson. For the course of the day, liberal Britain schmoozed the carcass of Oscar Wilde, and as the celebrations continued, its conservative counterpart attempted to stamp on the coffin lid.

1. SWITCH ROOM OF A CENTRAL OFFICE WORKED BY SLIPPER BOARD SYSTEM.—2. SWITCH ROOM OF A CENTRAL OFFICE WORKED BY PEG BOARD SYST
TELEPHONE FROM THE HOUSE
THE TELEPHONE

19 The Telephone Exchange in London (*The Graphic*, 1883)

'His behaviour often hovered dangerously close to being that of a paedophile,' snorted the *Daily Telegraph*, and these assertions were quoted gleefully on the website of the far-right British National Party.[2]

Merlin Holland's essay 'Biography and The Art of Lying' (1997) illustrates how the memory of his grandfather has been appropriated by charting the accumulation of myths around one well-known incident in the Wilde life story: the playwright's wobbly moment outside Swan and Edgar's department store. Wilde scholars will know it from Richard Ellmann's *Oscar Wilde* (1987), which describes how its subject was struck by an overwhelming sense of dread as he emerged into the street from the shop and caught sight of 'the painted boys on the pavement'.[3] The story dates back to 1930 and Ada Leverson, who probably heard it from Wilde's close friend Reggie Turner. In Leverson's version, 'a curious, very young, but hard-eyed creature appeared, looked at him, gave a sort of laugh, and passed on. He felt, he said, "as if an icy hand had clutched at his heart". He had a sudden presentiment. He saw a vision of folly, misery and ruin.'[4] The sex of this 'creature' remains unstated: Hesketh Pearson's 1946 biography of Wilde assumes it to be a woman, Stanley Weintraub's 1965 biography of Turner, however transfers the event inside Swan and Edgar and reinvents the 'creature' as a gang of young male shop assistants. Richard Ellmann returns to the pavement in front of the shop, and decisively envisages the passer-by as a gang of rouged renters. Brian Gilbert's film, the script for which was based on Ellmann's biography, depicts a group of unpainted male prostitutes lolling against some railings. Scouting for a cab, Stephen Fry's Wilde makes eye contact with one of their number. 'Looking for someone?' asks the lad (helpfully identified as 'Rent Boy' in the closing credits). Fry stares helplessly across the street. His expression is unreadable. Is he mortified? Aroused? Confused? *Wilde the Novel* (1997) – a prose-fiction adaptation of Gilbert's script by Stefan Rudnicki – helps to clarify the moment:

> Oscar wanted to turn away, to ignore the lad, but the handsome rentboy looked at him so knowingly, so openly, that Oscar for a moment couldn't so much as move ... The easy camaraderie he had always enjoyed with younger men was an admitted fact, but there was something happening here that did not fit the mould Oscar sought.
>
> Before his eye passed a panorama of destruction. He saw the

edifice of his life, which he had so carefully raised, crack and split and crumble, only to expose another image behind it: this raised eyebrow, this knowing face, this mere rentboy. Impossible.[5]

In the telling and retelling, a vague premonition has become a terror-struck homosexual awakening. An edition of the BBC arts programme *Omnibus* transmitted to coincide with the opening of Gilbert's film went even further, claiming that Wilde 'caught a glimpse of the rentboys – the boy prostitutes – leaning against the railings of Piccadilly ... It was as though he knew he'd been hooked into the world of homosexual prostitution.' We even got to see a shot of the railings.

Obliging as a late-Victorian telegraph boy, Oscar Wilde will be anything you want him to be: Irish nationalist, postmodernist, socialist, socialite, pedagogue, paedophile, playwright, major-minor writer, a saint iconised on bookmarks, notelettes, calendars, T-shirts and fridge magnets. Most of all, he is a locus for our anti-Victorianism. In the press notes for Gilbert's film, Stephen Fry applauded Wilde's epigrams as 'reversals of Victorian platitudes'. The back cover blurb for an anthology of quotations, *Nothing ... Except My Genius* (1987), described Wilde as 'lampooning the starchy morality of Victorian society'.[6] Fry's preface asserts that Wilde's 'imprisonment allowed late-Victorian England to roll up into a sack the work he had done and hurl it like a poxed odalisque into the Bosphorus ... A hundred years later it is Victorian life that is disgraced in our eyes, and Wilde now stands as the Crown Prince of Bohemia.'[7] In the introduction to his play *St Oscar* (1989), Terry Eagleton celebrated Wilde as 'a remorseless debunker of the high-toned gravitas of Victorian England'.[8] Oscar Wilde, the honorary Modern: too ironic, too desiring, too like us to be considered a *bona fide* Victorian.

Just as Wilde has been conscripted into the cause of post-war liberalism, those other Victorians – the ones who didn't walk down Piccadilly with a lily in their hand – have been mobilised to fight the battles of the right. The nineteenth century has become a rich source of rhetoric for the enemies of the left, and those in the centre attempting to resist the ideological polarities that dominated the twentieth century. In 1983, Margaret Thatcher famously declared her allegiance to the works of Samuel Smiles, appealing to a spirit of self-discipline that she believed had been erased by the welfare state. In 1996, Tony Blair described himself as a Christian Socialist, in order to create a continuity between

New Labour and a progressive political tradition that predated the formation of his own party. In the wake of these remarks, commentators at both ends of the political spectrum suggested that, in the post-Cold War world, British politics was in the process of assuming an explicitly Victorian form, reorientating itself around a new liberal consensus. The debate has been taking place on both sides of the Atlantic. In the United States, the right has looked to the Victorians for justification and inspiration. Taking his cue from Gertrude Himmelfarb's nostalgic celebration of Victorian self-reliance, *The Demoralization of Society* (1995), the former speaker of the House of Representatives, Newt Gingrich, celebrated the 'moral leadership' of the Victorians, their willingness 'to look at people in the face and say, "You should be ashamed when you get drunk in public; you ought to be ashamed if you're a drug addict." '[9] Himmelfarb backed him in these assertions: 'The Victorians were, candidly and proudly, "moralists". In recent years that has almost become a term of derision. Yet contemplating our own society, we may be prepared to take a more favorable view of Victorian moralism.'[10] Applying these ideas to his doomy brand of speculative demography, Charles Murray has predicted a western world divided into a restive underclass ('new rabble') and an economically and morally self-sufficient overclass ('the new Victorians'), which he regards as 'an optimistic forecast for those who share in it'.[11]

This attitude to the Victorians is a form of sentimentality: the expression of a desire to go back to the past, to return to a world uncomplicated by welfare, feminism, multiculturalism. In Britain, it has merged with a less fundamentalist attitude to the past, a conservative nostalgia visible on the streets in the form of faux-Victorian litter bins and lamp posts, and legible on the supermarket shelves, where tokens of the Victorian age are used to confer a bogus sense of tradition upon mass-produced food products. Factory lines such as Bendick's Victorian Mints and Brontë Biscuits use retro packaging to invoke an attractive home-made quality that has no connection with the mechanical processes which are truly responsible for their existence. Mrs Beeton's Cakes, for example, uses a famous Victorian name to suggest reassuring domesticity, when in fact these E-number-stuffed confections are constructed on an industrial estate on the outskirts of Cardiff. ('Our mission [is] to bring interest to the cake fixture,' snaps the rather less fanciful promotional material of their parent company, Memory Lane Cakes.)

You can trace this attitude back to John Betjeman – though he cannot be blamed for its consequences. From the 1950s until his death, Betjeman was an advocate for Victorian architecture and poetry. His work was cute and valuable, but it was also a form of wilful perversity, a rebellion against the prescriptive good taste of the prevailing orthodoxy. He was enthusiastic about Gilbert Scott and Henry Newbolt in the same way that some people go wild for Barbie dolls or Elvis mirrors. That said, his objections to modernity were undogmatic and nuanced – he was, after all, a paid-up member of Modern Architecture Research, the English section of CIAM, the Comité International d'Architecture Moderne, an outfit founded by Le Corbusier and his acolytes. Betjeman's attitudes, however, disseminated throughout a long career in television, achieved a strong resonance with the resurgent middle-classes in the 1980s – the retro-gressives of the dwarf conifer belt, people who fantasised that the nineteenth century was a place where being as mean-minded, greedy and philistine as they were was broadly celebrated. For these people, Victorian Britain was a Tory paradise ruined by the arrival of Walter Gropius, the blacks and the gays, but which, with enough diligence, could be recreated on their own Tudorbethan close, behind PVC leaded windows, blindfolded with a copy of the *Daily Mail*. The bad standing of the Victorians with Britain's liberal intellectual classes exists in an inverse ratio to the vague approval which they receive from the inhabitants of Llandrindod Wells.

What is to be done? Is there any way to liberate the Victorians from this position? To extricate them from the approval of reactionaries and the hindsighted moralism of the progressives? Only perhaps to say that, one day, when the Victorians are no longer needed to fulfil this role, it will happen to us. In the next few decades of the twenty-first century, the stereotypes about the twentieth will begin to accrue and ossify. At the moment, we are near enough to the last century to perceive social and cultural differences in the character of each decade. In 1900, the same was true of the nineteenth century. By 1918, such distinctions had become fuzzy. What stereotypes will our grandchildren and great-grandchildren use to punish us for our shortcomings? Here are a few suggestions. They will shake their heads at our long cold war and two hot wars. They will deride the empty language of the free market, of management theory, of consumption, that has colonised much of public utterance, just as we deride the religiose and patrician language that seems so prevalent in Victorian culture. They will roll their eyes at TV clips of crankily

Thatcherite head teachers referring to their pupils as 'customers', and believe that this was widespread practice. When Britain elects its first black prime minister, she and her wife may denounce us for imagining that the twentieth century achieved anything in the field of racial equality, and highlight the glaring inconsistencies in our laws dealing with immigration, gender and sexual orientation. And the litany of clichés will accumulate. The New Wilhelmines will imagine, perhaps, that their forebears all wore red braces, slugged champagne and dealt on the stock exchange via mobile phones the size of a house brick – and classroom material such as *Wall Street* or *Bonfire of the Vanities* will back up the assertion. They will stroll through the tumbledown ghettos of the post-war suburbs and wonder how people could have consented to live in such dismal, kitsch environments. They will shudder at our reliance upon fossil fuels, our use of radiotherapy, the Cambridge Diet, chemical anti-depressants, Angel Theology and *The Road Less Travelled*. Just imagine what future academics, pursuing the arguments of the twenty-first century through the textual detritus of the twentieth, could do with editorials from middlebrow tabloids and selective quotes from Mary Whitehouse, Enoch Powell, Paul Johnson and Laura Doyle. Imagine what they might make of a period of British history that produced factory farms, football hooliganism and the Moors murderers. Whatever form it takes, their derision will be nasty. And, as is demonstrated by the experiences of those Victorians who found themselves living on, voiceless, in the twentieth century, there will be nothing we can do to stop it.

When Lytton Strachey declared that 'The history of the Victorian Age will never be written: we know too much about it,' he was only half right.[12] Certainly, one of the problems of working with Victorian culture is that so much of it survives: a jungle composed of records, documents, handbills, books, pamphlets, newspapers, diaries and wax cylinders awaits the researcher. And, to follow that analogy, those working in the field have tended to stick to the paths cut by those who have already passed the same way. However, as I hope this book has demonstrated, a secondary problem exacerbates this: we have systematically forgotten many of the most interesting and distinctive aspects of the period, and much of what we think we know about it is utterly false, fabricated in the twentieth century and lazily accepted as truth ever since.

There is a mass of material in archives, libraries, private collections, waiting to be dragged back into public cognisance – a world of exciting, utterly forgotten stories, a huge cast of equally neglected personalities. I have tried to accommodate some of these disregarded people and events in this book, but there are thousands of others whom we have lost, whom judicious biographers and historians might restore to the nineteenth-century narrative. Why is Arthur Wharton, the first black British professional footballer, who kept goal for Sheffield United, Preston North End and Rotherham throughout the 1880s and 90s, not a national hero? Who remembers Captain Thomas Mayne Reid, a political revolutionary who created the Wild West genre and built himself a hacienda in Gerrards Cross? Why has obscurity swallowed up Mary Seacole, a Jamaican nurse who, at her own expense, set up a hospital service at Balaclava and was as celebrated in her day as Florence Nightingale? Or Thomas Peckett Prest, the hack who created the murderous character of Sweeney Todd, and who died penniless in Islington? Who remembers the Blondin Donkey, the lauded tightrope-walking mule of the 1880s? (No editor of *The Diary of a Nobody* has ever noticed that it is this creature that Charles Pooter is impersonating during a game of charades.) Why is it not more widely known that, by 1873, the Kentish Town branch of Sainsbury's had a coin-operated vending machine nicknamed the 'mechanical cow' that dispensed milk to after-hours shoppers? That the first colour illustrated newspaper was published in the 1850s? That in 1868, the world's first international cricket match was played between an English side and an Australian team composed entirely of Aboriginal players? Or that in 1869 there were image-capable telegraphs?

What prevents these facts from circulating more widely when so many baseless clichés about the Victorians have enjoyed such vigorous life? There is a simple answer to this question. The Victorians are the people against whom we have defined ourselves. We are who we are because we are not the Victorians. And if we concede that they moulded our culture, defined our sensibilities, built a world for us to live in – rather than being the figures against whom we rebelled in order to create those things for ourselves – then we undermine one of the founding myths of modernity. This is why we so rarely see the several extant photographs of Victoria laughing like a skunk, why she is most famous for a quote she never said, why the bogus story of her ignorance of lesbianism has to be repeated over and over again, why chintz-swathed piano legs and Ruskin yelping at the sight of his young bride's pubic hair are commonly invoked to characterise the period. If the Victorians are caricatured as cruel, hypocritical, repressive, intolerant, prudish and cheerless, then it makes all post-Victorian wife-beating, child abuse, social injustice and personal dullness more easy to cope with. If you think hard enough about the deprivations suffered by the crossing sweepers who slept in doorways on nineteenth-century city streets, that allows you to recognise *Big Issue* sellers as something else entirely.

Millions of us still occupy the streets of Victorian Britain. Commuters are discharged through the same underground tunnels, reading many of the same newspapers and novels. Colonies of graphic designers and HTML programmers have established themselves in the bodies of Victorian industrial units and Board Schools. Their theatres and music halls are still our places of entertainment. Most of our museums, libraries and universities are theirs. Our cities are theirs. A bus pass is all you need to explore Victorian Britain. Stand in the High Streets of Deptford or Didsbury, dawdle down the Pentonville Road or Sauchiehall Street, and raise your eyes above the level of the shop windows, and you are looking squarely at the Victorian past. Legions of dead Victorians, men and women as smart as you or I, lived in these lighted rooms.

I can see them: Ah Sing and Hannah Johnston, lying back on their divan and breathing in the poppy fumes of Shadwell; Joseph Merrick and Tom Norman, splitting a tidy day's takings on the Whitechapel Road; Blondin in his retirement at Ealing, turning a little somersault for a passer-by who remembered, long ago, gazing up at his tiny figure pushing a lion across the tightrope; William Dugdale, proofing another page of pornography and dreaming of a British Revolution. And beyond these figures, the unknown and unknowable dead, moving through the same brick tunnels which take me to work, scrumming for a drink in the same crush bars, gazing into the same shop windows, walking the same pavements, having the same desires, and feeling less bad about having them. Why do we hate these people? Or if not hate them, patronise them with our contemptuous sentiment? They made us – good and bad – what we are today. We are the Victorians. We should love them. We should thank them. We should love them.

Notes

Introduction

1 'I am happy now that Charles calls on my bedchamber less frequently than of old. As it is, I now endure but two calls a week and when I hear his steps outside my door I lie down on my bed, close my eyes, open my legs, and think of England.' Lady Hillingham, private journal (1912), quoted in Jonathan Gathorne-Hardy, *The Rise and Fall of the British Nanny* (London: Hodder and Stoughton, 1972), p. 71. The phrase is commonly attributed to Queen Victoria: 'As Queen Victoria advised her daughter on the eve of her wedding, "Lie back and think of England."', Steve Payne, 'Lie Back and Think of England', *Toronto Sun* (29 December 1999), p. 92. '... changes in sexual communication from Queen Victoria's discrete [sic] advice to newlywed brides – "Just lie back and think of England" – to the swarm of TV crews lighting up the intimate affairs of princesses and presidents', press release for TV documentary series *Sexual Century*, first broadcast on the History Television channel, 14 February 2000.

2 A few examples: 'We got in just in time for a quick Scrabble game before supper ... I was soon slotting in edh and vum with the best of them although when ax went down I found myself quickly adding an e, like a Victorian prude wrapping a skirt around the piano legs', Jenny McClean, 'Wordplay round the Cotswolds', *Independent* (4 May 1996), p. 19. 'Just as the Victorians were so prudish they covered up piano legs with skirts, some old-time woodworkers were offended by the sight of end grain', Jack Warner, 'Woodworking: Changes in the weather can affect breadboard edge', *Atlanta Journal and Constitution* (30 January 1999), p. 13. 'I think they are more like Victorian matrons, aghast at Mr Clinton's rampaging piano leg, and preferring simply to draw a discreet veil over it', Mark Steyn, 'The shape of things to come', 'Comment', *Sunday Telegraph* (19 October 1997), p. 1. 'The very thought may send the current Congressional majority reeling like so many Victorian young ladies confronted with the sight of an undraped piano leg', Martin Walker, 'Butter and Guns: America's Cold War Economic Diplomacy', *Washington Monthly* (1 April 1997), p. 58. 'Here was a world in which not just ladies' ankles but the legs of their dressing-tables must remain always concealed, for fear not only that such a sight would arouse men, but also that it should upset women, for whom sex was a taboo', Deborah Orr, 'Sex in the 21st Century', *Independent* (6 March 2001), Review, p.1

[233]

3 Harman Grisewood (ed.), *Ideas and Beliefs of the Victorians: A Historical Revaluation of the Victorian Age* (London: Sylvan Press, 1949), p. 351.

4 Ibid., p. 363.

5 E. Jane Dickson, 'Unlacing the Victorian Corset,' *Radio Times* (20–26 January 2001), p. 19.

6 Rosemarie Morgan, ed., Thomas Hardy, *Far from the Madding Crowd* (Harmondsworth: Penguin, 2000 [1874], p. xxix.

7 Stephen Bayley, *General Knowledge* (London: Booth-Clibborn Editions, 1999), p. 38.

8 Richard Sennett, *The Fall of Public Man* (London: Faber and Faber, 1986), p. 167.

9 'The Victorians loved covering up everything with little mats, generally decorated with flimsy tassels or pompoms, care apparently being taken to select a material which might be relied upon to attract the greatest quantity of dust', Nevill (1930), p. 29.

10 Frederick Marryat, *A Diary in America* (London: Longman, Orme, Brown, Green and Longans, 1839), ii, pp. 245–6.

11 Ibid., ii, pp. 246–7.

12 J. R. Planché, *Buckstone's Voyage Round the Globe* (London: T. H. Lacy, c.1854), p. 21.

13 Nicolaas Rupke, *Richard Owen, Victorian Naturalist* (New Haven, Connecticut: Yale University Press, 1994), pp. 227–8.

14 *Tomahawk*, ii (1868), p. 139.

15 Maryatt (1839), i, p. 8.

16 'Captain Marry-It', *Lie-ary on America, with Yarns on its Institutions* (Baltimore, Maryland: Turners, 1840), p. 20.

17 E. P. Thompson, *The Making of the English Working Class* (Harmondsworth: Penguin, 1980 [1963]), p. 12.

18 Lytton Strachey, *Eminent Victorians* (Harmondsworth: Penguin, 1948 [1918]), p. 165.

19 *Times Literary Supplement* (11 July 1918), p. 325.

20 Virginia Woolf, ed. Anne Olivier Bell, *The Diary of Virginia Woolf*, i (Harmondsworth: Penguin, 1979 [1977]), 166. A few days earlier she reflected on the 'horrible sense of community which the war produces, as if we all sat in a third class railway carriage together' (p. 153). For Mary Ward, see John Sutherland, *Mrs Humphry Ward* (Oxford: Clarendon Press, 1990).

21 'Megatheria', *Times Literary Supplement* (16 May 1918), p. 230.

22 See Virginia Woolf, *The Question of Things Happening: Collected Letters* ii (London: Hogarth Press, 1976), 13.

23 J. A. Bridges, *Victorian Recollections* (London: G. Bell and Sons, 1919), p. v.

24 Ibid.

25 Grace James, *The Pork Pie Hat* (London: Samuel French, 1922), p. 9.

26 'R.D.', *Less Eminent Victorians* (London: Peter Davies, 1927), p. vi.

27 Cecily Sidgwick, *Victorian* (London: Hutchinson, 1922), p.7.

28 Caryl Brahms, S. J. Simon, *Don't Mr Disraeli* (Harmondsworth: Penguin, 1949 [1940]), pp. 114, 88.

29 Barbara Shaw, *A Mid-Victorian Trifle* (London: Samuel French, 1940), p. 12.

30 For Tod Slaughter, see Jeffrey Richards, 'Tod Slaughter and the Cinema of Excess', in Jeffrey Richards (ed.), *The Unknown 1930s: An Alternative History of the British Cinema, 1929–1939* (London: I. B. Tauris, 1998), pp. 138–159. For Hammer and anti-Victorianism, see Robert Mighall, 'Vampires and Victorians: Count Dracula and the Return of the Repressive Hypothesis', in Gary Day, *Varieties of Victorianism* (New York: St Martin's Press, pp. 236–49).

31 Stephen Coleridge, *Famous Victorians I Have Known* (London: Simpkin Marshall, 1928), p. 121.

32 Ralph Nevill, *The Gay Victorians* (London: Eveleigh, Nash and Grayson, 1930), pp. 1, 34, 17.

33 Herman Ausubel, *The Late Victorians* (Toronto: Anvil, 1955), p. 91.

34 William Acton, *Functions and Disorders of the Reproductive Organs* (London: John Churchill, 1865 [1857]), p. 133.

35 Daniel Pool, *What Jane Austen Ate and Charles Dickens Knew* (London: Robinson, 1998), pp. 167–8.

1 The Sensation Seekers

1 'A Mere Phantom', *The Magic Lantern: How to buy it and how to use it* (London: C. L. Brinkman, 1866), p. v.

2 Thomas Richards, *The Commodity Culture of Victorian England: Advertising and Spectacle 1851–1914* (Stanford, California: Stanford University Press 1990), p. 57.

3 Earl of Malmesbury, *Private Diaries and Correspondences* (1779), i, p. 257 (Winchester HRO 9M73); *Illustrated London News* (25 May 1861), p. 1; [unsigned article], 'The Enigma Novel', *Spectator* lix (1861), p. 1428; [Henry Mansel], 'Sensation Novels', *Quarterly Review* cxiii (1863), p. 482; [unsigned article], 'The Queen's English', *Edinburgh Review* cxx (1864), p. 53; W. M. Thackeray, 'On Two Roundabout Papers I Intended to Write', *Cornhill* iv (1861), p. 379.

4 See John McCormick, *Dion Boucicault (1820–1890)* (Cambridge: Chadwyck-Healey, 1987), p. 44.

5 *The Times* (24 September 1861), p. 12; *Punch* xl (1861), p. 226; ibid., xi (1861), p. 226.

6 Roger Fulford (ed.), *Dearest Child: Letters between Queen Victoria and the Princess Royal 1858–61* (London, 1964), p. 305.

7 George Linnaeus Banks, *Blondin: His Life and Performances* (London, 1862), p. 38.

8 Toronto *Daily Globe* (1 July 1859), p. 2; Niagara *Daily Gazette* (1 July 1859), p. 3; Troy *Daily Times* (2 July 1859), p. 2; *Daily Gazette* (ibid.); *Daily Globe* (ibid.), *Daily Times* (ibid.).

9 Buffalo *Morning Express* (25 August 1859), p. 2

10 Justice Jarvis Blume, *Across Niagara on a Man's Back* (Chicago: privately published, *c.*1899), p. 9.

11 Quoted in 'A Reporter's Challenge to Mr Blondin', *Lockport Daily Advertiser and Democrat* (27 September 1859), p. 2.

12 'The Great American Snake Caught', *The Times* (18 September 1855), p. 5; 'Astonishing Feat at Niagara', *The Times* (7 April 1859), p. 12.

13 Banks (1862), pp. 59, 60, 84.

14 Charles Dickens, 'Old Rome in Crystal', *All the Year Round* v (1861), p. 324; 'Johnson and Blondin', *Punch* xl (1861), pp. 246–7; *Oxford Chronicle and Berks & Bucks Gazette* (8 June 1861), p. 5.

15 W. F. Deedes, 'It is Our Problem, Not the Prince's', *Daily Telegraph* (11 December 1993), p. 19; Simon Jenkins, 'Welcome to London's Age of Sensation', *London Evening Standard* (2 September 1999), p. 13; *The Boy Detective, or The Crimes of London* (London: Newsagent's Publishing Company, 1865–6), p. 87.

16 Unidentified newspaper cutting, *Entertainments, etc.*, box 6, John Johnson Collection, Bodleian Library, Oxford; *ILN* xxxviii (1861), p. 604; *Fun* (1 May 1869).

17 Johnson, *Entertainments, etc.* box 6; *The Times* (8 July 1861), p. 6; ibid., (5 December 1861), p. 4; 'The Female Blondin', ibid., (1 November 1862), p. 10.

18 *Punch* xlv (1 August 1863), p. 42.

19 Ibid., (2 July 1870), p. 7.

20 Blume (*c.*1899), p. 16.

2 The First Picture Show

1 Virginia Woolf, ed. Anne Olivier Bell, *The Diary of Virginia Woolf*, i (Harmondsworth: Penguin, 1979), p. 18.

2 Jonathan Law (ed.), *Brewer's Cinema* (London: Cassell, 1995), p. 346; David Thomson, *A Biographical Dictionary of Film* (London, André Deutsch, 1995), p. 460; Méliès quoted in David Puttnam and Neil Watson, *The Undeclared War* (London: Harper Collins, 1997), p. 18; 'The Prince's Derby', *Strand* xii (1896), p. 136.

3 J. Miller Barr, 'Animated Pictures', *Popular Science Monthly* 52 (1897), p. 178.

4 'The Cinematograph', *The Times* (22 February 1896), p. 15.

5 Unsigned article, 'The Sensation Times', *Punch* xliv (1863), p. 193.

6 Quoted in Q. David Bowers, *Thanhouser Films: An Encyclopedia and History*, CD-ROM, (Portland, Orgeon: Thanhouser, 1999).

7 Ray Allister, *Friese-Greene: Close-up of an Inventor* (London: Marsland Publications, 1948), pp. 48–9.

8 Ibid., p. 47.

9 William Rothenstein, *Men and Memories* (London: Faber and Faber, 1931), I, p. 311.

10 'The Cinematograph. Hubert von Herkomer's Views', *Daily Telegraph* (21 December 1912), p. 9.

11 Richard Little Purdy and Michael Millgate (eds.), *The Collected Letters of Thomas Hardy* (Oxford: Clarendon Press, 1984), iv, pp. 324, 329, 140.

12 Ibid., vi, p. 143, iv, p. 312.

13 Ibid., vi, p. 93.

14 Norman J. Atkins, *Thomas Hardy and the Hardy Players* (Guernsey: Toucan Press, 1980), p. 10.

15 *Collected Letters of Thomas Hardy*, iv, p. 302, vi, p. 72; Harry Furniss, *Our Lady Cinema* (Bristol: J. W. Arrowsmith, 1914), p. 45.

16 *Film Fun* (December 1915), p. 22.

17 C. L. Graham, *How to Write Cinema Picture Plays* (Cinema Playwriting School, London, 1913), pp. 2–3.

18 Channing Pollock, 'Swinging the Censor', *Picturegoer* ix (March 1916), p. 69.

19 *Kinematography Yearbook* (London: Kinematograph and Lantern Weekly, 1914), p. 15.

3 The Boer War, Brought to You by Bovril

1 *The Times* (3 June 1864), p. 13; ibid., (1 June 1864), p. 11

2 Ibid. (1 July 1864), p. 12.

3 *London Journal and Weekly Record of Literature, Science and Art* (28 December 1850), p. 287, ibid. (10 March 1866), p. 160; ibid. (13 January 1877), p. 31; ibid. (28 December 1850), p. 287.

4 Ibid. (22 June 1850), p. 256.

5 *The Times* (2 February 1853), p. 1.

6 Ibid. (11 February 1853), p. 1.

7 Ibid. (15 January 1854), p. 1.

8 See *Puffs and Mysteries; or, The Romance of Advertising* (London: W. Kent and Co., 1855), p. 66; H. Sampson, *The History of Advertising* (London: Chatto and Windus, 1874), pp. 295, 298, 297–8.

9 See Merlin Holland, *The Wilde Album* (London: Fourth Estate, 1997), colour II, p. 3.

10 *The Era* (4 May 1879), p. 18.

11 See Peter Bailey, 'Champagne Charlie: Performance and Ideology in the Music Hall Swell Song,' in J. S. Bratton (ed.), *Music Hall: Performance & Style* (Milton Keynes: Open University Press, 1986), p. 56.

12 [Henry Court], *Successful Advertising: or, the economical way of reaching the people*, (London: The Half-Price Closed Letter Co., 1892), p. 5.

13 *The Times* (18 November 1892), p. 10; ibid. (21 November 1892), p. 10; ibid. (22 November 1892), p. 11; ibid. (23 November 1892), p. 14; ibid. (25 November 1892), p. 14.

14 Hester Lacey, 'Making a Splash', *Independent on Sunday*, Sunday Review (13 February 2000), p. 21.

15 See T. R. Nevett, *Advertising in Britain, a History* (London: Heinemann, 1982), p. 72

16 Ibid., p. 35

17 George Gentle, *Hints on Advertising, Adapted to the Times* (London: privately published, 1870), p. 13.

18 'The Puffing System', *The Times* (24 January 1894), p. 7.

19 *Publicity. An Essay on Advertising. By an Adept of 35 Years' Experience* (London: G.S. Brown, 1878), pp. 26–7.

20 'Sure to be Healthy, Wealthy and Wise', *All the Year Round* i (1859), p. 8.

21 'Small Shot. Trap Advertising', *All the Year Round* ii (1859), p. 251.

22 See Paul Hadley, *The History of Bovril Advertising* (London: Bovril, 1972), p. 13.

23 For Thomas Lipton, see Thomas Lipton, *Leaves from the Lipton Logs* (London: Hutchinson and Co, 1931); James Mackay, *The Man Who Invented Himself: A Life of Thomas Lipton* (Edinburgh: Mainstream, 1998); E. S. Turner, *The Shocking History of Advertising* (Harmondsworth: Penguin, 1965), pp. 98, 113.

24 Lipton (1931), p. 124.

25 Ibid., p. 125.

26 Ibid., p. 126.

27 Mark Borkowski, *Improperganda: The Art of the Publicity Stunt* (London: Vision On, 2000), p. 9.

4 The Gutter and the Stars

1 Merlin Holland, *The Wilde Album* (London: Fourth Estate, 1997), p. 17.

2 William A. Cohen, *Sex Scandal* (Durham: Duke University Press, 1989), p. 2.

3 For Cleveland, see Alyn Brodsky, *Grover Cleveland: A Study in Character* (New York: St Martin's Press, 2000).

4 Matthew Arnold, 'Civilization in the United States', *Nineteenth Century* xxiii (1888), p. 490.

5 Ibid., p. 491.

6 Matthew Arnold, 'Up to Easter', *Nineteenth Century* xii (1887), pp. 638–9.

7 Josephine Butler, *Personal Reminiscences of a Great Crusade* (London: Horace Marshall, 1896) p. 375.

8 W. T. Stead, *The Armstrong Case* (London: W.T. Stead, 1885), p. 9.

9 W. T. Stead, 'Government by Journalism', *Contemporary Review* xlix (1886), p. 672.

10 For Stead, pornography and Gothic fiction, see Judith Walkowitz, *City of Dreadful Delight* (London: Virago, 1992).

11 *Pall Mall Gazette* (6 July 1885), p. 1.

12 Stead (1886), p. 671.

13 William McGlashan, *England on her Defence* (Newcastle: John Barnes, 1885), p. 3; 'An Oxford BA', *A letter to the Editor of the Pall Mall Gazette* (London: Jackson Gaskill, 1885), p. 4.

14 *Pall Mall Gazette* (8 July 1885), p. 1.

15 T. P. O'Connor, 'The New Journalism', *New Review* i (1889), p. 434.

16 See John Goodbody, '*The Star*: Its Role in the Rise of New Journalism', in Joel H. Wiener (ed.), *Papers for the Millions: The New Journalism in Britain* (New York: Greenwood Press, 1988), p. 148.

17 W. T. Stead, 'The Future of Journalism', *Contemporary Review* i (1886), pp. 670–1.

18 See John Pilger, 'Years ago, Murdoch said that "You tell these bloody politicians whatever they want to hear" and afterwards "you don't worry about it"', *New Statesman* (18 September 1998), p. 2.

19 Mark Woods, 'Monica Cancels Trip to Oz for "Laws" Interview', *Variety* (6 November 2000), p. 1.

5 I Knew My Doctor Was a Serial Killer Because . . .

1 For the details of the Palmer case, see *The Queen v. Palmer. Verbatim Report of the Trial of William Palmer* (London: J. Allen, 1856); *Illustrated Life and Career of William Palmer of Rugeley* (London: Ward and Lock, 1856); Rev Thomas Palmer, *A Letter to the Lord Chief Justice Campbell* (London: T. Taylor, 1856); *The Times Report of the Trial of William Palmer* (London: Ward and Lock, 1856); George Fletcher, *The Life and Career of Dr William Palmer of Rugeley* (London: Fisher Unwin, 1925); Robert Graves, *They Hanged My Saintly Billy* (New York: Doubleday, 1957).

2 *They Hanged My Saintly Billy*, p. 310.

3 For details of the Cleft Chin case, see 'Girl and Man Accuse Each Other in Cleft Chin Case', *News of the World* (21 January 1945), p. 3; 'A Girl Condemned to the Gallows Goes to Church', ibid. (28 January 1945), pp. 3, 5.

4 George Orwell, ed. Sonia Orwell, Ian Angus, *Collected Essays, Journalism and Letters* (Harmondsworth: Penguin, 1970), iv, p.127.

5 Ibid.

6 *Manchester Evening News* website www.men.co.uk; Tina Jackson, 'The families still mourn. The nation's still in shock. The book's now out', *Big Issue* (21 February 2000), p. 32; Mikaela Sitford, *Addicted to Murder: The True Story of Dr Harold Shipman* (London: Virgin, 2000), pp. 114, 117, 126; Brian Whittle, Jean Ritchie, *Prescription for Murder: The True Story of Mass Murderer Dr Harold Frederick Shipman* (London: Warner Books, 2000), pp. xiii, 199.

7 *Shocking Tragedy at Penge!*, Crime broadside in the Borowitz True Crime Collection, University of Kent State, Ohio, vol. 1.

8 *A Particular Account . . .* (Gateshead: W. Stephenson, 1825), Borowitz Collection, vol. 1.

9 *Horrible Case . . .* (Halifax: J. Lister, 1833), Borowitz Collection, vol. 1.

10 *Another Case . . .* (London: J. Pitts, n.d.), Borowitz Collection, vol. 1.

11 Quoted in Howard Engel, *Lord High Executioner* (London: Robson Books, 1998), p. 49.

12 Quoted in Pauline Chapman, *Madame Tussaud's Chamber of Horrors: Two Hundred Years of Crime* (London: Constable, 1984), p. 66.

13 Charles Dickens Jnr, *Dickens's Dictionary of London 1893* (London: Charles Dickens and Evans, 1893), p. 261.

14 Unsigned article, 'A Visit to Madame Tussaud's Wax-Work', the *Spectator* lix (1861), p. 1397.

15 Mary Elizabeth Braddon, *Three Times Dead!!! or The Secret of the Heath* (Beverley: William Empson, 1860), p. 123.

16 Orwell (1970), p. 124.

17 Quoted in Stewart P. Evans and Keith Skinner, *The Ultimate Jack the Ripper Sourcebook* (London: Robinson, 1996), p. 22.

18 'An Autumn Evening in Whitechapel', *Daily News* (27 September 1888), p. 9.

19 *The Life and Career of Dr William Palmer of Rugeley*, (1925), p. 19. George Fletcher heard Mrs Palmer use these words on a visit to Rugeley made shortly after the execution.

6 Last Exit to Shadwell

1 See 'A Curious Burial', *East London Observer* (11 January 1890).

2 Charles Dickens, *The Mystery of Edwin Drood* (Harmondsworth: Penguin, 1985 [1870]), p. 38.

3 James Platt, 'Chinese London and Its Opium Dens', *Gentleman's Magazine* 279 (1895), p. 273.

4 See Frederic Kitton, *The Novels of Charles Dickens* (London: Elliot Stock, 1897), p. 230.

5 James T. Fields, *In and Out of Doors with Charles Dickens* (Boston: James R. Osgood and Co, 1876), pp. 105–6.

6 Sax Rohmer, *The Mystery of Dr Fu-Manchu* (London, 1913), chapter 2.

7 'Opium Den Raid, Chinaman's Three Savage Guardians', *Star* (18 February 1930).

8 Thomas Burke, *Nights in Town* (London: George Allen and Unwin, 1915), p. 87.

9 Joseph Salter, *The Asiatic in England* (London: Seeley, Jackson and Halliday, 1873), p. 34; Rev Harry Jones, *East and West London* (London: Smith, Elder and Son, 1875), p. 240.

10 James Greenwood, *The Wilds of London* (London: Chatto and Windus, 1874), p. 2.

11 George Herbert Mitchell, *Down in Limehouse* (London: S. Martin and Co., 1925), p. 21.

12 'Opium-Smoking in London', *London City Mission Magazine*, reprinted in *Friend of China* iii (1877), p. 20.

13 Platt (1895), p. 275.

14 Percy Fitzgerald, *Memories of Charles Dickens* (London: Simpkin, Marshall and Co., 1913), p. 262.

15 *Sleep Scenes; Or, Dreams of a Laudanum Drinker* (London: Simpkin, Marshall and Co., 1868), p. 7.

16 Owen Howell, *The Dream of the Opium Eater* (London: George King Matthews, *c.*1850), p. 16.

17 See J. F. B. Tinling, *The Poppy-Plague and England's Crime* (London: Elliot Stock, 1876), pp. 6–7.

18 Benjamin Slater, *Memories of Mitcham* (Mitcham, 1911), pp. 22–3.

19 See Virginia Berridge, *Opium and the People* (London: Free Association Books, 1999), pp. 38–48.

20 'Report by Dr Hunter on the excessive mortality of infants in rural districts of England', *Sixth Report of the Medical Officer of the Privy Council, 1863*, Parliamentary Papers (1864), xxvii , Appendix 14, p. 459.

21 *Morning Chronicle* (26 December 1850), quoted in Berridge (1999), pp. 40–2.

22 Tinling (1876), p. 15.

23 *The Celestial Empire* (London: Grant and Girffiths, 1863), p. 60.

24 E. Impey, *A Report on the Cultivation, Preparation and Adulteration of Malwa Opium* (Bombay Times Press, Bombay, 1848), p. 7.

25 See *Self-Cure of Love of Liquor and the Opium Habit* (New York: Jessey Haney and Co., 1876), p. 88.

26 [Unsigned article], 'Breakfast in Bed', *Temple Bar* viii (1863), p. 77.

27 Louis Lewin, *Phantastica: A Classic Survey on the Use and Abuse of Mind-Altering Plants* (Rochester, Vermont: Park Street Press, 1998 [1924]), p. 218.

28 Platt (1895), p. 277.

7 The Archaeology of Good Behaviour

1 Tony Burmester, *Culture Fix: Programme 17*, first broadcast on BBC Knowledge in May 2000.

2 Stephanie Clifford, 'Profiles in Politics', *Equity* (Spring 2000).

3 *Manners of Modern Society* (London: Casell, Petter and Galpin, 1879), p. 65.

4 Mme [Marie] Bayard (ed.), *Hints on Etiquette* (London: Weldon and Co., 1884), p. 20.

5 Isabella Beeton, *The Book of Household Management* (London: S. O. Beeton, 1861), p. 817.

6 Jerome K. Jerome, *Three Men in a Boat* (Harmondsworth: Penguin, 1999 [1889]), p. 27.

7 Elizabeth Gaskell, *Wives and Daughters* (Harmondsworth: Penguin, 1996 [1866]), p. 213.

8 See 'A Family Chat on Cheese', *Cassell's Family Magazine* v (1878), pp. 287–9.

9 C. M. Aikman, *Milk. Its Nature and Composition* (London: Adam and Charles Black, 1895), p. 154.

10 'A Lady', *The Ladies' Guide to Etiquette* (London: H. Elliot, 1855), p. 14; *Habits of Good Society* (London: James Hogg, 1859), p. 259; Mark Lemon, *Jack in the Green* (London: T. H. Lacy, 1850), p. 8; *Manners and Tone of*

Good Society (London: Frederick Warne, 1879), p. 99; Lady Agnes Grove, *The Social Fetich* (London: Smith and Elder, 1907), pp. 12–13.

11 Sir Henry Bessemer, *Sir Henry Bessemer, FRS. An Autobiography* (London: Engineering, 1905), p. 136.

12 Beeton (1861), pp. 135, 197, 174.

13 *Etiquette for All* (Glasgow: George Watson, 1861), p. 6; *The Gentleman's Guide to Etiquette* (London: H. Elliot, 1855), p. 4; 'Mentor', *Always* (London: Routledge, 1884), pp. 20–1.

14 *The Young Ladies' Journal* xvii (1879), p. 415.

15 *Etiquette for All*, pp. 6, 2; FWR and Lord Charles X, *The Laws and Bye-Laws of Good Society: A Code of Modern Etiquette* (London: Simpkin and Marshall, 1867), p. 2; *The Gentleman's Manual of Modern Etiquette* (London: Paul Jerrard and Son, c.1864), pp. v–vi.

16 Harold R. Hardless, *The Indian Gentleman's Guide to English Etiquette, Conversation and Correspondence* (Chunar, The Sanctuary Press, 1920), p. 7.

17 *All About Etiquette* (London: Ward, Lock and Co., 1879), p. 39.

18 Henry P. Willis, *Etiquette and The Usages of Society* (New York: Dick and Fitzgerald, 1860), p. 17.

19 'The Lounger in Society', *The Glass of Fashion* (London: John Hogg, 1881), p. vi.

20 Eliza Ware Farrar, *The Young Lady's Friend* (Boston: American Stationer's Company, 1836), quoted in Margaret Visser, *The Rituals of Dinner* (Harmondsworth: Penguin, 1991), p. 192.

21 *The Habits of Good Society*, p. 20.

22 *A Manual Compiled under the Sanction of the London Swimming Club* (London: W.H. Leverell, 1861), p. 8.

23 The best analysis of the relationship between Margaret Thatcher and the nineteenth century is Raphael Samuel's 'Mrs Thatcher and Victorian Values' in *Island Stories: Unravelling Britain* (London: London, 1998), pp. 330–48.

8 Check Out Your Chintz

1 Nancy Evans, 'Designers Help Cure Decorating Mistakes', *London Free Press* (9 January 2000), p. 3; W. C. Edmundson, P. V. Sukhatme and S. A. Edmundson, *Diet, Disease and Development* (New Delhi: Macmillan, 1992); Edward Jones and Christopher Woodward (eds.), *A Guide to the Architecture of London* (London: Seven Dials, 2000), p. 119.

2 George Faulkner Armitage, *Health Lectures (for the People)* (Manchester: John Heywood, 1886) p. 118.

3 Wilkie Collins, *Basil* (London: Sampson Low, 1862 [1852]), p. 61.

4 Frances Trollope, *Paris and the Parisians in 1835* (London: Bentley, 1836), i, p. 231.

5 Virginia Woolf, *Orlando* (Oxford: World's Classics, 1998 [1928]), pp. 218–19.

6 'Elsa','Furnishing Economies', *Practical Housekeeping and Furnishing* i (1892), p. 38.

7 M. L. Frith, 'To those About to Furnish', *Englishwoman* i (1895), p. 403.

8 Quoted in Asa Briggs, *Victorian Things* (Harmondsworth: Penguin, 1990), p. 248.

9 'M. E.', 'Enquire Within', *Ladies' Home Journal* i (1890), p. 5.

10 W. Pett Ridge, *Outside the Radius: Stories of a London Suburb* (London: Hodder and Stoughton, 1899), p. 5.

11 Charles Dickens, *Great Expectations* (Harmondsworth: Penguin, 1965 [1861]), p. 230.

12 F. G. Trafford, *City and Suburb* (London: Charles J. Skeet, 1861), i, p.57.

13 Mabel Keningdale Cook, 'Domestic Arrangements. Suburban Wives', *Woman* (23 March 1872), p. 209.

14 George and Weedon Grossmith, *The Diary of a Nobody* (Oxford: World's Classics, 1995 [1892]), pp. 20–22.

15 R. Andom [Alfred Walter Barratt], *Martha and I* (London: Jarrold and Sons, 1898), p. 33.

16 'Elsa' (1892), p. 38.

17 'M.E.' (1890), p. 5.

18 For the Marshalls' DIY projects, see Zuzanna Shonfield, *The Precariously Privileged* (Oxford: Oxford University Press, 1987), pp. 86–8.

19 Hartfrid Neunzert, *Mansel Lewis and Hubert Herkomer* (Landsberg a. Lech: Kunstgeschichtliches aus Landsberg a. Lech, 1999), p. 136.

20 R. K. Philip, *The Practical Housewife* (London: Houlston and Sons, c. 1890 [1855]), p. 7.

21 Armitage (1886), p. 127.

22 Charles Eastlake, *Hints on Household Taste* (London: Longmans, Green and Co., 1868).

23 John Ruskin, ed. T. Cook, Alexander Wedderburn, *Works* x (London: George Allen, 1903–12), p. 196.

24 William Morris, *Hopes and Fears for Art* (London: Ellis and White, 1882), p. 108.

25 Dorothy Peel, *The New Home* (London: Constable and Co., 1898), p. ix.

26 Peter Thornton, *Authentic Decor: The Domestic Interior, 1620–1920* (London: Seven Dials, 2001), p. 210.

9 A Defence of the Freak Show

1 A. H. Saxon, *P. T. Barnum, The Legend and the Man* (New York: Columbia University Press, 1989), p. 120.

2 'Lord' George Sanger, *Seventy Years a Showman* (London: Arthur Pearson, 1927), p. 51.

3 C. J. S. Thompson, *The Mystery and Lore of Monsters* (London: Williams and Norgate, 1930), p. 180.

4 Handbill, *Human Freaks* box 2, John Johnson Collection, Bodleian Library, Oxford.

5 *Morning Herald* (15 February 1815), quoted in Ricky Jay, *Learned Pigs and Fireproof Women* (New York: Farrar, Strauss and Giroux, 1986), p. 33.

6 Francis Buckland, *Curiosities of Natural History. 3rd series* (London: 1868), ii, p. 42

7 Handbill, *Human Freaks* box 1, Johnson Collection.

8 *Entertainments* box 3, Johnson Collection.

9 *Illustrated London News* xxxvi (16 April 1859), p. 383.

10 *Human Freaks* box 4, Johnson Collection.

11 Ibid.

12 Ibid.

13 *Illustrated London News* xxxvi (16 April 1859), p. 383.

14 *Illustrated London News* xxxvi (28 May 1859), p. 471.

15 *Punch* xxxviii (1860), p. 19.

16 Charles Allston Collins, *The Eye-Witness, and his evidence about many wonderful things* (London: Bentley, 1860), p. 158.

17 Sanger (1927), p. 92.

18 Joseph Carey Merrick, *The Life and Adventures of Joseph Carey Merrick* (Leicester: 1884), cover.

19 Clarence L. Dean, *Book of Marvels in the Barnum and Bailey Greatest Show on Earth* (London, 1899), p. 7. The extent of Wilberforce's involvement in this process is not clear. Certainly his biographer George Russell did not think it worth mentioning in his life of the canon. See George W. E. Russell, *Basil Wilberforce. A Memoir* (London: John Murray, 1917).

20 *Book of Marvels in the Barnum and Bailey Greatest Show on Earth*, p. 7

21 Ibid., p. 13.

22 'Opening of Barnum's Show', *The Times* (12 November 1889), p. 7.

23 Raphael Samuel, *Theatres of Memory* (London: Verso, 1996), p. 389.

24 Tom Norman, letter, *World's Fair* (24 February 1923).

25 Tom Norman, unpublished MS, *This is Tom Norman: Sixty-Five Years a Showman and Auctioneer*, quoted in Michael Howell, Peter Ford, *The True History of the Elephant Man*, 3rd edition (Penguin, Harmondsworth, 1992), p. 81

26 Ibid., p. 83.

27 Framley Steelcroft, 'Some Peculiar Entertainment', *Strand* xi (1896), p. 468.

28 Ibid., p. 333

29 George Middleton, *Circus Memoirs* (Los Angeles: George Rice, 1913), p. 73.

30 Pickering material from the author's collection.

31 Thompson (1930), p. 240.

32 'Opening of Barnum's Show', p. 7.

33 Michael Wynn-Jones, 'Fox wanted to call me Ricardo and discover me in Mexico', *Radio Times* (1 January 1972), p. 6.

34 Valentia Steer, *The Romance of the Cinema* (London: C. Arthur Pearson, 1913), p. 14.

35 Patricia Bosworth, *Diane Arbus* (New York: Alfred A. Knopf, 1984), p. 162.

36 Rebecca Johnson, 'Jerry Springer Under Siege', *Good Housekeeping* 227 (1 September 1998), p. 115.

37 John Miller, 'Brazil wrestles with onslaught of shock TV', *Reuters* (29 December 1998). See also 'Jerry Springer, meet 'Ratinho': Brazilian talk-show host joins in on fights, features such guests as "elephant boy" ', *Dallas Morning News* (14 April 1998), p. 7.

38 Violet and Daisy Hilton, *The Intimate Hilton Sisters: Siamese Twins* (1942), quoted in Robert Bogdan, *Freak Show* (Chicago: University of Chicago Press, 1988), p. 173.

39 *Human Freaks* box 4, Johnson Collection.

10 Presumed Innocent

1 John Locke, *Some Thoughts Concerning Education* (Oxford: Clarendon Press, 1998 [1693]), pp. 115, 9.

2 Mary Martha Sherwood, *The History of the Fairchild Family* (London: Ward, Lock and Tyler, 1876), p. iii–v.

3 *The History of the Fairchild Family* (London: Hatchard and Co., 1865), i. 152, 57.

4 Ibid, iii. 35.

5 John Ryle, *Thoughts for Parents*, (London: William Hunt and Co., 1886), p. 8.

6 Ibid, pp. 9–10.

7 I have taken the details of the Fanny Adams murder from *The Alton Murder!* (London: Illustrated Police News, 1867).

8 Ibid, p. 15.

9 Natasha Walter, 'Review of the Year: Home – Sarah Payne', *Independent*, (29 December 2000), p. 6.

10 David Edwards, 'Tears for a Princess', Brighton *Evening Argus* (1 September 2000), p. 6.

11 *The Alton Murder!*, p. 16.

12 E. Jane Dickson, 'The Other Side of the Curtain', *Daily Telegraph* (22 December 1998), p. 17; Paul Taylor, 'The Trouble with Alice', *The Independent* (10 November 1994), p. 26; Elizabeth Wasserman, 'Sex Abuse Experts Puzzled', *Newsday* (17 January 1993), p. 4.

13 See Iain Gale, 'Portrait of the Artist as an Accused Man', *Independent* (15 February 1994), p. 25.

14 Edgar Jepson, *Memories of a Victorian* (London: Victor Gollancz, 1933), p. 219.

15 Pamela Tamarkin Reis and Laurel Bradley, 'Victorian Centrefold: Another Look at Millais's *Cherry Ripe*', *Victorian Studies* xxxv (1992), pp. 201–6; Robert M. Polhemus, 'John Millais's Children: Faith, Erotics and *The Woodsman's Daughter*', *Victorian Studies* xxxvii (1994), pp. 433–50.

16 Anne Higonnet, *Pictures of Innocence: The History and Crisis of Ideal Childhood* (London: Thames and Hudson, 1998), p. 132.

17 William Baker and William M. Clarke, eds. *The Letters of Wilkie Collins* (London: Macmillan, 1999), ii. 512–13.

18 Ibid, pp. 503, 501, 507, 508.

19 Ibid, p. 534.

20 Wilkie Collins, *Heart and Science* (London: Chatto and Windus, 1888), i. 157.

21 Ernest Dowson, ed. Desmond Flower, Henry Maas, *The Letters of Ernest Dowson* (London: Cassell, 1967), p. 213.

11 Whatever Happened to Patriarchy?

1 Harry Brod, *The Making of Masculinities: The New Men's Studies* (Boston: Allen and Unwin, 1987), p. 40.

2 Susan Faludi, *Stiffed: The Betrayal of Modern Man* (London: Vintage, 1999), p. 14.

3 Virginia Woolf, 'Three Guineas', in *A Room of One's Own/Three Guineas* (Harmondsworth: Penguin, 2000 [1938]), pp. 227–8.

4 Reay Tannahill, *Sex in History* (London: Abacus, 1989), p. 344.

5 Mark Jagasia, 'I dumped Damon because he wanted a Victorian wife', *Daily Express* (26 March 2000), p. 29.

6 Barry Miles, *Jack Kerouac: King of the Beats. A Portrait* (London: Virgin, 1999), p. 6.

7 Frederick Burkhardt, Sydney Smith (eds.), *The Correspondence of Charles Darwin* vi (Cambridge: Cambridge University Press, 1990), p. xviii.

8 John Ruskin, *Sesame and Lilies* (London: Smith, Elder and Co., 1865), pp. 146–7, 149.

9 Kate Millett, *Sexual Politics* (London: Virago, 1977), p. 94.

10 Ruskin (1865), p. 124.

11 William Byron Forbush, *The Queens of Avalon* (Boston, Massachusetts: The Knights of King Arthur, 1925), p. 1.

12 Millett (1977), p. 89.

13 Quoted in William James (ed.), *The Order of Release: The Story of John Ruskin, Effie Gray and John Everett Millais* (London: John Murray, 1948), pp. 49–50, 85.

14 Millett (1977), p. 91.

15 Adna Ferrin Webber, *The Growth of Cities in the Nineteenth Century: a study in statistics* (Ithica, New York: Cornell University Press, 1963 [1899]), pp. 275–6.

16 *Hints on Etiquette*, p. 36.

17 Coventry Patmore, *The Angel in the House* (London: John W. Parker, 1854) i, p. 125.

18 John Tosh, *A Man's Place: Masculinity and the Middle-Class Home in Victorian England* (New Haven, Connecticut: Yale University Press, 1999), p. 195.

19 W. H. Davenport Adams, *The Boy Makes the Man* (London: T. Nelson and Sons, 1867), p. 121.

20 *Punch* xxxviii (1860), p. 178.

21 Rev A. K. Boyd, 'A Young Man: His Home and Friends', in A. H. Charteris, *A Young Man* (Edinburgh: Macriven and Wallace), pp. 97, 99.

22 *The Boy Detective; or, The Crimes of London. A Romance of Modern Times* (London: Newsagents' Publishing Company, 1865-6), p. 3.

23 Ibid., p. 27.

24 Irving Lyons, *The Boy Pirate; or, Life on the Ocean* (London: Newsagents' Publishing Company, 1864-5), pp. 21, 52.

25 'Galloping Dick, the Boy Highwayman', *Tyburn Tree* i (c.1865), p. 2.

26 C. L. Robertson, 'Cases Illustrating the use of Digitalis in the Treatment of Mania', *Journal of Mental Science* ix (1863), pp. 550, 552-2.

27 John Millar, *Hints on Insanity* (London: Henry Renshaw, 1861), pp. 85, 83.

12 Monomaniacs of Love

1 Quoted in Stephen Calloway, *Aubrey Beardsley* (London: V&A Publications, 1998), p. 138.

2 Quoted in Matthew Sturgis, *Aubrey Beardsley* (London: HarperCollins, 1998), p. 160.

3 Paul Johnson, 'An Obscene Picture and the Question: Will Decency or Decadence Triumph in British Life?', *Daily Mail* (20 September 1997), p. 10.

4 Rupert Hart-Davis, ed., *The Letters of Oscar Wilde* (London: Hart-Davis, 1962), pp. 630-1.

5 Calloway (1998), p. 141.

6 Stephen Marcus, *The Other Victorians: A Study of Sexuality and Pornography in Mid-Nineteenth-Century England* (London: Weidenfeld and Nicolson, 1966), p. 263.

7 [Charles Edward Hutchinson], *Boy-Worship* (Oxford: privately printed, 1880), pp. 10, 9.

8 Quoted in Richard Ellmann, *Oscar Wilde* (London: Hamish Hamilton, 1987), p. 364.

9 *The Pearl* i (1879), pp. 37, 39, 97; ibid. iii (1881), p. 123.

10 Wilkie Collins, *Armadale* (Oxford: World's Classics, 1989 [1866]), pp. 94-5.

11 *American Journal of Psychology* vii (1895), p. 216.

12 Xavier Mayne, *The Intersexes* (Rome: privately published, 1908), p. 443.

13 Edward Carpenter, *The Intermediate Sex* (London: Swan Sonnenschein, 1908), pp. 31, 30.

14 'Walter', *My Secret Life* (London: Wordsworth, 1995 [c.1880]), i, p.134.

15 'Pisanus Fraxi' [Henry Spencer Ashbee], *Index Librorium Prohibitum* (London: privately published, 1877), p. 28.

16 *The Pearl* i (1879), p. 32.

17 48 and 49 VIC, Cap 69, clause 11.

18 Bonnie Zimmerman (ed.), *Lesbian Histories and Cultures* (New York: Garland Publishing, 2000), p. 401.

19 'What the Butler Did', *The Times* (30 December 2000), p. 29; E. Jane Dickson, 'Unlacing the Victorian Corset', *Radio Times* (20-26 January 2001), p. 20.

20 'Pisanus Fraxi' [Henry Spencer Ashbee], *Centuria Librorum Absconditorum* (London: privately published, 1879), p. 410.

21 Xavier Mayne, *The Intersexes*, pp. 634–63.

22 H. Montgomery Hyde, *Famous Trials, Seventh Series: Oscar Wilde* (Harmondsworth: Penguin, 1962), p. 326.

23 Phyllis Grosskurth, *John Addington Symonds: A Biography* (London, 1964), p. 275.

24 Herbert M. Scheuller and Robert L Peters (eds.), *The Letters of John Addington Symonds* (Detroit, 1967–9), iii, p. 381.

25 *The Monomaniac of Love* (London: Provost and Co., 1878), i, pp. 16, 79; Xavier Mayne, *The Intersexes*, p. 364; *The Monomaniac of Love*, i, p.72. In one volume of *The Pearl*, under the heading 'Amenities in Leicester Square', the editor printed the bon mot 'girl to ponce: Go along, you bloody Mary Ann, and tighten your arsehole with alum' (iii, p. 128). Similarly, a commentator recalled in 1895: 'I remember when residing in Oxford having pointed out to me in "the High" more than one professional catamite; just as waiting for a bus at Piccadilly Circus a few years later I heard prostitutes jocosely apostrophizing the Mary-Anns who plied their beastly trade upon the pavement beside the women', *Reynolds' Newspaper* (2 June 1895), p. 1.

26 Matthew Arnold, *Culture and Anarchy* (Cambridge: Cambridge University Press, 1993 [1869], pp. 58–80; Algernon Charles Swinburne, ed. Cecil Y. Lang, *Swinburne's Letters* vi (Newhaven, Connecticut: Yale University Press, 1962), p. 165.

27 Maurice Kenealy, *The Tichborne Tragedy* (London, 1913), p. 235. Perhaps to protect the dignity of its hero, David Yates's likeable film of the case, *The Tichborne Claimant* (1998), makes this defect a freakishly *large* penis.

28 Lord Chief Justice Sir James Cockburn, *The Tichborne Trial; the summing up of the Lord Chief Justice of England* (London: Ward, Lock and Tyler, 1874), p. 101.

29 Robert Molesworth Gurnell, *What Did Dr. David Wilson Say?* (London: privately published, 1874), p. 5.

30 Philip Henderson, *Swinburne: The Portrait of a Poet* (London: Routledge & Kegan Paul, 1974), pp. 151–2.

31 Xavier Mayne, *The Interesexes*, p. 36.

32 Quoted in Calloway (1998), pp. 205–6..

13 Prince Albert's Prince Albert

1 Virginia Woolf, ed. Jeanne Schulkind, *Moments of Being* (San Diego: Harvest, 1985), pp. 195–6.

2 Gertrude Himmelfarb, *Manners and Morals Among the Victorians* (London: I. B. Tauris, 1989), p. 42.

3 Ibid., p. 43.

4 Ronald Pearsall, *The Worm in the Bud* (London: Weidenfeld and Nicolson, 1976), p. xiv.

5 Fraser Harrison, *The Dark Angel: Aspects of Victorian Sexuality* (London: Fontana, 1979), p. 56.

6 Michel Foucault, trans. Robert Hurley, *The History of Sexuality: An Introduction* (Harmondsworth: Pelican, 1981), p. 22.

7 Gayle S. Rubin, 'Thinking Sex: Notes for a Radical Theory of the Politics of Sexuality', in Linda S. Kauffman (ed.), *American Feminist Thought at Century's End: A Reader* (Oxford: Blackwell, 1993), p. 4.

8 L. Emmet Holt, *The Diseases of Infancy and Childhood* (New York: D. Appleton and Co., 1936), p. 780.

9 Rubin in Kauffman (1993), p. 4.

10 Fraser Harrison (1979), p. 273.

11 'Europe, History of', *Encyclopaedia Britannica* (London: Britannica, 2000, CD-ROM).

12 Christopher Wood, *Victorian Panorama* (London: Faber and Faber, 1976), p. 135.

13 Henry Hartshorne, *The Household Cyclopedia* (New York: Thomas Kelly, 1881), p. 142.

14 Alfred Field Henery, *Manly Vigour* (Manchester: privately printed, 1861), p. 14.

15 Caroline Ann Smedley, *Ladies' Manual of Practical Hydropathy* (London: James Blackwood, c.1880), p. 26

16 Gathorne-Hardy (1972), pp. 92-3.

17 See Ian Gibson, *The Erotomaniac* (London: Faber, 2001), pp. 215-8; *My Secret Life*, i, p. 5.

18 George Gissing, *The Odd Women* (Oxford: World's Classics, 2000 [1893]), pp. 107-8.

19 *My Secret Life*, v, 1937.

20 See Slajov Zizek, 'Desire: Drive + Truth. Knowledge', *Umbra* i (1997), p. 152; Alex Chapple, *The Passion of John Ruskin* (1994).

21 See *The Passion of John Ruskin*.

22 Quoted in John Batchelor, *John Ruskin: No Wealth but Life* (London: Chatto and Windus, 2000), p. 135.

23 Mary Lutyens, *Young Mrs Ruskin in Venice* (New York: Vanguard Press, 1965), p. 21.

24 Batchelor (2000), p. 135.

25 John Everett Millais to William Holman Hunt, 25 August 1854, ALS in Bowerswell Collection, MA 1338, Pierpoint Morgan Library, New York.

26 Quoted in Vivien Noakes, *Edward Lear 1812-1888* (London: Royal Academy/Weidenfeld and Nicolson, 1985), p. 21.

27 Pauline Clarke, *The Eye of the Needle* (Nuneaton: privately published, 1994), p. 96.

28 Doug Malloy, 'Body Piercings', in *Modern Primitives: An Investigation of Contemporary Adornment and Ritual* (San Francisco: Search Publications, 1989), p. 25.

29 Queen Victoria, ed. Viscount Esher, *The Girlhood of Queen Victoria: A Selection from Her Majesty's Diaries between the years 1832 and 1840* (London: John Murray, 1912), ii, p. 263.
30 *My Secret Life*, i, p. 242.
31 Ibid., i, p. 243.

Conclusion

1   E. M. Forster, *Maurice* (London: Penguin, 1972 [1971]), p. 136.
2   Christopher Hart, 'Oscar Wilde: More Sinner than Saint', *Daily Telegraph* (17 October 1997), p. 28.
3   Richard Ellmann (1987), p. 258.
4   Ada Leverson, *Letters to the Sphinx from Oscar Wilde* (London: Duckworth, 1930), p. 44.
5   Stefan Rudnicki, *Wilde the Novel* (London: Orion, 1997), p. 100.
6   Alaister Rolfe, ed., *Nothing . . . Except My Genius* (Harmondsworth: Penguin, 1997), back cover.
7   Ibid., p. xiv.
8   Terry Eagleton, *St Oscar* (Derry: Field Day, 1989), p. x.
9   Cheryl Wetzstein, 'Thinkers from both the right and left back endorse shame', *Washington Times* (20 March 1995), p. 1.
10 Gertrude Himmelfarb, 'The Value of Victorian Virtues', *St Louis Post-Despatch* (7 May 1995), p. 3.
11 Charles Murray, 'The Next British Revolution', *Public Interest*, 1 January 1995.
12 Strachey (1948), p. 9.

Acknowledgements

My thanks are due to Matthew Beaumont, Maggie O'Farrell, Kate Flint, Ruth Metzstein, Barry Milligan, Peter Sweasey and Chris Willis, who read some or all of this book during the writing process, and gave me the advantage of their immense cleverness and their friendship. I am indebted to my editors at the *Independent on Sunday* and the *Independent* – particularly Suzi Feay, Marcus Field, Simon O'Hagan, Mike Higgins, Lisa Markwell and Andrew Tuck – who have allowed me to write numerous articles about the Victorians over the last few years. I am grateful to Emily Rustin for exemplary research assistance, to Helen Bevis for advice on nineteenth-century cutlery, to Mark Lee Rotenberg for sharing his knowledge of pornographic magic lantern slides, to Patrick Leary and the many subscribers of the Victoria Internet discussion list, to the staff of the British Library, Bodleian Library, Pierpoint Morgan Library, both Niagara Falls Public Libraries, and the Mile End Local History Library (whose librarians are in a class of their own). I owe particular debts of thanks to Tobias Jones, for introducing me to Walter Donohue, my incomparable and unflappable editor, to Jon Riley for his support and encouragement, and to my agent Simon Trewin and his assistant Sarah Ballard, for advice, enthusiasm and lunch. This book would not have been possible without my parents, Toni and David Sweet – in many more ways than the obvious one – or Robert Mighall, who knows that this book is a direct result of every conversation about the Victorians we've ever had, or my wife, Nicola, for giving me the benefit of her insight, knowledge and proof-reading skills – and for marrying me two months before the delivery date.

Index

Page references in *italics* are to illustrations.

Pg